Psychological Care in Physical Illness

Psychological Care in Physical Illness

Second edition

Keith A. Nichols

Senior Lecturer
Department of Psychology
University of Exeter, and
Principal Clinical Psychologist
Royal Devon and Exeter Hospital

CHAPMAN & HALL

London · Glasgow · Weinheim · New York · Tokyo · Melbourne · Madras

Published by Chapman & Hall, 2-6 Boundary Row, London SE1 8HN, UK

Chapman & Hall, 2-6 Boundary Row, London SE1 8HN, UK

Blackie Academic & Professional, Wester Cleddens Road, Bishopbriggs, Glasgow G64 2NZ, UK

Chapman & Hall GmbH, Pappelallee 3, 69469 Weinheim, Germany

Chapman & Hall USA., 115 Fifth Avenue, New York, NY 10003, USA

Chapman & Hall Japan, ITP-Japan, Kyowa Building, 3F, 2-2-1 Hirakawacho, Chiyoda-ku, Tokyo 102, Japan

Chapman & Hall Australia, 102 Dodds Street, South Melbourne, Victoria 3205, Australia

Chapman & Hall India, R. Seshadri, 32 Second Main Road, CIT East, Madras 600 035, India

Distributed in the USA and Canada by Singular Publishing Group Inc., 4284 41st Street, San Diego, California 92105

First edition 1984
Reprinted 1987, 1991

Second edition 1993
Reprinted 1996

© 1984 Keith A. Nichols, 1993 Chapman & Hall

Typeset in 10/12pt Palatino by MFK Typesetting Ltd, Austin House, Bridge Street, Hitchin, Herts SG5 2DE
Printed in Great Britain by Hartnolls Ltd, Bodmin, Cornwall

ISBN 0 412 43560 8

A Catalogue record for this book is available from the British Library

Library of Congress Cataloging-in-Publication Data available

∞ Printed on permanent acid-free text paper, manufactured in accordance with ANSI/NISO Z39.48-1992 and ANSI/NISO Z39.48-1984 (Permanence of Paper).

Contents

Acknowledgements		vii
Introduction		ix
1	When there is no psychological care	1
2	Illness, distress and neglect	11
3	Developing a scheme of psychological care	45
4	Informational and educational care	58
5	Emotional care and monitoring psychological state	96
6	Counselling and therapy	142
7	Self-care and preventive support for nurses and therapists	170
8	Overview and dealing with reality	185
	Epilogue: 'Alone with illness'	201
Appendices		213
Bibliography		220
Index		226

Acknowledgements

My wife, Lorna Sealy, has been an enormous help to me in refining this second edition. She has also contributed a much-valued chapter.

Polly Woodhams, the Clinical Nurse Manager at Exeter Renal Unit, has applied the basic notions of psychological care within her unit and shown that nurses can be very capable in developing and implementing the basic approach. Polly has also contributed much by way of discussion and first-hand experience, and has been very clear about what is practical and realistic within a busy unit and what is not. Her support has been invaluable.

The case studies presented in this book are composites and do not refer to the exact histories of specific people.

Introduction

Although this book gives special consideration to nurses it is designed to be relevant to all the health care professions. The emphasis on nurses is because, with their particular role and their large numbers, they are in the best position to provide much of the psychological care that ill and injured people need. I therefore outline a scheme of psychological care for use by nurses. However, there is also a great need for the various therapist professions to develop certain aspects of psychological care and their position is also kept very much in mind.

My assumption is that members of the medical profession need to understand the objectives and techniques of psychological care but will not usually be able to undertake this work themselves. Even so, as I write, doctors are in my mind too. I hope that the contents will serve as a useful guide for trainee and working doctors on the activities of nursing and therapist colleagues who are providing psychological care. Ideally, this will enable them to integrate with the work – an important and valuable contribution.

Similarly, clinical psychologists and psychiatrists working in the health psychology field often assist nurses and therapists by teaching various aspects of psychological care. The material to follow is mainly in the 'how to do it' mode. It ought to be of use as a back-up to such course work.

In 1983, at the time of writing the first edition of this book, I had never come across a properly operated scheme of psychological care in any general hospital. My belief then was that a high proportion of the staff in general hospitals seemed either unaware of the need for psychological care of the ill and injured, or were unsure about how to deliver it. As a result, many people suffered much needless stress.

Nine years have passed. Now, in 1992, as I have mused on the path to follow with this second edition, there has been a degree of stock-taking. I have had to consider what has changed. In so doing, I have also had to reflect on whether my own views have altered during the passage of time.

Certainly there have been changes and, against the rather dark view which I took in 1983, it is good to be able to say that, in many ways, things have changed for the better. Improvements in the provision of psychological care within hospitals are, to a large extent, dependent on the nursing profession (although in some circumstances it is the therapist professions which are best placed to give such care). Thus, it is an encouragement to note that articles in nursing journals urging improved psychological care are now commonplace. Similarly, the present-day training of nurses and therapists is often slanted towards 'whole person' care and, in my experience, recently qualified staff tend to be much more psychologically aware. Changes in certain organizational aspects of nursing have made it easier to implement the type of clinical developments required for effective psychological care. For example, the era of the 'nursing process', with its inherent concern for the psychosocial context of illness, has been followed by innovations such as team nursing and primary nursing, with the emphasis being on individualized patient care. This has made it so much easier to devise schemes for psychological care. Lastly, a recent work indicates a trend towards establishing nursing as a form of therapy. McMahon (1991) describes an approach to nursing which includes healing activities of a physical, emotional, spiritual, mental and environmental nature. Again, such a trend is very much in accord with the notion of psychological care and makes its introduction that much easier.

Another type of change, which appears to be ongoing, concerns the image nurses have of themselves. There seems to me to be a slow shift towards the sense of nursing being a non-apologetic, equal, autonomous profession. This is very good news because now nurses will specify the content and depth of the care they offer. In other words, nurses and not other professions (such as the medical profession) will decide whether or not to include psychological care as part of their routine procedures.

These developments have been brought to life for me in my contact with the Renal Unit at Exeter. I have had the pleasure of watching the effective combination of primary nursing and elements of the scheme of psychological care which is outlined in Chapter 3. Under the guidance of my nursing colleague, Polly Woodhams (Clinical Nurse Manager), real strides have been made in demonstrating that nurses are very able and very enthusiastic in the provision of basic psychological care. I will frequently refer to this unit to provide examples of how psychological care can be developed to suit the particular needs of any specialty.

I have also had the experience of working with occupational therapists, speech therapists and physiotherapists over recent years and find that members of these professions are also increasingly psychologically minded, and often keen to give psychological care. At other times, I have had the assistance of social workers who already have training in some of the basic psychological care skills.

Thus, the main overall change since 1983 is that increasing numbers of wards and units in different hospitals have introduced elements of psychological care into their service objectives. In general, though, they will have acted on an individual basis and never as a whole hospital. It is still common to find two wards operating side by side, one of which is striving to introduce psychological care while the other is still locked into a form of nursing which excludes it. Similarly, certain specialties seem to be ahead of others in general psychological awareness. I think, for example, of those working in the field of diabetes, wherein nurse specialists are often also trained in counselling skills and where a routine component of nursing care is education, information and support.

There are two negative elements that qualify this somewhat up-beat account. First, in Britain at least, the recent political emphasis on increasing apparent cost-effectiveness by rushing more acute cases through the hospitals, together with the so-called market economy, means that the 'centre of effort' in hospitals seems to have shifted from quality of patient care towards money care. The innovations of psychological care now have to be 'sold' to accountants in a boardroom, as well as to the health care professionals. It is a less easy task. Secondly, I have to say that it is still very easy to come by 'horror stories'. Interestingly, of those that have come to me recently, the majority have to do with outpatient clinics. For example, only last week a colleague of mine attended an outpatient clinic following a viral infection which had left significant hearing loss. Expecting some form of treatment, he was surprised when nothing was said to him about intervention but, having had a general assessment and audiogram, he was told to come back in a year and simply given an information pack entitled *Learning to live with deafness* and told that there were regular lip-reading classes available should he feel the need. He reeled out of the clinic in shock and anxiety to experience one of the worst nights of his life. In my view, this was a callous disgrace and a clear example of psychological negligence. No specific information, no follow-up for support and adjustment, no discussion – he was just abandoned with the news.

Having made this review, it is to my surprise that I find that the statement of my position and objectives which opened the introduction to the first edition of this book still serves to make clear my current objectives and why I am still so concerned with them. I would like to quote a section from the original introduction:

"Myrtle Dellbridge struck me as a somewhat unusual name. To be honest though, she was not an unusual woman, living a fairly ordinary life in an ordinary North Devon town. She achieved little that was exceptional in her 40 or so years save a valiant struggle against the hardships associated with total kidney failure which overtook her in mid-life. I met her a month or so after her transplanted kidney had also failed. Her experience was, I suppose, much the same as many other people whom I have since met but at the time, in 1977, it felt to me as if she had been dealt with rather savagely by the determinants of fate.

Myrtle had mastered the complex technique of haemodialysis and had adjusted with patience and courage to the deprivations and discomforts involved. She was noted for her cheeriness towards other people and clearly had made enormous efforts to put aside her personal grief and make the best of things. Like many people surviving by dialysis, she longed for a transplant and, to everyone's delight, a matching kidney did materialize and was successfully grafted. It worked well and Myrtle experienced some months which were akin to resurrection. Before that she had been weak, low on energy, dreadfully constrained by the routines of dialysis and assaulted by the nagging minor physical discomforts and illnesses brought about by uraemia. Following the transplant, though, she was her old self – a busy, energized extrovert. Tragically, her time in this comparative paradise was limited to 7 months, at which point an influenza infection led to the failure of the transplanted kidney and she was plunged once more into the grey world of survival by dialysis. Coping with the overwhelming disappointment and sense of loss required of Myrtle personal resources which she could not give. The effort of adjustment and acceptance had been found once, but this second blow broke her emotionally.

I used to visit her once or twice a week. She had been 'referred'. Without any sense of drama I can say that Myrtle unwittingly engendered a profound effect on me and fuelled my already growing interest in the psychological needs of people who are seriously ill or injured. What intruded upon me most powerfully was experiencing how isolated she was with the weight of her sadness. She was in decline, her spirit broken, conscious of the realization that she no longer wanted to carry on, and attempting to deal with her fears of death together with the intense grief of a mother saying goodbye to her child and husband. The staff in the Kidney Unit at that time were kindly and concerned but, it seemed to me, a hundred miles away in terms of understanding her experiences. She was truly alone, surrounded by caring people who were unable to offer the kind of care she needed – that is, companionship and understanding. They wanted to 'cure' her with antidepressants, persuade, cajole, in some way shake her into struggling on again. It was a difficult experience for me as a psychologist. One could quite easily understand why the staff were like this. They had very strong needs too – they also needed protection and care.

At the same time, I found it hard not to be angry and condemning, caught up as I was in Myrtle's distress.

This same conflict of loyalties and this same anger has nagged away for years now. Time and again I meet with people in general hospitals who are in great need of psychological care because they are undergoing great psychological trauma as a consequence of a serious illness or accident. Yet that need, I believe, is usually neither seen nor met – general hospitals do not offer this kind of care on a widespread and formal basis. I will go further and say that the typical general hospital, although supposedly a caring institution, paradoxically manages to be a centre of psychological neglect which actually generates psychological damage in a proportion of its clients. These are rather attacking claims to make and clearly there is need of substantiation. Accordingly, the earlier part of this book presents some of the large volume of material and experiences which back up such claims. I have also included a chapter written by the wife of a man who died while in kidney failure, as an extended personal example of an era in medical care which, I hope to persuade you, must come to an end (see Epilogue by Lorna Sealy).

I assume that most readers will either be training or employed as nurses, doctors or therapists, and I write deliberately to burden you with a dilemma. It is this. You must decide whether the position I take is yet another fashionable complaint which will get itself talked out and abandoned, or are we dealing with an issue which matters very much and requires from all of us working in the hospitals an openness to development and a willingness to implement new practices? My mind is made up, so what matters now is how you react. I will put before you the idea of caring as opposed to technical medicine, where caring medicine is a composite of educational, psychological and medical procedures, and where preventive psychological care is absorbed into the practices of the various professions involved as part of the everyday routines. The bulk of the book is given over to describing this approach under such headings as 'emotional care' and 'informational care'. I hope that you will grasp the dilemma and clarify your own position in the debate. If you agree that the insensitive, technical medicine so prevalent today is a needless addition to the difficulties which seriously ill people and their families already face, then the burden of implementing change also falls on you. You must take your share of the responsibility to shift the emphasis.

Deciding how to present the practices of psychological care was problematic. The training phase in psychological work can be frustrating because there are dozens of books which talk in generalities and give various theories on systems of therapy, but few tell you what to actually do. My experiences when teaching nurses and speech therapists during the last few years suggest that they have a particularly strong need for basic, down-to-earth instruction. This has tipped the balance and the book sets out to meet that need directly. What you will find is straightforward instruction aimed at the individual nurse on the ward, or therapist in the clinic. This is presented by making the temporary assumption of an ideal setting, that is, adequate time, facilities and the attribution of importance to the work by medical and other staff. The intention is to show what happens between an individual nurse and her client when psychological care is being conducted. This is the starting point, and if it fires the interest of senior staff in managerial positions it will be their task to think out the requirements of organizing such care on a wider basis. It will also be for them to assess the benefits.

A somewhat hard-headed medical administrator recently said to me, 'What arguments are there in terms of cost-effectiveness or increased turnover of patients if you introduce this sort of thing?' Well, there *are* arguments and evidence which demonstrate actual physical and financial benefits, but I did not need them in order to force him to concede. My reply was, 'Imagine your wife needs some distressing surgery. There are two units available; one is technically good but being traditional puts little effort into keeping patients informed or caring for them at an emotional level. The other has staff who, as well as medical competence, have also been trained in the basic skills of psychological care. They will care for her emotionally in a professional way and offer counselling in any difficulties arising. Which unit will you choose and why?' He replied, 'Point taken.' I hope you will feel that way too."

CHAPTER 1

When there is no Psychological Care

A CASE HISTORY

I want you to meet someone with me and see him through a psychologist's eyes. In medical terms he is just an 'average patient' but for us he will provide a good example of the ways in which doctors and nurses may unwittingly neglect the psychological needs of the people they care for and, on occasions, actually damage them psychologically. This damaging effect is not usually intentional or malicious, but it is a product of the ways in which the medical and nursing professions have developed. In particular, it is a consequence of a way of perceiving people and relating to them, which is known as the 'medical style of relating'.

We join Alan on a day three years ago when he is due in at the physiotherapy department of his district orthopaedic hospital for a mid-morning appointment. He has not arrived and now, at the beginning of the afternoon, he is in his bedroom at home sleeping in a restless haze produced by a generous salad of various painkillers and sedatives. He has not gone to physiotherapy because he knows that he will break down emotionally when he is there, just as he has done all week with his fiancée and other people who have looked in to see him. He is ashamed and embarrassed by his sudden loss of emotional control, which began shortly after his last visit to the hospital two weeks before. At 23, it is the last thing he expects. He despises himself for it and his instinct is to hide away.

How did Alan get like this? The story started with a road accident some years before which caused extensive damage to his left femur. He was cared for by the staff at the orthopaedic hospital and eventually, after a lengthy time in plaster, was out and about. As the months passed, though, he ran into increasing difficulties with stiffness and pain in the hip joint which progressively worsened. The medical team tried their best but there was no way round the hard fact that the head of the femur was breaking up and Alan was being slowly crippled. He

1

was aware of this happening and began to show his fright and frustration at the hospital. He worried that his job as a trainee car salesman was in jeopardy and believed that his fiancée and other friends were losing patience with his interminable problems and pain, which now had a history of nearly three years.

Alan's consultant knew also that he could not go on as he was and that a decision on surgical procedure had to be made. He requested that Alan attend a joint clinic with other orthopaedic specialists for a final review of the options. For reasons that he now cannot clearly remember, Alan deliberately missed this appointment: 'I was genuinely terrified; three or more of them all standing over you and talking as if you were not there and I knew they were going to make me have a big operation.' The joint clinic decided that the best course was to fuse his femur to the hip joint – that is, an arthrodesis of the hip. Accordingly a letter was sent giving the news and arrangements. Alan did keep his next appointment and after a brief discussion of the planned operation a trial period in plaster was organized for a few days' duration as a way of simulating the effect of the operation. He then agreed to go ahead. He was encouraged by what he remembered from his meetings with the consultant and had built up some optimistic expectations. Above all, he believed, the pain would go after the operation and after three years of it, he was desperate for this. He then could expect to spend some months in hospital and maybe six months in plaster, after which his job could be resumed. He would have a stiff hip but it would be possible to learn how to deal with that and then his mobility would be tolerably good. With these thoughts in mind, full of hope and confidence, he entered hospital in June 1978, three years after his accident.

Comment (1)

Now we should freeze the story for a moment and look at the ingredients of the situation. In what state is Alan embarking on this course? As a person, he is typical of a young man from southern England, average in education but quick-witted, not really sure where his future lies, insecure about many things but taking great comfort from two elements in life, namely his job, which he feels is the beginning of a ladder, and his membership of a close circle of friends similar to himself. He spends much time with them as they move around as a group, often on motorcycles, visiting other towns or dances and pubs. Alan's sense of worth is high in this group but it is based on a psychological make-up which renders him very vulnerable at this moment. He feels secure and accepted as long as he is the same and in no way (to use his language) freaky. Also, to remain a close member of the group it is important for him to be able to join the group in its changing pattern of activities, to be capable of pursuing the latest impulse with them.

It would be unfair to say that Alan has been given false expectations of the arthrodesis operation. No-one has set out to fool him. *However, it is the case that Alan's ideas about how he will be after the operation are, at this point, very unrealistic and badly worked out. He has had no help with this side of the business and without its being noticed, a gross discrepancy has developed between his expectations and the realities of undergoing surgery like this. He is being allowed to undergo the operation with knowledge only of the best possible outcome and has not been prepared for other possibilities.* These include: the risks of continued pain, of the bones not fusing and a second operation being required, of a year or more in plaster. Added to this he has in no way been prepared for the powerful emotional consequences of being disabled. Nor has provision been made in advance to help him with this.

Why is he so unprepared for these possibilities? The consultant claimed to have warned him of them at some point and clearly felt his duty had been discharged. But anxious people who are searching for relief to pain are not accurate listeners and often recall just the positive and hopeful side of a doctor's communications. Unless their view of events to come is frequently checked and corrected, they may idealize the situation, eventually creating unrealistic beliefs. Added to this, many doctors do not feel comfortable with anxious, dependent patients. In encounters with people such as Alan they will attempt to avoid raising anxieties further by playing down the possibilities of difficulties and failure. The business of preparing people for the whole range of outcomes to an operation like the arthrodesis of a hip, which will include information on possible complications or even failure, is often left undone. Simple, idealized versions are presented with the rationalization that patients are better off without additional worries. It may be a well-meant gesture, but you can see that it has introduced a second area of vulnerability for Alan. He is not aware of how things might go wrong and what he will have to deal with as he confronts his disability. He is being left to cope with the outcome of his operation on his own. If there are problems he will feel betrayed, frightened, angry and shaken by the power of his emotional reactions.

THE HISTORY CONTINUED

No doubt you can anticipate the next stage in this narrative. The operation was undertaken in normal circumstances. Technically it appeared to be a success and Alan joined a ward full of orthopaedic cases to begin his months in plaster. He was attended by kindly but busy nurses with brief, regular visits by one or other of the medical team and occasional contacts by a social worker and a physiotherapist. His fiancée, mother and friends visited frequently. As weeks passed, however, the nurses began to notice some worrying changes. Alan was more irritable now and inclined to be withdrawn and depressed. There were several strange incidents in which he became violently angry and broke his plaster, others in which he was clearly drunk and abusive. The staff became wary and uneasy. He was not expected to be a perfect patient, but surely this behaviour was unreasonable. They sensed an anger, an instability and an *accusation*, which was unnerving.

These fears were dealt with by categorizing him as a 'difficult' case, a disturbed personality. The doctors and nurses were, of course, concerned but also became angry and exasperated in return. Some tried to approach him to discover what was wrong but were unable to get far and often felt rejected by Alan's angry manner. Things slowly worsened. He complained of pain from the wound, openly speaking of being depressed. The medical social worker felt that he might be clinically depressed so the possibility of calling in outside help was raised. After some discussion, it was agreed to call in a clinical psychologist who worked in the locality. Note, by the way, that this was the first moment in this case history when help from someone specializing in psychological care was seen as necessary. Before such help was sought, it was necessary for Alan to deteriorate to a level which attracted attention to his difficulties and led the staff to label him as disturbed. *The implication was that psychological care was to be called for if he became a psychological casualty, but not in order to prevent it happening.*

It would be pleasing for me if I could introduce the psychologist as the saviour in the story. This was not to be the case, however. The psychologist was involved too late to make a major contribution – the damage was already done. Anyway, he made errors in judgement which reduced his effectiveness later on. Nevertheless, the two of them got off to a good start. The psychologist called to see Alan several times in the space of two weeks. He offered a counselling style of interaction, that is, with the emphasis on helping Alan express what was in his thoughts and what feelings were associated with these. There was little by way of advice or the interpretations of deep psychotherapy at this point, but because Alan felt that he was being listened to without demands or judgement, he was able to relax and explore exactly what was disturbing him.

Somehow he had expected the pain to go away as if by magic. It had not done so, however, and a despairing feeling that something had gone wrong and that he would never be free of pain was growing by the day. There was also an angry, resentful feeling that sometimes got out of control and made him want to smash things or hurt himself. He was not sure who this was really directed against. Sometimes it was himself, sometimes the surgeon and staff. It was at its worst during restless nights on the ward, when he visualized himself in the future on the beach, say, with his friends, at a disco perhaps, or involved in sexual encounters. He saw himself as a clumsy cripple with a wasted leg. The leg was, in fact, made shorter than he had expected and that, together with the problem of not being able to move it would, he believed, interfere with so many activities. His group would want to move off and do things but he would be slow and awkward. In his fantasy he was a nuisance and an oddity, thus breaking one of his most important personal rules. The sad image of so many favourite experiences in which he would no longer feel comfortable, or which would be physically impossible, increasingly intruded on him. These sadnesses alternated with the angry periods and often left him in quiet tears.

Two things were happening. First, because of his own values, he was bitterly turning against himself in self-blame and self-rejection. He had, of course, started grieving – rightly so, for a bit of him had died, taking with it, it seemed, access to his group and favoured activities. *It was not a weakness nor a neurotic instability on his part but a normal, quite predictable psychological process. A process, though, which no-one had forewarned him about and no-one had watched for in order to help him with it. He was alone with this most powerful of emotional upheavals, not knowing what was happening and surrounded by nurses and doctors who, though they meant well, lacked understanding of the process and were resentful with Alan for his behaviour. To them he was being inconsiderate and unreasonable, making their jobs difficult.*

As Alan's experiences were unfolded in these conversations with the psychologist, it became clear that the last few weeks in hospital had forced a complex problem onto him. How was he to endure the interminable weeks of boring ward routine when he was immobilized in plaster, in physical and psychological pain, and feeling alienated from the staff and from himself? His instinct was to turn to self-medication to blot things out. It began with alcohol taken together with hoarded painkillers and sleeping tablets. Later, friends brought in other drugs and a solution began to emerge. He could survive by taking lengthy periods of escape during which he no longer felt pain or cared about the future. It seemed ideal to him. From our vantage point now we might feel sympathy, yet it was clearly a disadvantageous solution since he was not confronting his problems. He was not beginning the work of adaptation and adjustment, he was simply setting everything aside. When he was not able to withdraw in this way his thoughts became more depressed and the emotion more painful. It was during these times that he was difficult with the nurses. Inevitably the urge to exploit every means of escape grew. It was a damaging learning experience, in that he was rehearsing a pattern of defence by drug-induced withdrawal which was later to become unshakably strong.

Comment (2)

If we may take a second pause here, it is instructive to ask how someone in a supposedly caring institution surrounded by caring people can become so isolated with personal problems and be forced to find his own solutions? Why was he not helped from the beginning?

In replying to the question I want to stress again that the motive here is not to make accusations or attribute blame. Nobody wished Alan other than well, and all the staff involved were concerned to see him recover. However, the case demonstrates one of the key points to be developed in this book, namely, no matter how well-intentioned doctors and nurses might be, when they practise with the view that medicine is primarily to do with physical treatment and where they maintain the distant, impersonal, medical style of relating which depersonalizes people into 'patients', then the psychological needs of seriously ill people will neither be properly recognized and valued, nor be properly met.

In contrast, where the focus of attention is *care, as distinct from just physical treatment*, then there will be an equal concern for the educational, psychological and social aspects of illness, in which case the psychological needs will automatically be recognized and provision made to meet these whenever possible. It is overly simplistic, but we might say that the contrast is between two very different approaches – treating bodies versus caring for people. In short, the answer to the question 'how did it happen?' is that Alan's psychological needs were neglected because they were not seen. The focus of attention was elsewhere and the feeling of the staff was, on the whole, that emotional disturbance in physical illness is an unfortunate complication – something of a nuisance which crops up with the occasional unlucky or weaker patient.

You may think that this is an unreasonable and old-fashioned view. You may want to say 'yes, but it is not like that so much these days'. But as we will see later, the evidence is that this impersonal, treatment-oriented style still lingers in many hospital departments and there are powerful sociological and psychological forces which allow it to remain.

THE HISTORY CONCLUDED

The contact with the psychologist appeared to have a stabilizing effect. Reports from the ward staff indicated less 'disturbed' behaviour. At the same time, the news from Alan was not good. The leg continued to be most painful, particularly when any weight was placed on it and, worse, he reported that small movements from the hip could be made within the plaster. These claims, though, were generally dismissed by staff as resulting from imagination and being too tense about things.

After four months in total on the ward, Alan began pressing his doctors for their agreement to a transfer into his own home. The feeling was that he could cope with the estimated two more months in plaster better at home than in hospital. The doctors acquiesced. It was at this point that the psychologist misjudged things. His belief was that the move home was a positive event which would result in Alan feeling less isolated and so facilitate the psychological adjustments which had to be achieved. It was a mistake. As things turned out, the arthrodesis did not fuse and six months were to pass with Alan still in plaster, still in pain, relatively immobilized, and with the added problem of being out of contact with his consultant other than brief appraisals by one of the team in a busy outpatient's clinic every six to eight weeks. It became more obvious by the week that there was definite movement at the hip, which technically should by then have fused solid. The arthrodesis had failed.

Many changes took place in Alan's psychological state during this time. Most importantly, there was a growing sense that he had been cheated and abandoned. The difficulties were, after all, quite unexpected since he had not been forewarned. He became convinced the operation had failed, yet he was unable to obtain face-to-face confirmation on his outpatient visits. Four times he had to carry away the simple message of 'Give it another six weeks and we will have another look'. If, then, he could have shared the consultant's thoughts and sensed the genuine doubt as to whether fusion would ultimately occur, he might have seen this period of waiting in a more positive light. But communication was not good and he experienced a frustrating evasiveness. One registrar told him to prepare for the worst, but on the whole he was kept minimally informed. (Ideally the psychologist would have liaised and kept him informed, but he was a stranger from another department and effective channels of communication and, more importantly, trust, were not established. The medical team saw the psychological care as a parallel but relatively unconnected activity, and maintained much the same poverty of communication with the psychologist.)

In other words, Alan was stripped of the vital supportive link provided by regular effective communication with the medical and nursing staff responsible for his treatment. He could not know what they were thinking or whether they were aware of his plight because they had retreated from reach. At the time when he most needed their encouragement, their information, their advice and their support, it was cut off almost totally.

The transition from inpatient to outpatient has many risks and is a complex event for those who are seriously disabled and in pain. In this case it was handled in a routine medical manner, without wishing harm yet proving to be a critically damaging event. The staff just did not see the need for their continued contact and support as a major resource to oppose the drift into despondency and feelings of abandonment.

For a while Alan made some efforts to get out and about on crutches, but it was difficult, unrewarding and painful. Increasing amounts of time were spent just lying on his bed at home, resorting inevitably to whatever means of withdrawal and pain relief that came to hand. Seemingly his intolerance to pain grew, as did his resentment and anger towards the hospital staff. His despair mounted daily. He was now discovering, *on his own*, what one of the alternative outcomes to the surgery could be.

In the sessions with the psychologist, which continued at an interval of every two or three weeks, Alan's distress was evident. He had begun to abandon his links with the future. In particular, he let contact with his employers lapse although they had been holding his job open for him. He turned against many of his friends and stretched his fiancée's loyalty to its limits. Then, unexpectedly for him, he suddenly lost all emotional control. Without warning he would be gripped by periods of intense sadness in which he could not hold back tears and was unable to talk. There were one or two embarrassing incidents for him. In his eyes, to add to his weight of problems, he was now 'going mental'. It was truly frightening. The psychologist tried to increase his support by suggesting more sessions, but Alan withdrew saying that he could not face the journey in, or cope with seeing people at the day hospital when he could never be sure of his emotional state.

As an alternative move the psychologist tried to attract the surgeon's interest in Alan's plight. The surgeon, however, felt that although he was concerned by the situation, the arthrodesis must be given more time just in case it finally fused. He saw his brief as limited to orthopaedic problems and not concerned with psychological troubles. There was no recognition that the established manner of doing things in that particular hospital was one of the main sources of Alan's psychological difficulties.

Sadly, although inevitably perhaps, Alan turned increasingly to drugs as a solution. Initially it was relatively safe, orally taken painkillers and sedatives. However, in his locality there was a robust trade in drugs among young people and some had learned how to inject their drugs intravenously. Alan's earlier experiences when still in the hospital were that drug-induced escape seemed the best means at his disposal to deal with the physical pain and the oppressive despair that he felt. He was responsive, therefore, to the suggestion of trying an intravenously administered painkiller which had a morphine-like effect. The immediacy of the pain relief, and the escape to another

world that had nothing to do with plaster and being crippled, produced a profound effect in him. Before long the use of drugs became
an everyday event and the insidious changes in outlook and personality which this generated began to show.

There is little more to be learned in charting Alan's steady slide into
drug dependency and the ensuing problems. For the sake of completion you will probably like to know that about a year after the first
operation, a second attempt was made at the arthrodesis. If anything,
it was more traumatic for him than the first experience. However, the
bones did finally fuse.

So, to a conclusion. This case has been used to demonstrate that the
style of communicating with and relating to people in hospitals that
has become prevalent in the last few decades is, in *psychological terms*,
the opposite of good care. Alan was actually damaged by the approach
adopted in the management of his case by the doctors and nurses
involved. Yet they did not wish this, or even realize the effect they
were having. Fortunately, not many cases are as dramatic a demonstration as this one has been.

HOW SHOULD IT HAVE BEEN? THE VISION OF PSYCHOLOGICAL CARE

In an ideal world, Alan would have been admitted to a ward which ran
a scheme of psychological care, which would have been a component
of the overall nursing care plan. Such a scheme would have been dis-
tinctive in that it involved *planned* routine interventions of a preventive
nature. It would have been operated as a professional service, as
opposed to the nurses simply making an effort to be a bit more caring
and communicate better. The point of such work would have been to
'head off' as many of the problems as possible by anticipating them in
advance and preparing Alan properly for the stresses of the event.
Ideally, this scheme would have been integrated with primary nursing,
so that the primary nurse assigned to Alan would have been unam-
biguously entrusted with the responsibility for his psychological care.
This responsibility would have included educating him about the surgery, keeping him informed and checking his knowledge and beliefs
regularly, monitoring his psychological state, helping him with the
emotional burdens, calling in the assistance of a psychologist if this
was needed, and arranging supportive contact during his home-based
phases. Lastly, this psychological care would have been requested and
supported by the medical staff who would have done their best to integrate with it. Similarly, the physiotherapist and occupational therapist
would have been aware of the objectives and complemented these in
their work. In fact, in a rather labour-intensive case such as this the

occupational therapist may well have been engaged by the primary nurse to do some of the psychological care work personally.

Are the nurses and therapists trained?

Is there an *explicit* scheme of psychological care?

Is there an allocation of 'psychological duties' to staff?
Is it systematic?

Are there prepared materials?

Are there records of psychological and educational interventions?

Is there a *guarantee of psychological care for all* clients and/or caregivers?

Do medical staff coordinate there work with the psychological interventions?

Figure 1.1: "We already give psychological care on our unit"

Many times during recent years, especially when I have given a talk at a conference, medical or nursing staff from various hospitals have said to me 'actually, we already give psychological care on our ward'. To this I reply, 'I'm encouraged, but are we talking about the same thing?I'm not talking about nurses simply making the effort to be more caring but rather about a professionalized scheme of psychological care which meets the following criteria'. At this point I show Figure 1.1 as a slide.

Maybe, similarly, you would like to check if your ward or unit meets these criteria. If your answer is 'yes' there will not be much that is new for you in this book. If the answer is 'no', then I hope to convince you of the need for psychological care in your work and to be helpful in offering an approach in developing psychological care that you can modify to suit your local circumstances. Otherwise, as you receive surgical cases onto your ward, or renal failure cases onto your unit, or assist dying people in your community, or whatever health care role you fulfil, you and your colleagues may be regularly and unwittingly rerunning Alan's story with other patients.

CHAPTER 2

Illness, Distress and Neglect

'No woman can imagine what it is like to awake from an anaesthetic to discover that one of her breasts is gone, to find only bandages where a breast has been. It is such a traumatic experience that scars remain – forever on her body, sometimes for as long in her mind.' (Brand and van Keep, 1978.)

Much of this book is set out as a practical guide to those wanting to develop their skills in psychological care. This chapter stands apart in that it draws together some academic and theoretical material which provides a reasoned basis for urging the development of psychological care in medicine, particularly in general hospitals. Without a sound basis of knowledge and argument we would lack direction and conviction. Knowing what we are trying to move away from, and what we are trying to develop in its place, is half the battle, so I make no apology in giving space to a little academic work. You may choose to move ahead to the practical side first and look through this chapter later, which is reasonable enough, but I do think familiarity with the material below is important and that it should be worked through at some point.

The last chapter ended with some important questions. We have now to formulate these questions in full and make sure that there are some satisfactory answers. Each section below poses a question, develops it and then looks to some of the research and literature in this field for a reply.

DOES ILLNESS CAUSE PSYCHOLOGICAL DISTRESS OR DISTURBANCE?

It is easy enough to find individual case studies of people in considerable psychological difficulty as a result of illness or injury, and it is similarly easy to find instances of individual doctors or nurses who fail to see the need for a psychological side to their work and thus add to the distress of their patients. However, an impassioned argument based on case studies alone lacks real power, and it would fail to convince people who take a broad, critical perspective. Therefore, we must

11

ask what evidence exists indicating a high prevalence of psychological distress among the population of seriously ill and injured people?

In seeking a clear answer we run into a problem straight away, in the shape of a common psychological defence called denial. Some people gain respite from their distress by blocking out awareness of threat and loss and *repressing* thoughts that excite emotional response. Thus inaccuracies are introduced. Often people are in considerable distress but deny this to themselves and to researchers. The data collected will, therefore, be an underestimate of the true levels of distress. If I may give a couple of examples you will see the problem.

In a study involving 87 men who had sustained severe myocardial infarcts and had been admitted to a coronary care unit, Hackett and Cassem (1976) noted that 70% of these people showed clear signs of an initial denial of anxiety and fear. In interview, they were unable to acknowledge a fear of death and the situation they were in. Subsequently some two-thirds were able to look back and see that they had been very frightened but had resorted to various devices to block out recognition of this. In a more complicated study, Levine and Zigler (1975) used a technique for assessing denial which involved measuring the difference between people's assessment of how they actually see themselves (real self-image) and how they would like to be (ideal self-image). Comparisons were made with a control group of healthy people and three groups of seriously ill people. One group was of stroke victims, one of people with lung cancer and the remainder with coronary heart disease. The relevant finding to us is that these seriously ill people did not show significantly greater discrepancies between their real and ideal self-images than the control group, that is, they denied the implication of the damage they had sustained.

Initial denial is widely reported as a feature of serious illness in reports from many sectors of medicine. It is a normal, protective response which may collapse after a short while and so lead to a more accurate perception, and then perhaps depression or anxiety. We will return to this later but for our purposes now we must note that measures of psychological distress in general hospital populations may well *underestimate* actual levels of psychological disturbance because of the distorting effect of initial denial. I have experienced a powerful, first-hand demonstration of this effect in a survey of the psychosocial problems associated with survival by haemodialysis (Nichols and Springford, 1984). Several subjects reported very few problems and no emotional difficulties, although reports from the staff indicated a persistent crop of difficulties and clear signs of emotional distress.

Bearing all this in mind we must consider the following. The prevalence of psychological disturbance in the British population runs at approximately 9% (Goldberg and Huxley, 1980). However, studies of the population of general hospital patients reveal much higher levels. For example:

1. Moffic and Paykel (1975) screened 150 medical inpatients by means of the Beck depth of depression inventory. The overall prevalence of clinical depression was 28.7%. When considering the subcategory of seriously ill people alone, the proportion rose to 61% (although we must not lose sight of the fact that certain drug therapies induce depression).

2. Johnston (1980) charted the levels of anxiety in four separate groups undergoing surgical procedures of orthopaedic or gynaecological natures using the State Anxiety Inventory. The data revealed that high levels of anxiety occurred before admission to hospital and, with some people, the anxiety level went up *after* the operation. Generally, anxiety levels remained above normal levels until discharge from the hospital.

3. Maguire *et al.* (1974) screened by questionnaire and then interviewed 230 consecutive admissions to two medical wards. The sample included people with degenerative diseases (heart failure, emphysema, osteoarthritis, etc.), major infections, cancers and so on. Of these, 23% fell within the category 'psychiatrically ill,' i.e. they met the criteria for inclusion in formal psychiatric categories. This figure would not, therefore include the many who were in distress but not psychiatrically disturbed. Later, Hawton (1981) followed up this sample and on finding that after 18 months 90 of them had died, noticed that a higher proportion of those with psychiatric disorders died (38%) compared with those free of disorders (20%). About half of those identified as psychiatrically disordered had remained so during the 18 months.

4. It has for some while been realized that the population of women who ultimately need a hysterectomy include many who are 'fragile' psychologically. This is reflected in the very high incidence of psychological difficulties observed among such people. Gath *et al.* (1982) used a very full diagnostic interview schedule called the Present State Inventory to assess 147 women four weeks before surgery and at six and 18 months after a hysterectomy. Of these, 58% revealed psychological disturbance before surgery, with 38% remaining psychologically disturbed at six months and 29% at 18 months after their operation. (By 'psychologically disturbed', it is meant a range of anxiety-based and depressive-type disturbances sufficient in intensity to impair life to some degree and cause considerable anguish.)

5. Similarly, it is clear that breast cancer and mastectomy precipitate high levels of distress in many women which can persist for some considerable time. There is a large literature in this area which,

frankly, removes any doubt on the issue. Morris (1979) produced an excellent review of many studies which all demonstrate high levels of psychological distress in significant proportions in the samples studied. For example, Maguire *et al.* (1980) interviewed and compared 75 women who were subjected to a mastectomy with 50 who were diagnosed with breast lumps which proved to be benign. Thirty-one per cent of the women undergoing surgery were depressed and/or anxious to a level that merited treatment prior to the operation, and 25% were similarly afflicted one year later. In contrast, the level in the control group was 12%. Morris herself has several important studies which reveal that 22% of 69 breast cancer victims were moderately to severely depressed *two years* after mastectomy, compared with 8% in a control group with benign tumours. Thirty-two per cent of the cancer victims reported changes for the worse in sexual relations during the two-year period. Recent reviews by Maguire (1989) Jacobson and Holland (1991) and Fallowfield (1991) confirm the earlier research. Between approximately 25% and 40% of women with breast cancer will experience marked levels of anxiety during the diagnostic process and, later, on receiving surgery, chemotherapy and radiation therapy. The number who become stressed and distressed as opposed to being identified on research instruments as clinically anxious will, of course, be greater. Similar figures apply to levels of depression.

6. Other instances of disfigurements or loss of body parts reveal similar reactions. Murray-Parkes (1976) interviewed 47 people shortly after the amputation of an arm or leg, and again one year later. He summarized his findings, noting that 'one-third to a half showed moderate emotional disturbance 13 months after the amputation'. Wirsching *et al.* (1975) described high levels of distress in people undergoing a colostomy. Prior to surgery, 39% of the women patients were undermined by feelings of hopelessness, 50% by spells of depression and 35% by anxieties about survival. After surgery, depression was evident in 50%, and 10% had suicidal thoughts. Thomas *et al.* (1984) review various studies of the psychological impact of stoma surgery and also conducted their own investigation. They conclude: 'overall, some psychiatric disturbance occurs in more than one-half of the subjects three months postoperatively'.

7. Mayou *et al.* (1978) produced two studies of 100 people with coronary heart disease. Interviews were conducted while they were in hospital, after two months at home, and finally after one year dating from the infarction. Spouses were also assessed. During the phase in hospital, 78% of patients and 53% of spouses revealed

mild or moderate distress. At two months, 53% of the patients described moderate to severe distress (including tension, depression, phobic problems, etc.) and 55% of the spouses were similarly placed. One year later, Mayou described the psychological distress as considerable with tension, anxiety, depression and fatigue occurring with some frequency in the people who had suffered the coronary; 32% showed moderate distress and 32% marked distress.

8. As may be expected, kidney failure followed by a life surviving on haemodialysis or peritoneal dialysis brings great hardship. Among this population the incidence of psychological difficulties and basic human anguish is known to be high. Kaplan De Nour (1981), in a wide series of studies, found that 53% of a sample of dialysands experienced moderate to severe depression, and 30% considerable anxiety. My own survey at the Exeter Kidney Unit (Nichols and Springford, 1984) returned similar figures, for both dialysands and partners. In this survey, the people involved used a problem checklist to indicate their difficulties and were then interviewed by a research assistant for an expanded account. Figures 2.1 and 2.2 give

General psychosocial difficulties	% Agreeing
Angry that I can't do the things that I used to	50
Worrying a good deal about the future	50
I'm too moody	43
Craving for liquid	43
Feeling depressed much of the time	38
Feeling irritable much of the time	38
Feeling ruled by the dialysis machine	31
Constantly in fear of injections	31
No interest in life	31
The kidney problems have made me physically unattractive	25
Frightened of any more operations	25
Feeling anxious much of the time	25
Desperate for a transplant	25
Missing being able to travel very much	25
Sometimes wanting to take my life	19

Relationships

Feeling no good as a parent	60
Feeling that there is too much strain on my partner	57
I feel I'm spoiling my partner's life	50
I'm difficult to live with	43
Sexual relationships are difficult/have stopped	43
Feeling no good as a husband/wife	36
Feeling that I spoil my family's life	31

Figure 2.1: Percentage of dialysands agreeing with dialysis problem checklist statements

some examples of the stresses and interpersonal strains encountered in this form of treatment during the first year. The figures give the percentage of people who agreed that the problem stated was one which affected them at the time of the interview. Figure 2.1 applies to those receiving dialysis treatment and Figure 2.2 applies to their partners.

A recent study by Petrie (1989) found the rate of psychological disturbance among dialysis patients to be 43%.

Dialysis	**% Agreeing**
Worried that I won't be able to deal with an emergency	46
Feeling anxious about being in charge of the machine	31
Frightened I'll cause harm or even death during dialysis	31
Feeling anxious about putting needles in	23
Helping with dialysis is a strain – my own health is deteriorating	23
The staff don't realize how difficult life is	23
Feeling anxious while dialysis is in progress	23

General psychosocial difficulties	
Feeling depressed at how he/she has changed	61
Feeling exhausted	54
Finding his/her depression hard to bear	31
Upset by the way our sexual life has suffered/stopped	31
I badly need a holiday	31
Feeling trapped because he/she depends on me so much now	23
Resenting the way he/she won't do things for him/herself	23
Worried about his/her attitude to other people now	23
Worried about the effects the situation is having on the children	23
Finding his/her tempers hard to bear	23
The future looks bleak	23
I badly need to get away for a day or two but never can	23

Figure 2.2: Percentage of dialysands' partners agreeing with dialysis problem checklist statements

9. The *Lancet* (1979) ran a short but powerful article quoting various studies which estimate the level of psychological distress associated with general hospital patients as ranging between 30% and 60%. The conclusion was: 'We now have ample evidence of the high prevalence of undetected and untreated psychiatric disorders' (among general hospital patients). To this we must add that with some types of illness there is also a high prevalence of distress among the

close relatives. Bailey and Clarke (1989) give a useful review of additional studies.

I think now that the message is clear. There are dozens of such studies, but little will be learnt from adding more. Even if, as suggested, denial causes underestimation, there is still clear evidence of psychological distress or frank disorder among seriously ill people which typically runs at 30% or more at the time of hospitalization and during the first year after the event. We therefore need to be clear about what is responsible for this. Illness and injury usually bring two things with them: the experience of threat and the experience of loss. The threat may be complex, not just to do with the immediate problems of pain and immobilization, but also to do with losing control of events affecting one's own life. Having no control and not knowing how things will go in the future undermines personal security. How will a husband respond sexually after his wife's mastectomy? How will a job be kept with three times a week dialysis training? How can a car be driven with one arm? How can a family be supported after a stroke has brought early retirement? It is the not knowing and not having control over the threat that triggers anxiety.

As for the losses brought about by illness, these will, of course, relate to the type of illness and the life context in which they are sustained. It may be a body part or function that has literally gone. The uterus, for example, which takes with it the chance of children, or the body shape and appearance after burns or amputation. Speech and vision are obvious losses and, in the case of people in kidney failure, there is a less obvious loss of physical energy. The effect, however, is usually much wider than just physical changes. Serious illness so often leads to the loss of key roles in a person's life – occupational, social, sexual and within the family. The reaction to loss is grief. It is a powerful process that can quite change a person and can mean a year or more of deeply disturbed experience.

The most important thing to pass on to you is that as we list these things rather academically and dispassionately, we lose contact with the feelings of the event. It is all too easy to become detached and dismiss profound distress as 'attention seeking or neurotic behaviour'. *It is vital to understand that the emotional reactions which grip people in these personal crises can have a crushing power. For some, the anguish of the emotional reaction is harder to bear than the illness itself.* Project yourself for a moment into a fantasy centred around you. Imagine finding out that after a bout of influenza you have unexpectedly gone into total kidney failure. Imagine the implications for your career, your relationships, your future as a free person. If you can sense the fright then you are in touch with the reality of the situation. If not, then you have work to do before you can be effective in psychological care.

DO THE MEDICAL AND NURSING PROFESSIONS RECOGNIZE AND RESPOND TO THE PSYCHOLOGICAL DISTRESS EXPERIENCED BY PATIENTS AND THEIR PARTNERS?

Without doubt, there are some very psychologically minded doctors and nurses who are sensitive, natural counsellors. Some work hard at caring for their patients at all levels. I know several personally and I pay tribute to them. However, in our inquiry we have to ask whether this is typical. In general, do these two professions actually monitor the psychological state of their patients and does either make appropriate psychological interventions, or at least engage other professions to do so on their behalf? Sadly, the answer has to be that, at the time of writing, the majority of people in practice as hospital doctors or nurses appear to have had little training in the detection and management of the type of problem that concerns us. Also, they make little use of the professions who do specialize in psychological care – psychologists and psychiatrists, for example.

Groundless accusations? In the study by Moffic and Paykel (1975) which we encountered earlier, although the overall prevalence of clinical depression on the wards was 43 out of 150 (28.7%), only six of these were mentioned as depressed in their notes, four were receiving antidepressants and only two had been referred to the psychiatric service. In the survey by Maguire *et al.* (1974), 23% of inpatients were revealed to be suffering 'psychiatric illness' but only 12% were referred for help, with 'no evidence in the notes that their problems had been detected by medical staff, treated or dealt with in any other way'. In a later study, Maguire *et al.* (1980) trained a nurse to act as a counsellor to women undergoing mastectomy. She detected and referred 38 women needing psychological help in a group of 77. Tape-recorded interviews were assessed by trained psychological therapists to establish the total number of those in psychological difficulty, and it transpired that the nurse had detected 89%. In a control group run by the usual surgical and nursing team, however, only nine (22%) of 41 cases were detected and referred – *that is, most of those needing to be referred for help went unnoticed.*

In an interesting study by Brody (1980), 58 physicians of varying levels of experience were asked to conduct assessment interviews with 235 patients. They failed to detect 38% of psychological disturbances and 76% of recent stressful events.

In my own study of people involved with dialysis, nearly 50% of the subjects agreed that 'the staff do not realize how difficult life on dialysis is'. There was a clear need on the part of staff to see the treatment as worthwhile and their patients as suffering less than was apparent to unbiased observers, which again meant a diminished ability to notice patients' psychological difficulties and arrange help for them. Similarly,

Kaplan De Nour and Czaczkes (1974) investigated the accuracy of consultant nephrologists in assessing the state of the people dialysing under their care. Again there was clear evidence of an inability to notice the difficulties and distress of their patients.

Thus the trend of the literature in this area is quite clear: doctors do seem quite poor at recognizing the psychological needs of their clients and, in the majority of instances, these needs will go unnoticed or at least unattended to. As Lief and Fox (1963) wrote:

'a pathological process of overdetachment begins which may eventually lead them as mature physicians to perceive and treat their patients mechanistically. The process of overdetachment may not stop at the failure to see the patient as a person but go on to the unconscious fantasy that the best patient is the one who is completely submissive and passive.'

If, then, doctors are poor at noticing the psychological needs of their clients, if the nurses are as yet neither trained nor empowered to take the initiative and deal with the problems, if allied professions such as social workers also lack training and are overcommitted with other tasks, and if the hospitals have not made provision for psychological care by the setting up of departments of clinical psychology to develop this side of the hospital care, who looks after the proven psychological needs of the general hospital patient? The answer is obvious. In many cases nobody does. *The general hospitals are often places of psychological neglect.*

DOES THE BEHAVIOUR OF THE MEDICAL AND NURSING PROFESSIONS CREATE ADDITIONAL STRESS FOR PEOPLE IN HOSPITAL?

This is difficult territory because it may seem that I am waging a campaign of hostile accusation against doctors and nurses and I might lose your sympathy. This is my last wish. At the same time, though, there is no point in evading the issue and so, in a fair-minded and objective way, we have to pursue the inquiry to its end. I will, however, preface this section with an important point. While I plan to demonstrate that, in certain ways, doctors and nurses often do impose additional stress, I do not see this as a personal issue, a form of deliberate negligence or punitive behaviour consciously carried out by an individual nurse or doctor. It is more to do with how people are trained into their job and certain psychological factors (detailed in the next section) which have caused the professions to develop certain ways of behaving. As Byrne and Long (1976) surmised in their study of communication by doctors, 'Doctors, like any other professional group, are both a product and prisoner of the training system that produced them'. I also recognize, as I mentioned above, that at the present time improvements are on the increase within the nursing profession. A small but growing proportion of nurses are extremely active in the pursuit of psychological care. However, although the signs are hopeful, there is plenty of evidence that, so far, all is not yet well from the psychologist's viewpoint.

Ivan Illich (1976) wrote, 'The pain, dysfunction, disability and anguish resulting from technical medical intervention... *make the impact of medicine one of the most rapidly spreading epidemics of our time'* (my italics).

Illich is a bitter, uncompromising assessor of modern medical practice and occupies an extreme position as a critic, much more so than myself. Nevertheless, I have to say that I know what he means. In the last five years in my role as a psychologist working in the general hospital sector, I have met many people who have been greatly stressed by their encounter with 'medical behaviour', and some who have been undoubtedly damaged by it. So how does it happen? How is the stress created? I will examine the problems created by the medical profession under the two headings of communication and emotional aspects. The position of the nurses will be discussed later under a separate heading.

Stressful non-communication

A much discussed issue in medical sociology and social psychology is the so-called 'medical style of relating'. The basic idea is that in their training, and because of the setting in which they first work, young doctors are slowly shaped into a particular way of relating which is responsible for much damage. The profession is, of course, composed of many people with differing personalities and backgrounds, so in reality there will be quite a wide range of expression of the medical style of relating. Our aim here, though, is to establish what is most typical. For a good review of knowledge and research in this area I cannot improve on that given by Hauser (1981). I will also draw on the work of Ley (1982a and b) who deals specifically with the communication of medical information.

A key feature of the medical style of relating is the approach to collecting and giving back information, and the level of attention given to the general needs of patients. The overwhelming evidence of dozens of studies is that most doctors hold back information, or at least make little effort to transmit information in a way which makes it usable. Hence because many of the people who are involved in a significant way with doctors receive too little information, they are often dissatisfied and usually ill-informed. In terms of receiving information, 68% of some 700 patients questioned by Cartwright (cited in Hauser, 1981) found their doctors unhelpful. Korsch (Hauser, 1981) revealed that 50% of 800 mothers attending a children's clinic were left wondering what had caused their child's illness, and many of the doctors failed to give clear diagnostic and prognostic statements, and had also tended to disregard the mother's account of her worries concerning her child's illness and ignore her tension. In Ley's survey involving 12 studies of communication by doctors, the percentage of people found to be dissatisfied with the communication varied from a minimum of 21% from a sample of general practice patients to 57% of medical inpatients and 65% of coronary patients. Webb (cited in Ley, 1982a) demonstrated that in *none* of 50 consultations which were studied in depth did patients receive adequate information about treatment.

By the way, it is relevant here to challenge the myth that many patients do not wish to know much about their illness or their treatment. This belief has led to remarkable levels of non-communication. For example, Lipowski (1975) (cited by Wilson-Barnett, 1980) describes a survey which revealed 90% of 219 doctors as believing it was best not to tell people they had cancer (although, as Ley comments, there is a trend for the proportion of doctors holding this view to decline). In contrast, Wilson-Barnett (1980) cites two studies in which 87% and 93% of cancer patients preferred to be informed. Ley cites similar figures from other research and also points out that there was no evidence found of increased anxiety or depression when patients were given full information about their case, even to the extent of being given their case notes or helping compile them (Stevens *et al.* and Fishbach *et al.* (Ley, 1982b)). Ley concludes, 'It would appear from survey evidence that the majority of patients wish to know as much as possible about their illness, its causes, its treatments and its outcome'. There will always be individual exceptions, of course, and also those who for one reason or another cannot make use of, or understand, the information. The majority it seems, though, do wish to know and are dissatisfied and disturbed by not knowing. I will return to and reinforce this theme in Chapter 4.

Part of the explanation of withheld information is the controlling style of interaction commonly found in doctors. Byrne and Lang (1976) conducted an intensive study of general practitioners in which they analysed and classified the transactions taking place in 2500 consultations. The most common style observed was described as the 'doctor-centred' style, which applied to about 75% of the physicians. In this style, the conversation was controlled by the doctor, who tended to adopt an inflexible questioning pattern concerning physical symptoms, with the sole purpose of gathering key information to make medical

decisions. This blocked any opportunity for the patients to direct conversation to other concerns and meant that the physician was unre-
sponsive to their feelings and needs. Hauser finds three terms in the
literature which are used to describe this predominant style of interaction in doctors, namely, doctor-dominated, doctor-centred and bureaucratic task-oriented. The opposite style of relating is termed
person-oriented. You can see that in the doctor-centred style effective
communication is unlikely. There is little opportunity for an equal
exchange of information – the doctor receives information and the
patient gives it. The need on the part of the patient to receive information back is not met, nor is the doctor in a position to react to the
needs of the patient, since little contact can be made with them in this
kind of conversation.

For those of you who have a taste for straight sociological analysis,
Strong (1979) presented a study of children's clinics which supports
this general claim. His message is a similar one, based on the verbatim
analysis of doctor–patient transactions made over three and a half
years in nine Scottish clinics and several American children's clinics.
(In reality the children were the patients but they were basically
ignored and the communication was with the parents.) The prevailing
pattern of interaction was a ritualistic, bureaucratic format. The parents
gave and the doctors took absolute control over the situation and conversation. They would initiate and terminate conversations, control the
content, manipulate conversations by interruptions involving medical
procedures or physical activity of some sort, e.g. talking with other
staff, referring to notes or moving away. The parents remained
passive–dependent and used none of these devices. Much of this could
be seen as motivated by the pursuit of technical efficiency and the
limited availability of time for each case. The overall effect, though,
was that although the doctors obtained the basic medical information,
the actual communication with and care of the people involved was
badly impoverished.

Another study, which is also very relevant to our purposes, is that of
Millman (Hauser, 1981). She describes three very frequently occurring
interpersonal manoeuvres by doctors that were identified in a two-year
observational study in hospitals. They appeared to be primarily defensive moves as a buffer against being seen to be guilty of error:

1. *Withholding medical information.* The effect of such a strategy is to
   limit the power and autonomy of the patient since, with less knowledge of their condition, patients are in a weak position and are
   unable to recognize mistakes in diagnosis or treatment. This particular strategy is commented upon in depth by Waitzin and Stoeckle
   (1972), who claim that, 'A physician's ability to preserve his own

power over the patient ... depends largely on his ability to control the patient's uncertainty'. They go on to add, 'The postulated association between uncertainty and power may help explain physicians' reluctance to reveal information to dying patients. A physician's disclosure of fatal illness is equivalent to a declaration of his own powerlessness'.

2. *Refusal to evaluate or comment on the competence and performance of other doctors.* There is an almost universal creed among hospital doctors which again deprives patients and other professionals of information, and so defends the medical power position. It is readily observed when there has been a crisis of some sort which involves medical error.

3. *Discrediting the patient.* Where mistakes occur the communications about the event carry the message that in some way the patient is actually responsible. I have met this on many occasions with kidney patients. For example, '*You* did not react to that drug at all well, did you?' when a prescription error was made and, 'The reason you have heart pains is because you have been overdrinking'. This latter example occurred to a young man two days after a kidney transplant attempt. In fact, an error had been made, instructing nurses to encourage a consumption of 2000 ml of water a day, although the output from the recently transplanted kidney was only 1000 ml and falling off. The intake of fluid should have matched the output. Another common form of the defence is frequently encountered by orthopaedic patients who complain of back pain which does not yield to ready diagnosis. They are likely to receive the communication, 'We can find nothing wrong with you, it is probably psychological', the implication being that the experience of pain is not real and they do not merit attention.

A last type of defensive strategy which is worth noticing is described by Duff and Hollingshead (Hauser, 1981) and concerns the extent to which 'personal doctoring' is blocked. In the extreme form of the defence called 'committee sponsorship', the patient is never able to deal with the same doctor for any length of time. The experience is of an ever-changing sequence of medical staff making visits, varying from senior house officers to the consultant. In addition, we might add that, although the consultant is usually the decision-maker, he has one predominant characteristic: he is absent for most of the time. The use of absence and the system of making doctors interchangeable leaves the patient in a very weak position, blocking the chance of relationships forming and communication developing. This is not so in what Duff and Hollingshead called 'committed sponsorship' in which an individual doctor would take an interest in a case beyond that of the disease itself.

Is non-communication really a source of stress? By far the most frequent complaint I have heard over the years is: 'It's not knowing that upsets us – they don't tell you anything'.

Stressful avoidance of communication about feeling

Moving on now to the issue of personal feeling in doctor–patient relationships, the role of a doctor can involve some harrowing experiences and devastating conflicts. Thus, right from the beginning, trainee doctors are 'shaped' into ways of dealing with the problem. I talked with a doctor recently on this theme and she was recalling some of her training experiences. The emphasis had been to stand back and never get involved for, the tutors stressed, if you began to feel something for a patient, you lost objectivity and became motivated to do things which lead away from good medical practice (for example, overprescribing painkillers with a risk of drug dependency developing).

One of the strategies for developing this remoteness in medical students was public ridicule. Medical students were severely embarrassed by consultants in front of their colleagues (and sometimes patients) if they revealed sensitivity and concern for the personal experiences of the patient. Hauser found that the literature dealing with the interpersonal training or socialization of doctors confirmed this to be widespread practice. Lief and Fox (1963) wrote of the development of 'detached concern': it is the beginning of a change towards diminished feelings which eventually results in doctors seeing the people they care for in an incomplete, mechanistic way, symbolized by the label 'patient' as distinct from 'person'. Once started, the process may develop a momentum of its own and can result in overdetachment, a gross form of interpersonal insensitivity which can appear to observers to be akin to cruelty. Thus, doctors may relate in a way devoid of emotional contact or empathy with their patients. These are best seen, then, as pseudo relationships.

There is a strong argument, incidentally, that there are important benefits in the maintenance of 'detached concern', both for the individual doctor and for the good standards of medicine. The benefits are in terms of insulating the doctor from excessive and traumatizing contact with other people's distress. I am basically sympathetic with this argument and will give my reply to it in the last two sections of this chapter. However, I can never give support for the more extreme form of overdetachment, which can cause extensive psychological damage.

Maguire (1985a, b, 1989) has written on this theme in relation to both palliative care and care of cancer patients in general. He provides some useful examples and, based on extensive observation, concludes that doctors and nurses use distancing tactics which cut them off from the real feelings of their patients, thus leaving them isolated with their distress. The distancing tactics are conversational ploys which block a patient from expressing their true feelings or worries. These include jollying patients along, selective attention to narrow, physical aspects of a patient's condition, obstructing attempts at reassurance, and the use of leading questions which bias patients' answers towards a favourable outcome, e.g.

> **Doctor:** I can't find anything to worry about and you are looking well, so everything has turned out fine so far. No need for us to meet again for three months. Quite reassuring eh?

Such conversations close off the possibility of the patient sharing that she has had a bad few weeks with anxiety, has been losing sleep and that she feels frightened for her future. She is thus left isolated with her emotion, which is an additional source of stress.

In my early days of work as a psychological therapist within a renal unit, it was possible to see the impact of such styles of interaction on patients and their partners. Gathering the data from Nichols and Springford (1984) and combining this with the experience of 50 or more cases seen in therapy, patterns began to emerge. As a result, I began to divide the sources of stress for ill and injured people into two types, illness-induced stress and staff- or hospital-induced stress.

The staff in the Renal Unit at that time (both medical and nursing staff in this study) were kindly, dedicated, well intentioned and professional. Despite this, they unwittingly created much stress in the following ways:

- *Poor teaching*: Nurses had no training as teachers; teaching was non-systematic, often poor in quality; this created pressures and anxiety.
- *Inadequate general communication*: There was no scheme for ensuring that patients were kept informed (and that they understood) in the fast flow of events. Confusion and apprehension through loss of control were common.
- *Staff out of touch and lacking insight*: Listening skills were poor and there was minimal effort to make contact with the real needs and experiences of patients and their relatives. Staff exerted a 'pressure to be well and not be a nuisance', and were inclined to project wellbeing.
- *Staff were ill at ease with emotional reactions*: The normal, predictable reactions by patients and partners were treated like infections. Comprehension was poor and distancing was common, which caused further isolation and suffering.

- *Partners conscripted as medical auxiliaries*: There was little awareness by staff of the enormous burdens of home dialysis. Tremendous social and moral pressure was exerted to ensure that partners continued. Some were very distressed, some trapped and desperate.
- *Home dialysis families 'set adrift' on their own*: The loss of contact between the unit and those who had completed their training was marked.

Interestingly, Maguire (1989) wrote under the title, 'Problems in women undergoing surgery for breast cancer'. The first half of the article describes one of the main problems – their doctors did not or could not listen to them. They distanced themselves and stressed the women accordingly. Not only was the cancer a source of stress but the doctors helping them were also a source of stress because of their 'out of touchness'.

Overall, then, the evidence is that many doctors do add to the difficulties of their patients by the maintenance of pseudo relationships and defensive strategies of behaviour. At a time of high dependency and fright, when information is usually all-important, patients and their relatives find themselves dealing with a profession whose members have often been schooled into an impersonal, detached manner of functioning which emphasizes minimal levels of communication and inaccessibility.

Communication and styles of relating in nurses

Nursing, of course, is a very different profession, with a large majority of its members being young women most of whom, it seems, were attracted to nursing because of a natural tendency towards caring and nurture. Assessing the characteristic relationship style that nurses adopt is not easy at the moment, though, since the profession does appear to be in a state of transition.

Although nursing has developed alongside medicine, its character and history are dissimilar. Healers have always existed but nurses are a comparatively recent development, stemming in this country from the model delineated by Nightingale in the 19th century, with its heavy emphasis on discipline, hierarchical bureaucracy and regimentation, reminiscent of the Victorian values of the society in which it was conceived.

The nurse's role was effectively that of a servant, implementing medical instructions without question. Even today one hears nurses complain about doctors treating them as if they were some kind of 'handmaiden'. Although this style of nursing is disappearing fast, it is instructive to note what nursing is changing from and why it initially developed in the so-called task-oriented style. An investigation by

Menzies (1970) makes a good start. Her brief was to make a study of nurse behaviour and nurse relationships in a large London teaching hospital. There were 150 trained nurses and 550 student nurses. In her report, which was based solely on clinical observation, Menzies identified several features which had become predictable aspects of nursing organization and behaviour. Combining various of these together, the following characteristics emerge:

The splitting of nurse–patient relationships. Personal nursing was blocked by the practice of giving nurses a few tasks to perform on a large number of patients, rather than working with just a few patients and coping with the whole range of tasks.

Ritualistic task performance – the task-oriented approach. The attention of the nurses was directed to the performance of tasks rather than to the patients as individuals. The work tended to be undertaken in a ritualistic manner, that is, without variation or individual interpretation in relation to patients' needs. This again had a blocking effect on nurse–patient relationships.

Denial of feeling. The young nurses were tutored to hold back their feelings and not to get close or involved with the patients. They would receive rebukes from seniors of the 'pull yourself together' type if there were instances of emotionality.

The depersonalization of nurse and patient. The basic attitude taught to the students was that nurses were interchangeable with one another – it should not matter to nurse or patient which nurse dealt with which patient. They were all required to approach their job in a standard, regimented way, the uniform symbolizing their neutrality as individuals. The student nurses particularly were moved from ward to ward with notable frequency. The patients were similarly depersonalized by the nurses, perhaps referred to as 'the cancer in bed twelve'.

Hawker (1983) directed her attention to the relationship between nurses and relatives. She mentions various studies which indicate strategies of avoiding contact with relatives, including not noticing their efforts to attract attention, being very busily engaged on seemingly important tasks such that the visiting relative feels inhibited about interrupting her, and being inaccessible by engaging in tasks away from the ward when the relatives are visiting.

A recurring theme in these earlier studies is that of nurses being efficiently and busily engaged in tasks with a manner that discourages communication and relationships by imposing a barrier of activity.

Evidence also exists that nurses, like their medical colleagues, are preoccupied with the risk of making a mistake with the consequent threat of exposure to discipline by senior nurses and medical staff, and guilt towards the patient involved. Hawker (1983) cites Stein (1969, re-published 1978) as finding that 86.1% of a sample of nurses were overly concerned about the risk of making a mistake.

Another feature which I have observed repeatedly in various hospital settings, and have had verbally confirmed in many seminar discussions with nurses, is to do with responsibility *and taking clinical initiatives.* Basically nurses appear *actively to avoid being responsible for clinical decisions.* The effect of the ritualization of procedures is to take away the need for clinical initiative on the part of the nurse. An example of this was nurses on a children's ward insisting on doing a drug round regularly at 9.30 p.m. One child who had been fractious all day was beginning to doze off at 8.30 and her mother asked if the child might have her antibiotic syrup then. The nurses said no, as they would have to contact a doctor to check if it was alright and they felt things should be left to the usual procedure. They would wake the child up and cope with the reaction. Both the nurse and mother knew that giving the penicillin one hour early was of no consequence at all.

Again, Hawker (1983) cites studies which reveal that the average nurse passively implements the doctors' wishes even when the nurse believes the doctor to be wrong. However, the strategy of avoiding responsibility can be complex and devious, in that the nurse may manipulate and lead the doctor to make a certain decision (which she, the nurse, wishes) but will retain her position as 'not responsible' by subtle ploys. Stein (1978) wrote of this feature of professional relationships in an intriguing little article called 'The doctor–nurse game'. His various analyses indicated that, in many instances, senior nurses would give doctors selective information about patients which inevitably led to a particular treatment. The nurse effectively initiated the treatment but both she and the doctor colluded together to maintain the belief that it had been the doctor's decision. A further observation is that, in avoiding responsibility and avoiding challenging medical colleagues, nurses also become involved in the business of withholding information. Searching questions will often be parried with, 'You will have to check with your doctor, I cannot say'.

Such generalizations, based on nursing as it was ten years ago, must be accepted with considerable caution, for the research is very scant. As to the actual nature of relationships which do form and the content of communication between nurses and patients today, this is even thinner ice. The reality is that there is probably much more individual variation among nurses than doctors. The setting in which they work will produce variability. Compare, for example, the nurses' contact with patients in a small coronary care unit against that in a large general ward working under a full load with many short-stay patients.

The value of these older studies is that they may indicate the style of nursing relationship that can easily develop if nurses are not trained and empowered to deal with the emotional side of illness and take part in information exchange.

As I mentioned in the introduction, this is an era of rapid change in nursing. Whereas in the past the nursing establishment was locked in the task-oriented style of nursing, now the establishment is active in eradicating it. In the recent 'patient's charter' in the UK, patients are guaranteed the right of a named nurse to undertake their care. This is the focal point of the new movement of *patient-centred* nursing, the underlying principle being that a named and qualified nursing practitioner is accountable for the nursing care of a named patient (Woodhams, 1992). The nursing practices involved are developed within the terms of primary nursing (Pearson 1988) and therapeutic nursing (McMahon and Pearson 1991). It would be good to think that, one day, we will have 'primary doctoring', (Woodhams, 1992).

WHAT ARE THE ORIGINS OF THE MEDICAL MANNER OF RELATING AND WHAT PSYCHOSOCIAL FORCES MAINTAIN IT?

Many people are dissatisfied with the neglect of psychological care in hospitals. These people, and nurses in particular, are seeking to bring about improvement. As we prepare for changes it is clearly important for the people who wish to play a part in developing psychological care to understand why, after centuries of development, the medical profession failed to see the need for psychological care and why the nursing profession tended to collude with the medical profession in ignoring the psychological needs of the people it cared for. Such understanding is important because the psychological influences responsible for this situation probably still operate and will continue to obstruct developments unless they are exposed and consciously opposed. The basic idea being considered is that perhaps something shapes and maintains doctors and nurses in the patterns of behaviour that have just been described, rather than the possibility that the people in these professions are abnormally cold and unfeeling.

Some clues are to be found in certain differences evident in *hospice* care compared with the general hospitals. In hospice care, staff undergo training to produce behaviour which is visibly different from that in the institutions they are leaving. Figure 2.3 shows some of the differences. These are intriguing because they illustrate the two possibilities, before us. Either the staff in hospice care are rather different types of people, or the psychosocial conditions of hospice care *free* doctors and nurses from influences which produce the 'medical style of relating'. The converse is that there are certain pressures in general hospitals which mould and trap the majority of the medical and nursing staff in the medical style of relating. What might these

Medical style of relating common in general hospitals	Medical and nursing objectives in hospice care
Impersonal, insensitive, detached, authoritarian	Interpersonal closeness, giving comfort through companionship
Withholding information, defensive	Open communication, efforts made to keep the patient fully informed
Lack of awareness of patient's needs	Special attention given to identifying patient's needs
Lack of permission and lack of provision for the emotional component of illness	Staff trained to include emotional care as a central activity

Figure 2.3: Differences in hospital and hospice care

pressures be? We will look at each profession one last time with this question in mind.

Influences that shape the behaviour of doctors

Experiences in training and the development of personal defences

The medical student does not just learn medicine. He or she is trained into a way of thinking, a way of dealing with natural empathy and emotional responding, and a way of relating. In other words, the student is shaped into the norms of a new *subculture*, and the pressure to conform is intense. The early exposure to clinical responsibility towards the end of training and in the early years as a house officer are believed by some to have a damaging effect. Both Stein (1978) and Hauser (1981) write on this theme. They illustrate several conflicts that most physicians will experience all their working lives, but which may be traumatically intense during the early years of hospital work; for example, the feelings of compassion – horror even – at the suffering and mutilation associated with severe illness, which is heightened by the young doctor's personal responsibility towards a case. In such situations, older doctors will both model and advise detachment. It will be experienced as a 'safe haven' from the emotionally stirring contact with distress.

The young doctor is inexperienced and gets by on basic knowledge. To him, therefore, the dread of mistakes will be high. Senior staff, patients and their families, can all apply pressures which intensify the dread. In the event of a mistake, particularly if it is a damaging one, there is much difficulty to be faced from the people involved, together perhaps with guilt and the uncomfortable feeling of incompetence. Inevitably the young doctor is pushed towards the defensive strategies that were described in the previous section. These are anxiety-reducing and help defuse the tension. For many, the defences become entrenched behavioural patterns without which intolerable stresses would be suffered.

When training is complete and a doctor stands alone with clinical responsibility, there is no doubt that the need for personal defences remains high. *To be directly exposed to the fright, anger, dependency and trust of the more distressed patients, and at the same time to be responsible for the outcome of their illness or surgery is a burden that few could bear for long.* This is obviously doubly so in very serious illnesses, where the doctor's decision can have profound consequences. Jason Brice, a neuro-surgeon, recently described some of his experiences in *The Sunday Times*. He talked of the effect on him of deciding whether to operate on aneurysms or tumours in the brain when the operation involved the risk of brain damage and severe impairment.

> 'People say that surgeons are a bit cold, a bit autocratic and unsympathetic with patients. I suspect a lot of this is part of a psychological barrier we put up to protect ourselves...I some-times feel that the strain of living with the decisions you have made creates greater stress than the operation itself...If she had been younger I would have taken the chance and pressed on. It would have been better if I had because the tumour bled and com-pressed the brain and she woke up with ghastly and gross dis-abilities. She would have been better off dead.'

Without doubt, practising in the isolated and unsupported setting which many doctors face will provoke much emotional upheaval unless there are effective psychological defences, the most likely of these being denial, distancing and the blocking of personal feeling. It seems reasonable to argue that doctors do need defences if they are to bear the burden of clinical responsibility. *However, what is rarely recog-nized is that the price paid for these defences is the neglect of psychological care.* This is inevitable in that their own defences reduce the capacity of doc-tors to see distress in other people, but at the same time the very same doctors, because of their clinical responsibility, are the people in the role of 'managers'. Putting it simply, the psychological needs of the people in distress remain unheeded because many doctors are unable to see them and so do nothing to help. Maguire (1985a and b) gives further illustrations of this point.

Medical mistakes and the community – some speculation

The issue of mistakes has figured prominently in much of our discus-sion, so let's ask how did the whole business of medical mistakes turn into the apparent millstone that it has become? Enter the general com-munity – us, that is. Collectively we are the source of a strong pressure on the medical profession which I believe has shaped its development over the last century and, with the promise of new medical technology, is taking an even more powerful grip. The pressure is our clinging to the myth of *medical infallibility* and the consequent expectation of a per-fect, mistake-free medical service.

The psychology of the situation works out in the following fashion. The threat of serious illness and injury looms over us all, but in our society it is buffered by denial and a tendency to 'project' special powers onto the medical profession. This term projection refers to a defensive, perceptual response in which an object of perception is ex-perienced as having qualities which the perceiver needs to see rather than that it actually possesses. The suggestion here, then, is that by and large the general community diminishes the threat of illness by the projection of infallibility onto the medical and nursing professions. Thus, there is a secure feeling because casualty will mend broken bodies after accidents, the physicians and the scanners will spot the threatening tumours and aneurysms, the transplants will replace the failed kidneys or hearts. In short, the doctors will know what is wrong, what to do, and how to do it.

Of course, *people do not consciously think like this – it is a felt thing. Many people feel doctors are infallible.* This diminishes the threat of illness and death. It is a widely held, comforting myth which allows us to disown responsibility for our own health and pass this on to the fan-tasized powers of the medical profession.

Now for a very important point. In its development, the medical profession has opted to collude with this myth even though it clearly *is* a myth. The reality of medicine includes confusions, doubts, mis-diagnoses, treatments which fail, treatments which cause damage, pro-cedural mistakes of one sort or another, notes, X-rays and blood tests which somehow go astray, errors in surgery, and poor communication between doctors, nurses and departments. Hospitals are cumbersome, bureaucratic institutions. They inevitably have a high 'mistake rate'. Illich (1976) notes, 'The US Department of Health, Education and Wel-fare calculates that 7% of all patients suffer compensatable injuries while hospitalized . . . the frequency of reported accidents in hospitals is higher than in all industries but mines and high-rise construction'. He goes on to claim that one out of five people admitted to a research hospital acquire damage of one sort or another as a result of investi-gative procedures or treatment. Of course, the staff in hospitals are well aware of the mistake rate and will be able to identify individual doctors or surgeons as mistake-prone, or particular wards will be referred to in terms which recognize high mistake rates ('Oh, Exeter

Ward, it's chaos up there.'). However, two sets of needs bring pressure to bear to keep this knowledge within the confines of the professions.

First, the general community *resists* knowing about mistakes. The myth of infallibility is functional as a defence and thus conflicting knowledge will be rejected. When knowledge is forced into the open there is usually much anger and accusation, as we can see from the growing number of court cases and articles hostile to medicine in the press. For this reason, plus the risk of raising anxiety, it is often argued by doctors that people are generally better off if they do not know.

Secondly, the medical profession clearly finds it imperative to protect itself from exposure and works hard to prevent general recognition of the rather more human and fallible realities of medicine. Why this is so important is speculative. Several writers suggest that it is to do with power. Illich has no doubts on this point: in his eyes, medicine is a radical, power-conserving monopoly. It controls large sums of money (estimated at 8.4% of the gross national product (GNP) in the United States during 1975, with a similar figure for other western European countries including Britain), has ever-growing power over the individual in society (sanctioning illness, judging fitness for occupation, recreations, etc.), governs its own affairs and, like other powerful monopolies, works to remove from the general community any power or knowledge which would rival the monopoly. In short, much of the behaviour of the medical profession is the same as any political organization which seeks to preserve its own power. Thus, the common defensive strategies (keeping doctor–patient contacts unpredictable and to a minimum, maximizing uncertainty by withholding information, refusing to comment on other doctors' work, etc.) may be

Objectives and needs	Strategies and defences
Accept clinical responsibility but minimize inevitable interpersonal stresses and pressures.	Avoid real relationships with patients by means of detachment, minimizing contact by absence and the 'interchangeable' doctor system. Personal defences, *e.g.* denial, projection of well being, etc.
Preserve the power position of the medical profession and individual doctors.	Maximize autocratic control by use of 'legal responsibility' device, and exclude other professions from decision-making roles.
Maintain the image of mistake-free, infallible medicine.	Control patients by withholding information, refusing to comment on other doctors' decisions and discrediting patients.

Figure 2.4: Hypothesized psychological basis of medical behaviour

seen as behaviour which has *evolved to protect the profession from being 'found out'*, since being found out breaks the myth of infallibility and erodes power.

Such behaviour is handed on to new members of the profession who find that it gives a more comfortable, defended feeling. The defensive medical behaviour patterns are, therefore, functional defences which are entrenched and very hard to change. Figure 2.4 sets out some of these ideas in summary form, but remember that these ideas are to be treated as theory, not proven fact, and the point of developing the theme is to show that the medical style of relating does not originate from indifference or malice on the part of individual doctors, but is a way of behaving which has evolved in relation to stresses, needs and objectives.

Influences that shape the behaviour of nurses

The same exercise can be extended to the nursing profession, that is, to assess the needs and objectives of the profession and derive how these have led to the evolution of defensive strategies.

The sparsity of research on the nursing profession makes the exercise rather more problematic for me, added to which two other factors obscure the situation. First, as I argued above, there is likely to be more individual variability within the nursing profession and secondly, the wave of change gathering within the profession makes it difficult to be definitive, since needs are changing as the scope of nursing expands.

A good proportion of trainee nurses that I have met in the last year are increasingly psychologically minded in the conceptualization of their work, as are many of the nursing journals and conferences. This very much complicates a simple analysis of the type attempted here, since it implies a major psychosocial movement. However, if you will at least allow me to present some ideas on the nursing profession as it has been up until recent years, I will leave you to judge the relevance of this analysis to the present day.

From the material available, we have already constructed a profile of the standard nurse of past years. She had a leaning towards the 'task-oriented' approach, was disciplined, deferred to medical authority and rarely challenged this on behalf of her patients. Rather, she was anxiously preoccupied about making mistakes and, although kindly, remained distanced from the people she cared for.

What shaped nursing into this pattern? An important factor must be the interpersonal nature of nursing. The nurse is forced into extended face-to-face contact with the people for whom she cares. Unlike doctors, she is not free to distance herself by absence. She is often in close personal contact with patients, engaged in intimate tasks on the wards day by day. She personally receives the impact of her patients' psychological states. This can be a very variable experience, ranging through fright, worry, sadness, grief, depression, anger, frustration, impatience, euphoria, gratitude, affection, trust and dependency. The nurse will inevitably respond with her own feelings, perhaps echoing those of her patients, or at other times reacting to the patients' psychological states. Face-to-face nursing can be a hard job emotionally because relationships will inevitably form and these can produce conflicts and emotionally stirring experiences. Menzies writes, 'The core of the anxiety situation for the nurse lies in her relation with the patient. The closer and more concentrated the relationship, the more the nurse is likely to experience the impact of anxiety'.

Bearing this in mind, we will expect to find that, over the years, the nursing profession will have developed ways of defusing this situation and protecting its members from the risk of traumatic involvement. These solutions will not have been so much thought out as 'felt out', that is, patterns of behaving will have developed which will leave nurses feeling more emotionally comfortable. I believe that because of the close personal contact and the inevitability of relationships forming, the nursing profession, in the past, has defended itself by avoiding direct clinical responsibility. This is the opposite defence of the doctors. *The hypothesis is that if there is to be clinical responsibility then relationships will be minimized. If there are to be relationships, clinical responsibility will be minimized.* Thus, nurses often appear to push away responsibility and redirect it at the doctors. Traditionally they have implemented medical orders in a mechanical way and related to doctors in a manner which shapes and maintains the position of doctors as sole bearers of clinical responsibility. *By so doing, they avoid the conflicting combination of close personal contact combined with clinical responsibility.* (I will remind you of my recognition that in reality not all nurses adhere to this pattern of defence, but we are talking about the general features of nursing behaviour where the profession is regarded as a whole. Also, it is clear that younger nurses are often unsure of their role and so keep to a safe, narrower approach.)

Of course, even though nurses have accepted closer contact with patients, this does not mean open, trouble-free relationships. These are often difficult, hence defensive behaviours have developed. The task-oriented style, for example, offers a means by which relationships may be kept under control and the level of intensity reduced to tolerable levels, by splitting a nurse's attention between a number of patients and ensuring that she is busily preoccupied with tasks. The shift system and rotation of duties also produces a distancing effect, which is, of course, related to the idea of nurses being relatively impersonal, standard, interchangeable units. Personal defences are in evidence with nurses as well as doctors. The insulating effect of detachment and denial are quite clearly important. In other words, the traditional approach to nursing makes sense if it is viewed as a *solution* to certain interpersonal stresses inherent in the nurse–patient relationship.

Objectives and needs	Strategies and defences
Accept closer personal contact with patients and the inevitability of relationships forming.	Avoid clinical responsibility, act to maintain doctors as sole decision-making body, perpetuate anxiety at challenging doctors or taking initiatives.
Minimize the stresses and pressures within the relationships.	Reduce the depth of relationships by the mechanistic task-oriented approach, organize nurses as 'interchangeable', maintain an atmosphere of disciplined non-involvement and pressure of work. Personal defences of detachment and denial.
Collude with the medical profession in preserving the image of mistake-free, infallible medicine.	Foster an anxious preoccupation concerning mistakes. Support doctors by refusing to comment on their performance or act as an alternative source of information to patients.
Regulate medical behaviour by covert means.	'Shape' and maintain doctors in the autocratic style, influence their decisions by suggestion and manipulative reporting of observations.

Figure 2.5:   Hypothesized psychological basis of nursing behaviour

Other aspects we should note have to do with the nurse–doctor relationship. In avoiding clinical responsibility, the nursing profession has had to 'prop up' the medical profession in its acceptance of responsibility, and so has been responsible for strengthening and maintaining medical authority. This has meant collusion with medical behaviour, aimed at the defence of medical power and the image of mistake-free medicine. Nurses have kept their silence while seeing the harsh effect of the insensitive medical style of relating. This inhibition has been bolstered by the *use* of an exaggerated concern over their own mistakes and a consequent fear of taking initiatives. But we must remember Stein's point that nurses do also exert covert control by manipulative tactics. Figure 2.5 puts these ideas together.

Positive trends

Before leaving the topic of doctor–patient and nurse–patient relation ships we need to ask how relevant the preceding sections are. Do they not refer to a past era? I think that a better outlook would be to say that they refer to a passing era. Few people working in the health care professions will have problems in finding examples that will confirm that the distant and evasive style of relating is still common in hospitals. However, things are very definitely changing, and it is an equally common experience to find patients and their partners who feel that they *have* been cared for in an open, supportive manner, and have been kept well informed and encouraged to ask questions by both nurses and doctors. In the last few months I have received spontaneous positive comments from patients in a renal unit, on a coronary care rehabilitation programme, and being treated in a plastic and reconstructive surgery unit. This balances the regular spontaneous negative comments from some other specialties. We are nowhere near a point where self-congratulation is in order but, compared with the situation of ten or more years ago, things are very much on a positive trend. This certainly applies to nursing and there are some signs that it also applies to the rising generation of doctors.

Relationships between the nursing and the medical professions are changing too. In explaining aspects of therapeutic nursing Wright (1991) comments: 'The general aims of these and other principles suggested is to devolve the maximum power, control and accountability of nursing to those nurses who are in practice . . . For nurses to act therapeutically, they need not only a method of organizing care to do so, but a supportive organizational structure which facilitates them'.

I know of no examples wherein complete hospitals have achieved this move away from the 'handmaiden' ethos in nursing, but I could take you to several individual units in various hospitals which have achieved the conversion. In these units the nurses are respected as autonomous co-professionals, who offer a service which they have designed in terms of their own values and frames of reference.

Hazards

The logic of the above arguments centres on the notion that both doctors and nurses acquire defences against the stresses inherent in their jobs. One of the key defences is interpersonal distance from patients. This book is concerned to promote an approach to care termed psychological care, in which nurses especially and – to a degree – doctors, become much more closely involved with their patients – actually striving to narrow the interpersonal gap. Thus a very important question will be: does this not expose the nurses and doctors to more stress and so put them at greater risk? The answer is simple. Yes, it does. Therefore, the contents of Chapter 7 concerning self-care and support are of great importance to you if you are to become involved with psychological care.

DOES THE PSYCHOLOGICAL DISTRESS ASSOCIATED WITH PHYSICAL ILLNESS MATTER?

The theme developed in this chapter has been to do with the psychological effects of illness and injury on both patients and the people caring for them. We have noted that a significant proportion of ill and injured people do become psychologically stressed. It has also been noted that the stressors involved may be related to the direct effects of illness and injury, or to do with the organization of their care and the style of relating and information exchange that doctors and nurses adopt.

In this last section I want to return to the issue of the psychological reactions of people to their illness or injury. How concerned should we be about stress, distress and actual psychological disturbance in patients and their partners? Other than causing discomfort, do they really matter?

If I had extended the quotation from the *Lancet* given earlier by one more line, you would have read, 'We now have ample evidence of the high prevalence of undetected and untreated psychiatric disorders. Does it matter? *Probably it does.*' I will be more decisive on this point. It very definitely does matter in terms of physical recovery, the rate and the extent of rehabilitation, and the protection of people from psychic pain and anguish which makes a heavy burden on top of their physical discomforts. I shall examine the issue from several viewpoints.

The effect of psychological distress on physical health and recovery

The article in the *Lancet* makes the point that psychological distress has a negative effect on recovery from illness. What evidence is there for this? A large-scale investigation provided convincing evidence of this point some years ago. Querido (1959) studied 1630 patients admitted over a period of years to the municipal hospital in Amsterdam. Assessments were made of a physical, social and psychological nature, the latter being used to categorize the patients as either distressed or non-distressed (distressed signified 'social or psychic tensions too heavy to bear'). The relevant data for our purposes were collected six months after discharge. The patients were assessed as 'in a satisfactory or unsatisfactory medical condition', the latter category comprising a return of former symptoms or continued suffering of former complaints. Of the people who were assessed as psychologically distressed, 70.4% were in an unsatisfactory condition medically six months later, whereas of those classified as non-distressed, only 29.6% were in an unsatisfactory medical condition after the same time lapse.

Taking a different perspective, of the total 1630 cases, 1128 had been given a favourable medical prognosis, yet only 660 of these had lived up to this expectation. The majority of those who failed to improve were psychologically distressed. In fact, Querido counsels caution in leaping to dramatic conclusions. Nevertheless, he allows himself this statement: 'It is plain that such a mental attitude on the part of the patient reduces the efficiency of the hospital staff by almost a half'.

Wai *et al.* (1981) followed a group of 285 home dialysis patients for 18 months or more, and assessed a range of variables to test for any link with survival rates. Level of depression proved to be a significant predictor of physical survival, more so than physiological measures. Similarly, Ruberman *et al.* (1984) investigated factors influencing the three-year mortality rate in 2320 men who had experienced a first myocardial infarct. Those men assessed as being socially isolated and having a high degree of life stress had more than four times the risk of death from a second infarct. Note that the primary objective of psychological care as it is taught in this book is to prevent patients from becoming isolated with distressed feelings, and to reduce the stress of illness and hospitalization.

In recent years, there has been a growing interest in the relationship between psychological wellbeing and the functioning of the immune system. Basically, the notion is that immunocompetence is influenced by the prevailing hormonal bias in a person. It appears likely that certain psychological states, including long-term stress, long-term feelings of helplessness and hopelessness, and extended grief induce impaired immune efficiency via the hormones generated in such psychological states. Cortisol, in particular, is thought to affect the maturation and functioning of T-lymphocytes and natural killer cells.

O'Leary (1990) and Kennedy *et al.* (1988) reviewed the known links between acute and chronic stressors and immune function. The research included evidence of immunodeficiency in stressed caregivers who were looking after victims of Alzheimer's disease. Also (take note, young doctors), it included research which showed a fall-off in immunocompetence in medical students in their run up to exams.

If immune function is impaired, resistance to infection and also to the onset of cancer is reduced. Thus, if there is long-term stress associated with illness, injury or caregiving, then there may be secondary health effects as a result. In other words, everything needs to be done to reduce stress and maintain long-term support at times of serious illness or injury. An editorial in the *Lancet* (1985) took up this theme and noted that survival in cancer and the severity of autoimmune diseases such as rheumatoid arthritis are influenced by psychological state. The mediating variable, it was accepted, is quite likely to be immune functioning, which varies in relation to psychological state. Hence, as you will see, the editor regarded counselling and support during illness as an important determinant of outcome. This was quite a remarkable article, coming as it did from the 'bastions' of medicine.

Lastly, we'll take a glimpse of the expanding field concerning pre-surgical psychological states and the physical response to surgery. Evidence has accrued for some time now that recovery from surgery is influenced by the general psychological state of the patient prior to surgery. Here we are not just talking of emotional state but also levels of knowledge and prepared strategies for coping. Thus Ridgeway and Mathews (1982) in their study of various strategies for assisting people undergoing surgery, demonstrated that if the general psychological condition of women undergoing hysterectomy was modified by educational counselling or coaching in coping strategies, then in comparison to patients left on their own without such stress-reducing contact, there was less preoperative anxiety and worrying and (importantly) less need of analgesia as indicated by nursing records, and less postoperative pain. These differences held up after discharge, when it was shown that the groups without the supportive intervention experienced more pain and more symptoms. Similarly, Ray and Fitzgibbon (1981) found that preoperative stress was positively correlated with postoperative stress and pain in cholecystectomy patients.

Failure to comply with treatment

Another important facet in the relationship between psychological state and recovery from illness is the *failure to comply with necessary treatment regimens, dietary restrictions and behavioural requirements for the best chances of recovery*. Again, a reminder about the introductory case in Chapter 1. The subject, if you remember, became angry in his distress. He broke his plaster on a couple of occasions and probably reduced the chances of his arthrodesis healing, since he almost certainly stressed the recently pinned joint. With this and so many other cases, it is quite evident that because of low morale and depressed or angry feelings towards the situation, people behave in a way which is antagonistic to healing or disruptive to medical treatment.

Dialysis patients are high in the league of compliance problems. They have tremendously difficult restrictions on fluid intake to comply with, sometimes as little as 1000 ml/day. They must also regulate with great care the type and quantity of food they take. In fact, failure to comply with these restrictions is often an early sign of emotional disturbance. A good proportion of the cases referred to me for psychological therapy at the Exeter Kidney Unit were initially seen on the basis of their having difficulty in keeping to their fluid limits, thus becoming fluid overladen. Later, it became clear that this was just a sign of more profound difficulties of adjustment and grief.

The point here is that, when people do not understand, are out of communication with their doctors and nurses (even though in their presence), are low in morale or are emotionally disturbed, they often hazard their recovery and make new medical problems by abandoning the behaviour which gives them the best chance of recovery. Extending the example given, a dialysis patient who is restricted to drinking 500 ml of fluid a day but who drinks 1500 ml will accumulate 3000 ml of excess fluid in his body between dialysis sessions. Much of the fluid adds to the volume of the blood system and literally physically stretches the heart and vascular system. Eventually the muscular tissues of the heart change in response, and permanent damage is done. Some die of heart failure as a consequence of non-compliance with fluid limits, so wiping out the effort of physical care.

Kaplan De Nour (1981) noted that in a sample of 100 dialysands, about 75% were not able fully to comply with fluid and dietary regimens. This was associated with the observation that at least 50% had episodes of depression. Ley (1982b) in a very concise, useful review on matters related to compliance and communication, reports studies indicating that typical levels of non-compliance for diets and other forms of medical advice is about 50% of the population of patients. Ley cites Barofsky (1980), who established levels of non-compliance associated with specific drug treatments, e.g. antibiotics, 52%; antituberculosis, 43%; antihypertensive, 61%. In fact, some people give up their medical treatments because they directly cause psychological difficulties or unacceptable discomfort. The cost can be high for the individual and for the hospitals. Ley lists reliable surveys in which 20% of hospital admissions could be attributed to non-compliance with medical advice (see Chapter 4).

A final example from the field of diabetes. Unless diabetics maintain good self-care, especially in terms of diet and good blood-sugar control, then microvascular deterioration may develop. In the long term this leads to retinopathy, lower-limb circulatory problems and renal failure. Both Chase *et al.* (1989) and Brinchmann-Hansen *et al.* (1992) produced follow-up studies in which higher average blood-sugar levels were found to be correlated with more advanced retinopathy. Unfortunately, diet and blood-sugar control are usually early 'compliance casualties' of low morale, stress and emotional upheaval. Similarly, failure to understand the significance of self-care in diabetes can produce compliance failure and early microvascular problems such as renal failure.

The effect of psychological distress on doctor/nurse utilization

Balint (1964) argues that where neither the doctor nor the patient recognizes that the latter is in psychological trouble, then the two parties may spend much more time than normal in the business of physical investigation and treatment. People will engage a doctor's attention on matters of *physical* health as a means of securing supportive contact when, in fact, there may be no physical pathology present. Tessler *et al.* (1976) measured both psychological distress and the number of visits to a general practitioner made between this assessment and the passing of one year. There was a positive relationship between the presence of psychological distress and the consultation with a doctor on matters concerning apparent physical symptoms. Rather more alarmingly perhaps, Rawlings (1972) investigated the records of 235 people who were judged to be presenting psychological disorders. They turned out to be operation-prone, having logged 453 operations of which 50% revealed no disease process. Similarly, many cardiologists have spent much time conducting physical investigations of complaints and heart pains which are of a psychogenic nature.

The pain clinics and orthopaedic hospitals give excellent examples of this effect too. The postoperative experience of pain and the long-term pain from injuries to the spine – lower back pain – are known to be amplified by anxiety and depression. Presenting the physical complaint of pain may be an indirect way of presenting a state of psychological distress. Alternatively, the presence of anxiety or depression is known to increase the impact of pain and diminish adaptive behaviour (Bond, 1980; Sternbach, 1974). The exasperation that is a familiar experience with orthopaedic surgeons seems to originate from the fact that they encounter a good number of cases where they suspect complaints of pain are psychologically based, yet they cannot extend their ideas of care beyond that of physical treatment, so a state of impasse is created.

A rather interesting study by Schlesinger *et al.* (1983) compared the utilization of medical services in two groups of people. These were a group who received psychological assistance through a mental health care programme, and a second group who had no psychological assistance. The utilization of medical services (as indexed by medical insurance costs) in the group who were not receiving psychological care was significantly higher than those who did receive psychological care. In other words, relatively cheap psychological care cut down the demand for expensive medical treatment.

A position has been reached where we can point to three conclusions in answer to the question, 'does it matter?' It does matter, because:

1. Recovery from illness and mortality rates can be influenced by psychological distress.
2. Compliance with treatment regimens and medical advice can be diminished by psychological distress.
3. The level of utilization of medical and nursing services tends to increase where physical illness is associated with psychological stress. This places a burdensome and expensive demand on those

services and creates additional work, which is often irrelevant to the central problem.

GENUINE CARE – CARING VS. TECHNICAL MEDICINE

We need to think for a moment of the underlying moral philosophy of medicine and nursing. Without getting too involved, we have to ask what is the real point of it all? Two extreme alternatives should be named. The first I will label 'technical medicine' and the other 'caring medicine' to illustrate the point. The differences are probably obvious to you already. The aims of technical medicine are to deal with faulty body parts and functions and restore these physical systems to normal functioning, or at least to halt deterioration. Technical medicine does not include in its span of attention the personal needs of the individual beyond the minimum necessary to facilitate treatment regimens. To a large extent, the 'person in the body' is an inconvenience and an irrelevance, since the requirements for optimum technical medicine often clash with the requirements of the person. To this end, people and their needs are banished by turning them into something less distracting called 'patients'. A patient is not directly equivalent to a person and can be treated in ways which are less inconvenient for technical medicine.

Caring medicine, at the other end of the scale, involves educational, psychological, social and medical approaches. Here the aim is to minimize the trauma of illness by giving instruction and information, providing supportive intervention to help with psychological reactions and social difficulties when they arise, and, of course, standard medical procedures. The difference is that these procedures are not pursued without attention to the other needs, since this produces an outcome which is often psychologically, socially and morally unacceptable. Because in the pursuit of medical excellence technical medicine often proves to be the opposite of caring, it leads to the inevitable neglect of psychological needs and the likelihood of people being *made distressed* in addition to the effects of the illness.

Conversely, caring medicine is an ideal, with the aim of minimizing the damaging impact of illness and actively buffering the individual from additional stresses created by hospitalization and medical procedures. I recognize that it is an ideal and that arguments about manpower and resources must be heeded. Nevertheless, it seems quite indefensible to me that the medical and nursing professions should opt for technical medicine and remain uncaring in their basic approach. It is morally bizarre to create a set of problems and great distress as a consequence of a narrow attack on another set of problems, which, as we will see, is a very prevalent situation. People who are seriously ill or injured are vulnerable and powerless. Technical medicine, with its associated insensitivity, sometimes amounts to a psychological attack upon them, whereas caring medicine represents a recognition of their vulnerability and a balanced endeavour to meet all their needs.

The question we began with asked, 'does the psychological distress matter?' Here we find a different type of answer to those above. That is, it matters if there is a concern to be humane and to reduce distress in every possible way – and this surely is the only way. In order to be humane there must be psychological care. Our task now is to establish how this should be done. The next chapter gives you an overview.

CHAPTER 3

Developing a Scheme of Psychological Care

Hopefully, I will now have made clear why I consider the development of psychological care in the general hospitals to be so important. Our next step is to consider the basis for constructing a scheme of psychological care which you can put to use on your own ward or unit.

Please note the careful use of the word 'scheme'. You may remember from the first chapter that one of my criteria for the effective provision of psychological care is that an explicit scheme has to be in operation. This point needs emphasizing, because giving psychological care is not just a matter of being more caring in an interpersonal sense, but it involves various psychological interventions which must be organized to anticipate and integrate with medical events. If, at present, you believe that you are providing psychological care on your ward but have no answer to the question 'can you describe your scheme of psychological care?' then, for me at least, you need to think about upgrading things. Psychological care has to be planned out in advance, it cannot just be reactive.

FIVE PRINCIPLES FOR DEVELOPING PSYCHOLOGICAL CARE

One complication looms over us at this stage. Specialties, units or wards all have different types of work to do. They do this in varying contexts, with differing lengths of contact and with differing patterns of relationship with patients. For our purposes, this means that schemes of psychological care have to be individually tailored to cater for such differences. My aim here is to make clear general principles and practices which *you* must then interpret to fit your own circumstances. For example, the approach taken by the 33 nurses in our local renal unit, who serve a slowly changing population of about 200 patients (often over a period of ten or more years) will differ to some extent from that taken by the nurses in our gynaecological wards, with

45

their relatively fast turnover of many more patients. Even so, psychological care in these two units will need to be organized around common principles.

Having now spent some years exploring psychological care in various medical settings, I find that the following principles help to clarify the realities that any scheme of psychological care must deal with:

- Serious illness, disability or disfigurement *inevitably* cause psychological reactions or psychological disturbance, for which psychological care is necessary.
- Psychological care *underpins* the effectiveness of many physical treatments – it should not be seen as a luxury but as a basic component of treatment which carries equal priority.
- Psychological care should be designed in order to *minimize* the stressful impact of illness, injury and treatment. It should also be designed to *prevent* doctor/nurse/hospital-induced stress.
- Psychological care therefore needs to be *preventive* in emphasis dealing (where practical) with all patients and partners and not just 'psychological casualties'.
- Because of the numbers of patients involved, *nurses* and *therapists* have to be the front-line workers in psychological care.

These five principles state the rationale for this book. Although I am a clinical psychologist and, therefore, a psychological therapist by training, I am not arguing for hundreds of psychologists to be taken on by the general hospitals in order for them to provide individual psychological therapy for selected patients. Quite the opposite. One of the purposes of psychological care is to *reduce* the number of people who need psychological therapy as a result of illness or injury.

The central idea is straightforward. As part of the routine of ward or clinic life, the staff *normally present* should include certain basic psychological interventions in their work. These will be structured around the reality established in Chapter 2, namely, that physical illness and injury provoke parallel psychological reactions and, in many cases, actual psychological disturbance (that is, tension, anxiety-laden thought and overwhelming emotion). Unless these reactions are identified, respected and included within the care regimen, then not only is the quality of care impoverished but efforts to restore physical health may well be undermined. Similarly, the experiences of becoming ill or injured, being hospitalized and, possibly, disabled or disfigured, can all be very stressing. Such stress can either be reduced or amplified, depending on the type of care received. In short, we have a choice. It is that of a care regimen which is psychologically negligent versus a regimen of active, planned psychological care. In psychological care, the whole emphasis is therefore on the recognition and prevention of stress and psychological distress. Without this, many people are likely to become needlessly stressed during their encounter with illness and hospitals.

Getting away from the 'casualty' model

Without schemes of psychological care, hospitals have tended to fall back on the 'psychological casualty model'. The assumption in the casualty model is that people in hospital are basically fine unless they externalize distress or show disturbed behaviour, in which case they are singled out and regarded as psychological casualties. In such cases, an outside expert in the form of a psychologist or psychiatrist is called in to deal with the problem, or it is suppressed by drugs. In other words, before receiving psychological assistance, a person needs the 'ticket' of significant psychological distress; there is no attempt to prevent this distress in the first place.

This will not do. In many medical subcultures there is neither permission nor encouragement to show or communicate psychological distress – quite the opposite, in fact. Often, the emphasis, as we have seen in Chapter 2, is on staff *not* seeing, or denying, the psychological impact of serious illness, injury and hospitalization. In other words, the patients are encouraged by the general atmosphere to hide their feelings. Effectively, they are left alone to deal with their psychological reactions to illness *unless* they have some kind of breakdown. Well-run schemes of psychological care will make such a situation a thing of the past.

Implications – nurses as key workers in a two-tier system

Where does this lead us in terms of creating schemes of psychological care? An important implication is to do with the issue of who organizes and provides the psychological care. Clearly, it cannot be undertaken by a handful of outside 'experts'. For one thing, there are not enough of them. Although health psychology (a branch of clinical psychology) has developed enormously in recent years, in real terms the number of people in this profession is trivial. There are fewer than 2500 clinical psychologists of all specialties in post in the UK at present, and only a small proportion work as health psychologists. Psychiatrists working in the health psychology field are no more numerous. On the other hand, there are approximately 350 000 nurses working in the UK. They are present on a 24-hour basis throughout the hospitals. There are also smaller but significant numbers of occupational, speech, radio and physiotherapists. Medical social workers must also be kept in mind. It is therefore to the nurses, with a degree of assistance from the therapist and social work professions, that we must turn to for the actual provision of psychological care – *only they have sufficient numbers and contact with patients to handle the job on a day-to-day basis.*

There isn't enough time

None of these professions is short of things to do, of course. In fact, most will say they are already inundated with work and the likelihood of finding time to take on additional work is remote. Maybe. But let me make an initial comment on the issue of time through a short case illustration:

Case study

James was referred to a clinical psychologist following admission with dysrhythmia or, possibly, a second mycardial infarct. It emerged in the assessment interview that, when he had recently been discharged from his ward after treatment for his first infarct, there had been no effective instruction on how he should go about rehabilitation and self-care. No literature was offered, virtually no verbal instruction was given and no long-term support was arranged. There was no psychological care pro- gramme whatsoever (note: information and education are an intrinsic part of psychological care). As a result, James had set about creating his own rehabilitation programme which was based on the idea that 'I can overcome this by effort of will'. He was driving himself very hard physically, including running several miles a day. The problem was that he was doing this in the context of an ongoing divorce and was expressing much of his anger and adverse reactions through this exer- cise. He was thus stressing his heart.

Being rather disbelieving of the claim by James that no worthwhile information had been given to him, the psychologist checked with the nurses. They confirmed the position. It was a general medical ward and they were really exceptionally busy and just did not have time for post-coronary psychological care. James had been discharged with a few general instructions such as 'take things easy at first, then try a bit of exercise'. Notice one thing, though. *While the nurses could not find the time to give any meaningful psychological care, they did find the time to read- mit him for a whole week of general nursing care. This was enormously more time-expensive than providing two short post-coronary counselling sessions during the first admission – which could well have prevented this second admission.*

It would be impertinent for me, as someone who has never done a day's nursing in my life, to start organizing nurses' work for them. It does seem, though, that this case was handled with spectacular inefficiency, which was maintained by clinging to the familiar myth 'we are too busy.' This is of great significance in the general discussion of whether or not nurses should include psychological care in their work.

I have discussed the issue of time and the nursing workload with a considerable number of senior nurses. Interestingly, they almost always take a critical view of cases like this. Summing up their position, they say, 'Yes, the nurses are very busy – but busy doing what?' The implication is that in wards such as that on which James was nursed, the nurses are often required to give their time to low-priority tasks, or jobs which patients could well do for themselves, thereby leaving no time for other types of care. I am acutely aware of this in some of the outpatient settings in which I work. While nurses could readily be giving psychological care (especially educational and supportive counselling), they spend much of their time doing low-grade clerking work and making tea for the consultants.

These days I feel confident that nurses can take on psychological care because it is clearly an investment of time which will often save time. In considering its introduction, psychological care should not be seen as just another chore but as something of importance to be 'prioritized' in relation to all other demands. Sometimes, for any one patient, it will be top priority and take the time available. At other times, treatments, procedures and basic physical care must take priority. As a last comment on this point, I mention again having watched an enthusiastic senior nurse slowly introduce a scheme of psychological care into her nursing plan. This was not in a quiet ward where the nurses had little to do, but in a hard-pressed haemodialysis unit. It can be done and it is worth it.

Well then, you might reasonably ask, if nurses are carrying the burden of operating a scheme of psychological care what are clinical psychologists supposed to be doing to justify their existence? This is where the two-tier system comes in. Basically, the psychologist takes on the role of co-designer, trainer, adviser and associate psychological therapist to a scheme of psychological care which the nurses will run. That is, the psychologist is a resource and support person to the nurses. The last thing psychologists should do is to impose demands on nurses to provide psychological care and then 'disappear'. It has to be accepted that nurses are trained as nurses and are not in a position to meet demands of this type unassisted – although, in my own experience, they are usually enthusiastic to set up schemes like this. The approach we have adopted at Exeter Renal Unit has evolved on this cooperative basis. It may be helpful to recount a brief history of how the development took place.

My first contact with the unit was in 1978, when I was approached to help with a patient who was having psychological difficulties converting back to haemodialysis after a transplant failure. Once the contact was established, the unit and I slotted into a permanent working relationship wherein I was cast as psychological specialist on call, helping with psychological casualties in the haemodialysis and transplant programme. I was quite happy with this until, with the experience and research results outlined in Chapter 2, I began to realize that many of the problems which came to light in the therapy sessions resulted from the lack of those types of intervention from the staff which I now call psychological care. At that point, the unit became the 'patient' and changing the way things were done by nurses and doctors became the primary objective. Fortunately, I was not alone in seeing the shortcomings – the sister in charge was also painfully aware that things had to change (Woodhams, 1984). Accordingly, we worked together. Her basic position was 'we are trained as nurses, not psychologists, so there is no point in you just complaining about things, show us what needs to be done on the psychological side, set up some training and be around when we need help'. It seemed a fair deal. Thus, Polly Woodhams and I have worked together on the project since then. I have specified the psychological ideals and suggested possible approaches. She has taken these suggestions and converted them into something which is workable within the constraints and resources of her unit.

Thus, the approach to psychological care at Exeter Renal Unit has been a joint nurse–psychologist venture. I have been on hand to suggest, guide, train and, as part of the scheme, be available as a psychological therapist for those patients whose needs go beyond care into actual therapy.

THE ELEMENTS OF PSYCHOLOGICAL CARE

So, on to the nuts and bolts of it all. Figure 3.1 sets out the basic components of the full scheme of psychological care. At the centre of the scheme is the task of monitoring the psychological state and psychological needs of the patient. The outcome from this ongoing task determines what aspect of psychological care will be pursued at any one time, and also evokes consideration as to whether or not a patient's needs go beyond the care procedures and, thus, assistance with psychological therapy should be sought. Note, incidentally, that it will be the nurses running the scheme who will judge whether or not to involve the help of the psychologist, although ideally they will discuss the issue with both the patient involved and medical colleagues.

Most of the chapters which follow are written as 'tutorials' in each of the psychological care skills or strategies named in Figure 3.1. For the purposes of providing an overview, I will give a brief introduction to each of these in this chapter. Note that I will refer to nurses much of the time. Please understand that this is not meant to exclude other professions: I wish to encourage people from all the health care professions to develop their interests and skills in this work. However, I do this since my suggestion is that because of their numbers and pattern of contact with patients, nurses, in particular, should make psychological care an explicit component of their work. Keep in mind, though, that whether psychological care is given by a nurse, social worker, occupational therapist, speech therapist or whoever, the skills are the same.

When operated fully in a situation such as a renal unit, the scheme of psychological care comprises the following elements:

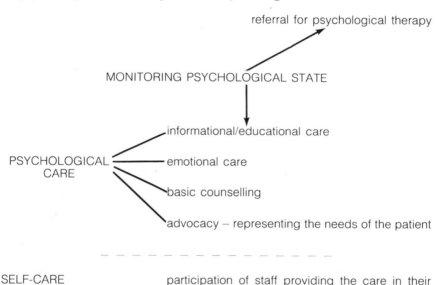

Figure 3.1: The psychological care scheme

Monitoring psychological care

The nurses become the psychological 'ears and eyes' of the unit. They are trained to be aware of the psychological condition of their patients and to check it regularly. They use a straightforward approach based on questions like 'how is he coping, are there signs of emotional change or distress, is he perceiving the situation in realistic terms and is the behaviour appropriate for the situation? What are the current anxieties and problems?'

A very brief written report (ideally, worked out with the patient) should be lodged with records every two weeks or so to encourage a proper formulation of observations and thoughts. Psychiatric classification is not wanted. What is required, however, is a constructive response from each nurse based on her observations. She is responsible for ensuring that action is taken with one or more of the care strategies given below.

Informational and educational care

Lack of information and understanding, together with inappropriate or contradictory information, becomes a major source of stress and distress for many people in general hospitals. Thus, a major contribution to stress reduction can be made through the full and regular provision of information. Consequently, informational/educational care is presented to nurses as the most basic element of psychological care.

The nurses are trained to regard information exchange as having much the same character as the physical routines of nursing, for example the regular turning of bedridden people. It is emphasized that information exchange cannot be done once and be considered complete. The objective in informational care is to maintain the information a patient and his partner hold at a level of accuracy and completeness such that they have realistic expectations about the course of events for them in the immediate future. This will include information on the procedures to be used, likely experiences, levels of pain and disability, side effects, the general thinking of the doctors with regard to the clinical problem, and an honest review of the possible outcomes. The important word here is 'maintain', because keeping people who are ill (and usually anxious) informed is a more difficult task than informing healthy people on everyday issues. Selective forgetting, anxious or hopeful distortion, misinterpretation and confusion, all rapidly erode the accuracy and completeness of information given in a medical setting. The nurses are endlessly reminded that 'something told does not automatically mean something heard and accurately remembered'. Thus, informational care involves routinely checking what a patient knows and intervening as necessary to build up and maintain information and understanding. In tutorials, we talk of 'professionalizing' information exchange by means of the IIFAC scheme (see Chapter 4) and by planning informational care so that it takes place after ward rounds or before procedures and treatments.

Supporting this effort, much work also goes into the preparation of educational materials for general educational purposes, so that standard information is delivered consistently and the time drain on nurses is minimized. This is especially important when patients have much to learn personally, as with home haemodialysis, after a diagnosis of diabetes, or following a myocardial infarct.

Emotional care

Training in emotional care is based on the premise that serious illness almost inevitably provokes emotional upheaval. However, in the majority of cases, these emotional responses are aspects of normal, predictable, emotional processes. We are, so to speak, designed to be anxious if we are exposed to threat, angry if frustrated, and to grieve if something of great importance to us is lost, whether it be a role in life, a relationship or part of our body. Therefore, such emotional activity should be expected, valued and respected, rather than construed as something alarming to be attacked and subdued by one means or another. Rather than bland reassurances, blocking strategies or immediate recourse to the drugs cupboard, care procedures are taught which facilitate the expression of feeling and so aid emotional processes – since expressing emotion is one of the main means of 'working through' to less emotionally laden states.

Emotional care is always made available should crises occur, but its real input is at the low-key, everyday preventive level. The nurse will take the initiative and regularly make time to ask her patients how things are and how they are feeling (emotionally, that is). She will inquire whether they have issues they would like to share and talk through. As a result, patients will not be isolated with their emotional reactions, nor should they be embarrassed, because the nurse will be at ease and communicate that sharing feelings is regarded as important – that it is valued by the staff.

In emotional care, the key skill is in providing a relationship and a setting which helps along the emotional processes set in motion by the impact of the illness or injury. A nurse giving emotional care aims to relate in a manner which communicates permission, acceptance and, above all, *safety*. Patients receiving her care should never feel a need to suppress emotion. They should never feel ashamed of their emotion nor believe themselves to be an oddity or a nuisance. With this close nurse–patient relationship as a basis, the distressed patient can choose (and it has to be their choice) to share their feelings and the thoughts or memories that have triggered them, with the nurse. Her role is to provide the patient with a genuine opportunity for the expression of feeling, the essence of which is the *experience of being listened to and understood*. It is through such expression of feeling that emotional processes can proceed. The provision of emotional care gives a sense of support and companionship, which can be invaluable to anxious or distressed people.

Counselling

As nurses become more experienced and confident with psychological work, the care role is extended to include basic counselling. Training is either internal or external by means of continuing nurse education courses. The counselling is of an elementary type and not intended as a substitute therapy. The aim in training is to shift nurses away from giving advice to an approach in which they assist a patient to talk through issues, help elaborate the perception of a situation and help clarify the options available in solving problems.

Representing the patient's psychological needs – advocacy and referral

Psychological care depends upon the nurse using her judgement and responding to the psychological needs of her patients. She takes initiatives, not in a competitive fashion that undermines medical authority, but rather in an open, collaborative manner. The nurse has to go beyond the passive role of monitoring psychological state, and 'do something about it'. Her role is that of representing each case in a flexible, negotiating way, acting on behalf of her patients, for example to acquire and relay information from a surgeon, or to make sure that presurgical anxieties are dealt with by adequate premedication and assistance from a psychologist with anxiety-management training. In this scheme, it is the nurse who will usually make the initial moves that lead to referral to a psychologist – after all, she more than anyone else is likely to know how the patient *really* is. That is her role in the scheme.

Personal support

Finally, nurses are taught to regard seeking support for themselves as a major professional responsibility. This is because involvement in this work requires regular exposure to the distress of others and, without adequate support, stress-related problems can slowly develop. The support systems advised are of both an individual and a group nature. A support network offers an immediate way of dealing with difficulties, and regular scheduled support meetings can be used as a means for dealing with less urgent business and for providing a safe place to monitor personal stress levels.

Where do therapists fit in?

Having indicated that the nursing profession is in the best position to take on the main part of regular psychological care work in hospitals, I want to emphasize again that this is not at all an excluding position. In some circumstances, therapists are the primary point of contact between a patient and the health services. After a stroke, for example, speech therapists may maintain lengthy relationships with the patients and their partners. In the coronary rehabilitation programme in which I assist, both the physiotherapist and the occupational therapist spend much time with the people on the programme, and are well placed to take on basic psychological care duties. In such situations, if the therapists do not take on responsibility for providing psychological care, the likelihood is that no-one will. It therefore falls to the therapists to challenge the psychological neglect by implementing the basic elements of a scheme of psychological care.

In similar terms, many therapists in my acquaintance have an interest in psychological care and would happily integrate with a programme run by nurses, undertaking some informational and supportive emotional care work, for example.

What part do doctors play?

In the scheme of psychological care developed above, the complementary role of the medical profession is crucial. Doctors can contribute in several ways. First, they can ensure that a service of psychological care is available, or at least being developed, for their patients. Secondly, they can ask to be kept informed on which nurse is providing psychological care for which patient and request occasional reports on progress. Thirdly, doctors must take a helping initiative with informational care by informing the nurses of the current medical plan for a patient and, thereafter, of any variation in this plan. Then the nurses can plan informational care effectively. Overall, unless doctors keep the targets of psychological care in mind and do their best to integrate their medical work with the psychological work of the nurses, they can do much to undermine a psychological care scheme.

On occasions, members of the medical profession may wish to be directly involved in psychological care work themselves. This is always welcome, assuming, that is, that the doctor has had appropriate training. In general, though, it is unlikely because of the huge case load that many bear and the resulting severe limitations on the time available for each patient under care. (I once asked an oncologist how much time he had available for individual patients. After thought, he said 'about one hour a year'.) Nevertheless, doctors do need some instruction in psychological care in order to value and complement the approach. Ideally, this is something which can be started at medical school.

Does the patient have an active role?

In our approach to psychological care at Exeter Renal Unit, we do not see the role of patient as simply that of a passive recipient of care. At times, for example before a kidney transplant, we need them to be active in engaging staff to answer specific questions to do with their case. This has led to the formulation of an informal 'contract' of psychological care which can be summarized as below.

We aim to create a situation in which:

1. We do not seek passive patients but people who are 'associates' in the health care team and are willing to take part in the planning and problem solving linked to their case whenever possible.
2. These people are asked to honour the following responsibilities in terms of education and self-care:
    (a) to use the informational care facility in order to keep informed, thus reducing the stress of not knowing and allowing them participation in medical objectives and decisions;
    (b) to use the educational facility in order to achieve self-sufficiency in dialysis techniques and an understanding of dietary and physical self-care strategies;
    (c) to use the emotional care and support facility in order to prevent isolation with stress and distress.

Although they will vary in detail for differing medical settings, similar 'contracts' will have relevance in most places where seriously ill or injured people are given care.

Community and practice nurses

All the talk thus far has been to do with general hospitals. Should this be interpreted as suggesting that psychological care belongs only in the hospitals? Emphatically no. However, my development work has been in the hospitals and my emphasis on the creation of a scheme run by a staff of nurses means that, as described, the exact approach to psychological care will not be suitable at the primary care level. However, as any readers who work as practice or community nurses will know, there is a great need for psychological care among some of your patients. The principles of psychological care will be the same, but, because of the very different nurse/staff ratios, the targets will have to be tailored to your local needs and circumstances. Selective individual work may prove to be more practical than the preventive contact with all patients envisaged, say, for a renal unit.

FINAL COMMENTS

Both nursing and medicine are still evolving, and so attitudes are changing. Whereas ten years ago much of the above was seen by some as attempting to undermine medical authority, I do not believe that this now applies. Also, ten years ago, this 'whole person approach' was, frankly, novel; even now it is not widespread, but what has changed is that few people challenge it these days – the issue is more one of *how* to implement rather than *whether* to implement.

In the UK, great energy has gone into changing the basic ethos of the health service into more of a market economy. In these terms, psychological care should be seen as an 'investment' which can save both staff time and medical expense in the long term.

The underlying motive in proposing schemes of psychological care is a move to improve the way health care professionals interact with their fellow human beings. In the past the treatment of 'patients' was often unacceptable. Once a person was labelled 'patient', attitudes towards them changed because 'patient' did not equal 'person'. There was an inherent devaluation. The disregard for patients – keeping them waiting, not informing, dismissal of emotional needs etc., was a symptom of this devaluing process. I used to challenge this by no longer using the title patient and substituting it with the term client. Now, with the market economy in health care, this has a degree of ambiguity and connotations which some colleagues find distasteful, thus I have abandoned the term client.

Irrespective of the terms in use, the principle on which psychological care is based is quite simply that patients are people who have psychological needs – probably the same needs as you or I would have in the identical situation. Therefore we need to meet these needs in a sensitive, supportive and courteous manner.

CHAPTER 4

Informational and Educational Care

MEDICAL COMMUNICATION – FACTS AND THEORY

Keeping people informed, communicating with them in an appropriate way on a regular basis, should be easy. Of all the hurdles to overcome with ill people in a hospital setting, surely this must be one of the simplest? After all, the topic of communication now makes frequent and prominent appearances in the literature of the nursing, medical and therapy professions. Trainee doctors are not excluded from exposure to such material either, since some medical schools go so far as to include tutorials in interview and communication skills in their curriculum; so we must examine what is done and how effective it appears to be.

Nursing (July, 1981) comprised twelve articles all constructed to teach the importance of communication in a hospital setting and to discuss the basic skills involved. These articles talk gently and encouragingly of the following principles. In communication, one must convey a feeling of having time, patience and involvement. The language must be appropriate and a basis of trust developed. The communicator must be familiar with patients' needs, be able to pick up cues, give the right kind of information at the right kind of pace and possess such conversational skills as reflection (expressing back to a person the ideas they have just spoken) and clarification. Listening skills need to be well developed in the professional communicator, such that inner feelings on the part of the patient are allowed expression without blocking or interruption. Then there is the important non-verbal component which also receives full attention. The way one touches another, looks at them, the posture and position adopted and the gestures made, all contribute to the skill of communication.

Why do these authors place so much stress on efforts at communication? Primarily because they see it as a buffer against the incubation of fear and confusion, allowing a person to collaborate and follow treatment through in a more relaxed manner. In other words, effective communication is a positive contribution to recovery. The series of articles ends with a set of five principles which I summarize as:

1. Each patient is unique, bringing differing needs and abilities, and therefore requiring an individual approach.
2. Communication skills are as necessary for the 'ordinary patient' as for those in specialized areas.
3. The type of communication must be assessed in relation to a person's particular state and needs.
4. Essential communication skills must be identified and taught to health care professionals.
5. Communication makes demands on the professional. The primary demand is involvement, and because of this there must be support.

This and many similar publications are, without doubt, very positive and useful contributions to the growth of communication skills within the medical and medically related professions. There is little doubt that training within the profession is sensitizing many people to the importance of communicating information to seriously ill or injured people. As you will have probably guessed, though, there is bad news too. The bad news is this: at the time that I write, if you or I were to be admitted to our local hospital, it is still highly likely that we would find ourselves the victims of poor communication and kept short of the type of information that really matters. Here are some typical examples of what seems to remain commonplace in the average hospital.

1. Extract from *The Sunday Times,* June 1983. A woman is describing her recent experiences in childbirth: 'I never wanted to be treated like a VIP but it was the most important and frightening thing that had ever happened to me and I felt that they just couldn't be bothered'.

   At each of her dozen or so antenatal checks, she was prodded by a different pair of hands. Finally, on the basis of an estimated date, doctors concluded that she was overdue. An induction was recommended and she was told that she was risking her baby's life if she refused.

   'I was flat on my back for 20 hours with electronic monitors, drips and then emergency oxygen, because the speed of contractions was causing distress. It terrified the life out of me.'

   After a difficult forceps delivery, performed, says Beverley, by a nervous junior doctor, 'My baby was cleaned up, wrapped and handed to me briefly. Then everyone just filed out of the room without a word. The drip was turned up so high that I was still contracting after the delivery. I found out after that they couldn't just turn it off, it had to be turned down gradually, but no-one would explain why I was in such terrible pain.' The bruising was dismissed by midwives as, 'what motherhood is about'.

2. Richards (1981). Another woman relates her experiences after an accident in the home: 'A brief visit from the surgeon dismissed the idea of an operation but revealed that I was to be admitted, and I finally reached the ward six and a half hours after entering casualty. By this time I was unable to take in what was said to me. I was put on complete bed rest and eventually gathered that I had broken the first lumbar vertebra. But it was not until the consultant appeared a week later that the injury itself and some of the possible consequences were explained. I was told that it was a serious injury – the vertebra was completely smashed and I was lucky not to have any nerve damage. I was also told it would be about six weeks before the fracture was sufficiently consolidated for me to move. Three weeks after admission more X–rays were taken of my back. The registrar showed them to me shortly before the consultant arrived, and explained that although the bones were starting to knit together it would be another two or three weeks before I could be moved.

When the consultant arrived late that afternoon, my first impression was that he had enjoyed a good lunch! He glanced at the X–rays, decided they were too dark to see and then announced that I should get up the next day. Having arrived late, he was in a hurry and unwilling to be engaged in discussion. It is, in any case, extremely difficult for a patient lying flat on her back to initiate a conversation, when she is separated by a blanket cage from the group of doctors and nurses talking among themselves at the foot of the bed. As common sense and reason, as well as all my earlier information, were against the possibility that my recovery time should suddenly be reduced by half, I decided not to take it seriously.

The next morning I was distressed at the arrival of a brisk physiotherapist announcing that she had come to get me up. Suddenly, all the pent-up anxiety about the possible consequences of things not properly explained focused on what I felt sure was an ill-considered decision. I wept profusely and refused to move until the decision was explained. I was left alone for some time, but later, when I tried to explain my anxiety to the staff nurse on duty, she reproached me as if I were a five-year-old, at the same time accusing me of childish behaviour.'

3. The experience related here was conveyed to me by a young woman who came to see me just an hour before I sat down to write this paragraph – an odd coincidence. She had just been discharged from the local hospital where she underwent minor abdominal surgery to remove an abscess: 'I was put in a cubicle after a nurse had

taken details and waited three hours before a doctor came. He could barely speak English but he said I would have to go to theatre to have it dealt with. The nurse put me in a bed in an empty side ward at midday. She did not know how long I would have to wait but thought they might want me at about 4 p.m. No-one would or could tell me what was happening. I waited without any further information until 11 p.m. when finally I was told I would be taken to the theatre. I had assumed that the operation would be done under local anaesthetic but suddenly it came out that it was to be a general anaesthetic. I felt very worried – maybe they had mistaken me for someone else, or misunderstood the problem. Nobody would tell me anything definite, it was really quite frightening and frustrating. Looking back on it I feel so angry towards them.'

4.   During one of my regular sessions at a pain relief clinic, a 61-year-old man angrily related the following experience to me: 'I never heard anything from them after the X-rays so I decided to go for a private consultation with a back specialist. He examined me without speaking (other than instructions). It took about ten minutes. Then he went across to the X-ray viewer and mused over them in silence. I said 'What do you think doctor, can you see the problem'. He walked back to his desk, glared at me and said, 'I ask the questions here, if you don't mind. All right that's all, I'll write to your doctor'.

Of course it is by no means always this bad, but clearly there is an odd situation here. Most people qualifying in nursing and the medically related professions *do* know of the importance of clear and regular communication. The objective of good communication seems to be valued and every so often, as described, relevant journals make powerful appeals for improved efforts and improved performance in communication. Yet recent research and the continuing stream of impressions suggest there is still something going wrong in terms of implementation.

In Chapter 2 we had a look at some theoretical issues accounting for the development of 'professional behaviour' in medicine, which include the psychosocial explanation of why the professions were inclined to be defensive and maintain poor levels of communication. These factors still operate to a varying degree and undoubtedly hold back progress. Even so, when good intentions do exist, things still do not seem to go well.

Let us assume for a moment that we could spend a while in a hospital department where the staff are highly enthused with the ideal of communication. They go about work in the usual way, simply trying a little harder with communication. Would we find that the common

shortcomings brought to light by various investigations were eradi-
cated? Probably not, and indeed this is quite likely to be a transitional
state that exists in a good proportion of hospitals today. Many professional staff in hospitals now seem keen to achieve better communication, yet there are still obstacles which seem to block the
breakthrough. That is, *positive motivation alone is not sufficient; there are*
practical problems to be overcome before standards of communication truly
improve. Accordingly, it should be helpful to take a quick look at some
of these practical problems before launching into a detailed account of
the approach which I have called informational care.

Hayward (1975) summarized some very relevant findings given in a
Ministry of Health report concerned with communication in hospitals.
Blending these with some points of my own, a set of answers can be
derived in reply to the question, 'given good motivation towards communication in hospitals, where do things still go wrong?' There are five
main points:

1. *Inadequate comprehensibility* – doctors and nurses often give information to people which is non-usable because it is not in a form
   which the individual can understand. Various factors influence the
   chances of good understanding being achieved. Prior knowledge of
   medical terminology and concepts is clearly important, as are actual
   intelligence and language or vocabulary differences (that is, the
   communicator may have a different style of using language compared with the recipient). When there are major discrepancies of
   this type, a session of well-meant communication may leave the
   recipient little better off. This explains why Ley (1982a) reports
   some of his own surveys revealing that approximately 50% of
   people interviewed after being given medical information did not
   understand what they had just been told concerning the diagnosis,
   aetiology and prognosis of the complaint involved. In psychological
   terms, this is sometimes referred to as egocentric conversation, that
   is, the conversational content means a lot to the communicator but
   not much to the recipient.
2. *Unfavourable context* – information may be well presented and com-
   prehensible, but that in itself does not guarantee good reception
   and retention. Anxious people are sometimes poor listeners, with a
   reduced capacity to take in information or question the person giving the information in order to achieve clarity. Thus, if attempts at
   communication are conducted in a social context which adds *social*
   tensions to the anxiety inherent in the situation of illness itself,
   then comprehension and retention are likely to be reduced. In addition to this, requests for repetition, consolidation and discussion of
   the information are harder to make. The terse, socially awkward
   atmosphere of a ward round is a typical example of heightened

social tension. In such a setting, the ability of the listener to absorb, understand and retain information is inevitably reduced. In short, some of the customary settings for communication in the hospital are likely to *reduce* many people's abilities to make use of the communication, the standard ward round and examination/consultation being the two most suspect situations.

3. *Inappropriate form and quantity* – in many non-medical settings, information which is of significance is recorded in writing as it is expounded verbally. The decisions of a committee, a pilot obtaining meteorological information and air traffic details, are good examples. The information is written down because it is vital and the 'vehicle' of spoken words alone is inadequate. However, if we were to conduct a random set of observations upon the transactions within the consulting room or ward round we would find very few people being given a written summary of the information they have just received. The information is presented verbally, without diagram and without a written record to assist the person to remember it. Quite often the information load may be high – possibly too high – and without aids, forgetting is then inevitable. The reliance on verbal information, delivered episodically in unpredictable quantity but with a predictable lack of additional aids, is a major hindrance to medical communication.

4. *No one person has responsibility for coordinating and relaying information* – in the average hospital the allocation of responsibility to keep people informed is haphazard in the extreme. Information is presented piecemeal, sometimes by doctors, sometimes by nurses. There is no one person who has a special responsibility to check what has been told and what is known, and who then works to bring a patient's information up to an appropriate level. It is the 'luck of the draw' which nurse or doctor you will see, whether or not they will tell you anything useful, and whether this confirms or contradicts what you have already been told. Such disorganization can only be resolved by having particular people assigned to the role of coordinating communication and guaranteeing minimum standards by regular contacts. As long ago as 1963, a Ministry of Health Report, *Communication between doctors, nurses and patients*, recommended the notion of personal responsibility for giving information. It does not seem important to specify the profession but the issue is that *someone* should have a clear role in giving information in each individual case.

Added to this problem is the variable quality of communication between doctors and nurses or other professionals. I say variable because each team will have differing strengths in this aspect of professionalism. In some less fortunate examples that I have encountered, the nurses would have been delighted to spend time with people in the wards building up their level of understanding and information, but were impaired because they had no means of getting clear information from medical colleagues themselves. Incidentally, this was not all the fault of the doctors – the nurses had played their part in creating the situation.

5. *Information is 'censored'* – because of a reluctance to tell people bad news, there is a general tendency to shelter them by giving only the more favourable bits of information. It is easy to talk of the hopes rather than the fears in a doctor's mind, and it is easier to give estimates of outcome based on things going well rather than the (in many cases) equally likely outcome of things going badly. The motive is benign but the impact can be destructive. When information is 'filtered' to allow only positive aspects to be exchanged, if a case then goes badly, this information will be experienced as misleading, or misconstrued as incompetence on the part of the staff. Either way, it erodes confidence and is another nail in the coffin of high-quality, open, honest communication.

Equally, I hope you can see that enthusiastic communication 'binges' are not the real solution. The vital requirement is a change in approach and that requires a basic change in attitude on the part of hospital staff.

To support these claims I must draw your attention to a helpful review of research into the inadequacies of communication in medicine, presented by Ley (1989). The following outcomes from the many studies he included are of relevance to us. Between 40% and 80% of people are dissatisfied with the information they receive from doctors, nurses or therapists. Despite increased interest in communications skills, this figure is the same as 20 years ago. Part of the problem is that people often do not understand the information they are given, they feel too inhibited to ask questions, they forget much of what they have been told, and false beliefs about their illness or treatment further erode retention. Thus, results from various studies showed that up to 69% of people did not fully understand the information given to them, and anyway, they forgot between 40% and 70% of the information very quickly. Age and intelligence were not important influences in forgetting, but an anxious need to know, previous medical knowledge and the perception of information as important did correlate with better retention, assuming that information was delivered well in the first place.

Ley considers the issue of compliance in relation to information, and refers to studies which reveal that 20% of readmissions to hospital are correlated with non-compliance. This can be costly. Some research cited suggests that the cost of compliance failure in America during the 1980s ran at somewhere between $400m and $800m dollars per year.

Department of Health, Education and Welfare figures showed that the *non*-compliance levels for antibiotic and cardiovascular drugs were 47.7% and 39.3% respectively.

However, Ley does give some good news and reviews research which shows that the following do have a positive impact on the understanding and retention of medical information by patients and their partners:

- Use of primacy effects (i.e. people recall best the first few things they are told at any one time)
- Stressing the importance of particular items of information
- Simplification – shorter words and sentences
- Labelling categories of information ('now I'm going to tell you about your drugs and after that I'll tell you about washing the wound')
- Repetition
- Specific rather than general information
- Additional interviews to check understanding and retention.

From this and other studies, it can be concluded that poorly informed patients are more likely to be stressed and angry, less likely to comply with treatment and dietary regimens and will cost the medical services more money and time.

CARING BY INFORMING – THE RATIONALE OF INFORMATIONAL CARE

Reynolds (1978), a medical student at the time, carried out an investigation on communication in a general hospital. She summarized her findings thus:

'One hundred patients on four general wards in a large teaching hospital were interviewed about the information they had received about their illness and what they had been told about the investigations they had undergone. Fifty-five of them expressed some dissatisfaction and fourteen were strongly dissatisfied. Twenty-four patients would have liked more explanation about why investigations were performed and thirty-eight thought they had not been told enough about the results of their investigations. *This lack of information led to anxiety and fear.* A patient summed this up by describing her feelings about one member of staff: "Mr. X. will talk to you. He doesn't make you feel that you're just another piece of furniture, he makes you feel you're an individual. I'd like to think that all doctors could be like that" . . . '.

Me too. I hope we can get to a point where all doctors, nurses and health care professionals evoke such a response. Caring by informing, or informational care is aimed at this.

What, then, are the overall objectives in informational care? These are set out in summary form in Figure 4.1. Information is seen as something which has to be *maintained*. It is necessary continually to check what patients and their partners know about the medical plan for them, and whether they have an accurate understanding of this plan, the treatments, any procedures, their diet and so on. The 'maintenance' work is basically that of reacting to the outcome of the check by providing more detail, updating or correction – that is, whatever is necessary in your judgement to maintain your patients in a state which can be confidently described as accurately informed. This maintenance effort is necessary

Aim: To maintain information and understanding at a level which

   (a) Produces *realistic* expectations

   (b) *Reduces* the stress which otherwise results from the confusion of 'not knowing'

   (c) Leads on to effective participation and self-care

Figure 4.1: Informational care in illness

because of the reasons highlighted in a phrase which has become the prompt line for informational care: 'something told does not mean something heard, understood and remembered'.

The problem for any one of us in a hospital is how to make sense of what is happening and how to build up enough knowledge and information to gain an accurate appraisal of the immediate future with its various medical possibilities. If a member of staff checked what we knew, corrected it, updated it, amplified it as required and actually went and found out answers to questions for which answers were not immediately to hand, we would experience this as a very caring regime. Worry would not be banished but the anxiety generated by *needless* uncertainty would go, and the experience of someone functioning in this way for our benefit would have a very supportive effect. There would be a sense of collaborating with the staff to deal with problems together.

An illustration of this was evident in the case study given in Chapter 1, the case of Alan and the arthrodesis. I stressed how isolated he had been with his failing arthrodesis. *He* did not know what was happening. Allow me to rerun a little of the story, telling it as if informational care was being practised. (I will deal just with the phase when he had been sent home after six months in hospital – he was in pain, but still clinging to the idea that time was all that was needed for the bone to fuse. He was, however, becoming rather desperate.)

Instead of the once every six to eight weeks' contact with a brief appointment for a physical examination and X-ray, there would have been recognition that, to a person in pain, frightened because his operation was not following the expected pattern, two months was far too long a gap to be left without checking on how he was coping and what he believed was happening. He needed contact at least every two or three weeks with someone informed about his case. This member of staff would have gone through and repeated the various thoughts on what might be happening with his hip joint, looked at the X-rays with him again and shared the medical speculations on the future outcome. Honest and frequent communications such as the following:

Doctor: 'The pain is not a good sign and it means that fusion is incomplete – you can see the gaps on the X-ray – we are powerless at this stage to do anything about it at all except encourage you to be patient and comply with the physiotherapist's instructions. Don't give up hope yet – sometimes these wounds do fuse after a long while of not knitting, so we are not stringing you along pointlessly. Ideally we will have to give it nine months in plaster, you have done six. We will go on with X-rays every six weeks and watch it carefully with you. It is in my mind that we may well need a second operation to repack the joint with bone chippings taken from elsewhere. If you like, I'll tell you about that now so that you don't get the wrong idea, and I'll just jot down a couple of notes for you to take away as a reminder . . . Being practical, I'd say the chances are 50/50 that a second operation will be needed. If on the next X-ray there is no improvement then I'd say more definitely that a second operation will be necessary, but I'll not commit us until the full nine months. I asked you last time to bring a list of any questions or worries you had – do you have it with you? Are you finding the level of pain tolerable – enough to go another six weeks?'

Two or three weeks later that doctor, or another member of the team, for example a well-informed nurse or physiotherapist, would meet with Alan again to check his understanding of the situation, go through the plan again, discuss any matters arising and check on his general level of morale. This pattern would continue until the medical problem was resolved in order to maintain, correct and update Alan's understanding. With contact of this nature, Alan would have felt cared for and seen that his situation was under control. Also, he would have felt that, inconvenient though it was, the best path was in fact being followed. However, 'normal' hospital routine and behaviour prevailed, allowing (not causing) a situation wherein he felt completely out of touch with his doctors and was bitterly convinced they were not concerned (did not even believe) that he was in so much pain.

This was not, of course, the case – they were aware and it did bother them. Unfortunately, though, the transfer of information was often little better than, 'mmm – I think we will have to give it another six weeks'. The gap between the ideal and the actual in this history indicates that the staff involved could not see how important staying in touch and keeping clients fully informed might be. They were kind, but unwittingly uncaring. As one of the medical team actually said when the need for this type of back-up was pointed out, 'Where are we going to find the time for these gossip sessions?' I have to tell you that the inability to understand how to care by informing and the failure to invest 15 minutes every two or three weeks in this work made it necessary to provide many hours of psychologist's time for Alan, a good number of consultations with his GP, an admission to a casualty department, and it certainly created the circumstances in which Alan was risking his life in his own attempts at pain-killing and sedation. Furthermore, because the same information-depriving approach had prevailed in the run-up to the operation and the following months, Alan's reactions were adverse and the resultant disturbed behaviour probably contributed to the failure of the arthrodesis in the first place – a heavy price indeed.

In case you feel I am being unreasonably critical, please understand that my motive in going through the less admirable aspects of this case example is *not to condemn, but to demonstrate with maximum clarity how the absence of informational care risks creating great anguish and causing much greater consumption of professional time in the long run.*

I will shortly give more examples of the type of intervention that is required in good informational care. Before that, there is one aspect of theory which must be dealt with in a little more depth. We have to consider the characteristics of both the people receiving information and those giving information, which affect quality, understanding and retention during and after information exchange.

FACTORS AFFECTING THE RETENTION OF INFORMATION

Communications to the ill and injured must take into account the high probability of psychological changes having been induced which *alter a person's ability to receive information*. Consequently, you cannot go about the task of giving information in an everyday fashion and reasonably expect to have much success. Both the hospital environment and the traumatic circumstances are likely to create the following sorts of impediment.

Dislocation and confusion

When you have worked in a department or ward for a few months it becomes thoroughly familiar. The geography, social structure, conventions and routines become totally absorbed. It is then hard to see it as unfamiliar and unknown, and all too easy to *project* familiarity – i.e. you experience your patients as finding it as familiar and homely as you now do. This projection of familiarity is misleading. In the first few days of admission (particularly an unexpected admission) or in the first few days of an internal transfer, say, from a ward to an intensive care unit following a kidney transplant, the known world is dislocated and substituted by an unknown (and sometimes alien) world. The result is a state of *confusion* in relation to people, places, routines, norms of interaction and behaviour. This applies especially to those experiencing a first admission to a hospital. As Heatherington (1964) describes:

'When the patient goes into hospital for the first time he has to make a sudden adjustment to a new kind of life. He has to fit in with a new timetable involving a modified sleeping schedule, he may have to adjust to a strange diet, and he has to get used to sharing a dormitory with complete strangers. He may see strange and frightening apparatus being wheeled about on trolleys; he may experience real pain or discomfort for the first time in his life. He may also meet death or disfigurement at close quarters for the first time. He may have to submit to the authority of nurses, some young enough to be his daughters, and will have to submit to the dictates of doctors, many of whom may be his own age or younger. The patient may not know all that is expected of him in the hospital ward. He does not know the rules. Can he smoke or not? Is it 'done' to speak to the man in the next bed? How does he get hold of a newspaper? Is he allowed to get out of bed to go to the lavatory? To whom should he speak about worries concerning his family at home? He may not know who is the appropriate person to ask: indeed he may not have a very clear idea of who is who in the ward. He tends to confuse the consultant and the junior house physician, the sister and the probationer nurse. At first he will not have learned what the various uniforms mean. Just because he sees more of the house physician than he does of the consultant, he may view the former as the doctor-in-charge.'

When we absorb information in our everyday world, we are usually absorbing the relatively familiar into the already known. A newly admitted patient, possibly of high intelligence and verbal skills but without prior experience of medical environments and language, cannot necessarily do this. A good number of people will be disoriented and confused in this way, struggling to make sense of what is happening and why, not knowing who is who and what can be expected of the staff. In this state, the ability to make use of medical information is likely to be diminished, since it cannot be readily assimilated into aspects of life that *are* familiar to the individual. People need time to learn the language and conventions of hospitals, to incorporate them into a 'known' world.

The extent to which this confusion disables people is enormously variable. Those with past experience of hospitals will have learned how to learn about new hospital environments; the uninitiated are likely to be more handicapped. In general, though, I cannot tell you what proportion of people are affected nor how long such effects persist. All I can do is warn you that you must expect this as a difficulty with new or newly moved patients and build in compensatory elements (specified later) to your informational care work.

Socioeducational gulf

Hospitals are effectively a separate subculture, necessarily using a set of concepts and corresponding vocabulary of their own. To participate within this subculture, one must either know the language and concepts or have ready access to an accurate translation into familiar terms. The temptation in communication within hospitals is to give a short measure in the translation to save time, which means overly simplified explanations that do not give genuine understanding. What translation, for example, would the wife of a seriously injured man admitted for intensive care in your hospital receive of the following: 'In ITU supported by a ventilator, with cardiac monitoring, an intravenous drip and penile catheter'. For the average citizen, unless there is a good translation of these terms which actually takes into account the level of knowledge, intelligence and verbal ability of the recipient, *much of what is told will be meaningless and wasted.* The only people to benefit will be the staff, who will feel some job satisfaction with the belief that they have kept people informed.

Adverse psychological states

It is not possible to give precise laws concerning the relationships between psychological state and the ability to listen, absorb and retain information. There is copious research, though, which confirms the obvious – namely, that emotional arousal and psychological shock produce an impaired ability to take in new information. For example, a relative in a fraught state, people who are dazed and frightened with the impact of unexpected entry into hospital, people who are very tense and inhibited during a consultation, people shaken by the disappointment of a medical failure – in all these instances you must expect disruption of the usual processes involved in information absorption. People are less able to listen with full attention: their attention is fragmented. They become preoccupied and distracted by an idea or experience of the moment which diverts attention, they find they cannot follow the full flow of an explanation, nor take in details. Later they may be remarkably blank about what has been said. Even short-term elevation of anxiety can have this disruptive effect. You can observe this in yourself, no doubt (do you remember how you were affected by anxiety in an oral or practical exam?). Thus people in states of emotional arousal require special techniques when information is being relayed to them.

Other factors may also influence a person's capacity to take in information. The illness itself may cause deficits, for example there is intellectual deterioration accompanying uraemia, and injuries to the head will often produce confusion and amnesia. Similarly, certain drugs take the edge off people's intellectual abilities. So do keep this aspect in mind before you even begin. Is the person you are about to inform functioning in a way which impairs their ability to receive information?

Selective listening and forgetting

If your experiences follow the same path as mine, then you will be impressed by the power of this effect. We have established that people in hospital harbour some sense of threat and often add to this an urgency to return to their own world. Their listening and remembering, therefore, is interspersed with fears, fantasies, hopes and strong personal needs. The effect of varied psychological states of this nature is analogous to a filter. *Certain information is easier to listen to and retain than other types, and some information has a high loss rate for an individual compared with other types.* Before expanding this, I think a short case example will be of help to you.

Case incident

Tony was a self-employed electrician. He was 34 and had two young children. He was an extremely self-sufficient man, priding himself on his ability to deal with the problems of his work on his own, running his business efficiently and independently. He was ill with influenza in the month of March last year. He worked on despite being ill, there being an important job to complete. Two days later he complained of pains in his back but he continued to work on, clearly finding it increasingly difficult. Then he noticed blood in his urine and became alarmed, so decided to call in to see his GP. A month later he was taken into a kidney unit in complete renal failure.

As with most people, the shock of the transition was tremendous. However, Tony was very tightly held in, bringing all his powers of self-reliance to deal with the situation. The nurses described him as brooding, silently angry, spending much time sitting thinking in his room.

After two weeks of peritoneal dialysis by machine, he began training with the bag system, CAPD. His information on this was standard, being given an overview of the training scheme and the outline plan for conversion to home dialysis in five to six weeks. The staff were reluctant to give exact timing because various obstacles can delay training. Things went well, the habit of self-sufficiency driving him to master the techniques and learn to overcome the snags quickly. However, after a week of training an incident occurred in which he exploded into violent anger. The sister in charge of the unit was chatting about his progress when it came to light that he was expecting to convert to home dialysis at the end of two weeks after the start of his CAPD training. The sister said that this was not possible, it would be at least four. 'But,' he said, 'the nurse told me I would be going in two weeks – you people just change things to suit yourself. The organization here is disgusting.' (Actually, he said a great deal more, in increasingly vehement terms, but we will not go into that just now.) The poor sister was somewhat taken aback. Only the day before, at a review discussion, it had been agreed that he would be ready in about three weeks' time, making a total of four. She 'knew' no-one had told Tony two weeks. Correspondingly, Tony 'knew' that someone had.

In retrospect it is easy to see what had happened and why. Tony found that the situation of being in hospital, dependent on others and not knowing much about dialysis treatment, was like being in a cage. He could not exercise his self-reliance – his great defence against anxiety. He was profoundly ill at ease and desperate to get away. He drove himself to achieve this end, learning all he could by talking with the nurses and other patients and fixing in his mind the objective of early conversion to dialysis at home. He found out that one patient had completed training on the bag system in two weeks, and decided that he could manage this too. However, he failed to take sufficient account of the differences in their respective positions, namely that his fellow trainee was converting to CAPD after five years of haemodialysis and was thoroughly experienced in the ways of life on dialysis, the sterile techniques, dietary principles and so on. Tony, meantime, could expect at least two weeks on conventional peritoneal dialysis and then a training period on CAPD, the *average* length of which was four weeks, assuming no complications. He had certainly been told this. It became a clear case of something told does not mean something heard, understood and remembered. One source of the discrepancy between Tony and the sister came from an earlier conversation which Tony had shortly after starting the CAPD training. He had carefully questioned a young nurse helping him with a bag change:

Tony: Do people sometimes finish training and go home after two weeks?
Nurse: Well, I think some do if they get on very quickly and know what they are doing.
Tony: How am I getting on, do you think?
Nurse: (sensing both Tony's anxiety and the pressure he was exerting) I think you're doing very well, really, for someone who has only been trying this technique for a few days.
Tony: I must get back to my business as soon as possible – do you think they'll let me go at the end of two weeks?
Nurse: I don't know, really. It's not for me to say. I should think you might be able to if you keep up like this. You should ask sister or the doctors tomorrow. I'll mention it to them, if you like.

Tony did not hear the qualification in this last reply including the suggestion that he should check with other staff. The next day he told his wife, 'The nurse said I might come home after two weeks.' He fixed this objective in his mind and several days later he 'knew that he had been told it would be two weeks'. He had blocked out the information given to him as he started the training.

You can see what was happening here. Some of Tony's questioning was manipulative. Through non-verbal means he was signalling the kind of answer he needed to hear. He was then responding only to selected elements of a statement – he was hearing what fed his hopes and soothed his agitation. This selected-out material was remembered with greater ease than the rest. Before long, he 'knew' that certain things were said to him, although in reality this knowledge departed considerably from the original information. There are very few of us who do not function like this from time to time: we hear what we want to hear and memories include certain modifications – it is, we should say, a very human trait. Be that as it may, it is also a very prevalent hazard to effective communication in a hospital setting, where there is the catalyst of anxiety and strong personal need.

As you begin to work in this general area, one idea must be burned into your consciousness – *something told does not mean something heard, understood and remembered*. The information you give has to run the gauntlet of the following active distorting processes:

• The patient is *searching* for certain types of communication and information, for example reassuring predictions.
• The patient has *powerful expectations* of certain types of information

related to angry, depressed, anxious and hopeful fantasies, which will distort the reception and recall of information received.

- *Blocking* response – an active rejection of information without conscious awareness that this has happened. The individual simply has no memory of the communication.
- Straightforward *forgetting*, because the person is either overloaded with information or because of comprehension problems.

Information drift

One of the disruptive aspects to communication in the hospital environment is the multiplicity of sources of information – medical staff, nursing staff, social workers, relatives who have conversed with these, other people resident in the ward, and so on. Information from differing sources almost inevitably means variations in the theme of important information. This variability, together with manipulative inquiring, seeking alternative views and simple gossip, can lead to the erosion of precise information and a progressive drift away from accuracy, not at all unlike the party game involving passing whispered messages from one person to another, which predictably goes badly astray.

Health beliefs

When we give people information it is not equivalent to feeding information into an empty computer memory: there will already be a great deal of material in the store. A composite of past learning (not necessarily accurate), attitudes and beliefs will have been accumulated. Naturally, this composite will affect the reception, retention of and reaction to the information we give. Put it another way: what you tell patients and partners may be held on to as life-saving information by some, whereas others may regard it as of dubious value and reject it. You have only to read briefly in the field of preventive health education to discover countless examples of the phenomenon. I do not plan to deal with this topic in depth, but will note that there is a large research literature available which takes its origin from the so-called health belief model of Becker (1974). Useful recent review articles are Becker and Rosenstock (1984) and Marteau (1989).

What pattern of influence do health beliefs have? They are especially likely to influence long-term health care behaviour such as the diet, exercise and behaviour change regimens recommended in diabetes care and post-coronary rehabilitation training. As Rutter (1989) writes, there are 'two principal variables: the value an individual places on a particular goal; and the individual's estimate of how likely it is that a given action will achieve that goal. For preventive health behaviour, the model suggests that there are three specific dimensions: perceived susceptibility, perceived severity and perceived benefits and barriers'. In plain language, this implies that people will react to what you tell them in relation to their judgement of its payoff and the personal cost of either following or not following advice. I can illustrate how arbitrary this can be by relating a brief conversation between myself and a builder who was recently doing some work on my house:

Self: Would you like a coffee?
Builder: No thanks mate, never touched it for years since I heard on the radio that it was bad for you.
Self: But what about that cigarette you always have in your mouth?
Builder: Oh no, a good ciggy won't do you any harm mate.

FACTORS AFFECTING INFORMATION EXCHANGE

You will remember, I hope, from Chapter 2, that the most obvious failure of information exchange between the medical profession and its patients is the *lack* of information exchange. The very prevalent habit of withholding information was accounted for by illustrating how, for purposes of (1) defence against criticism and exposure of errors, (2) the maintenance of an absolute power position in relation to the users of the hospital service, and (3) minimizing involvement with the distress of ill people, the ploy of holding back information evolved as virtually standard practice, and it is still quite common.

To this must be added factors including the difficulties of effective and consistent information exchange resulting from the high work load carried by the majority of doctors. I imagine that this particular problem has received a sufficient airing already and, since this book is primarily intended to convey the elements of good practice in psychological care, we must limit any further comment concerning the basic approach of the medical profession to noting likely behavioural characteristics, and remaining mindful that these characteristics may be antagonistic to good psychological care. Obviously, our present concern with the provision of information has to take into account this habit of withholding information. However, the idea in this chapter is to assume that a positive motivation to provide good communication and optimal information exchange *does* exist, and to examine what is likely still to go wrong.

Thus, imagine again that we could visit a unit where the doctors and nurses, without further preparation or thought, simply decided to try harder with the business of communication. What would we be likely to discover as the main obstacles to their success in actually giving their patients information? Consider yourself in the following situation: a young woman has been diagnosed as having suffered an episode of illness which has been positively identified as multiple sclerosis. The disease is expected to develop and she is likely to deteriorate badly over the next two or three years. She does not know this yet; she is sitting facing you and you have the job of replying to her question asking what the diagnosis might be.

What motives does this fantasy situation stir up in you? Unless you are unusual, there will be a feeling of awkwardness and a need to minimize the impact of the bad news on her. You will probably experience a wish to placate, to reassure, to give hope that the next episode will not happen for a long time, maybe never. That is how most of us feel: *our* needs are strong in such a situation too. Of course, the young woman does not want to hear, nor will she profit from hearing, the outcome of the investigation blurted out in an insensitive way. However, we will leave the issue of how best to convey such news until later. At this point, I want you to register that, for most of us, situations of this type create strong feelings which direct our behaviour. *Our instinct is to shelter people from bad news*, to offer hope and reassurance as a buffer against distress. Put more directly, our own anxieties in this situation are likely to direct a predominantly evasive and placatory style of communication. An example catches a doctor from our fantasized unit, where the effort to communicate is running on goodwill and instinct alone:

Doctor: Well, we have had your tests back now and we can't really be certain what is going to happen. So there is no point in worrying too much at present. Certainly you have had some form of nerve disorder which was responsible for the weakness in your legs and arms. There is a chance that your illness might have been an episode of multiple sclerosis. At this stage, though, it is best we think of it as inflammation of the spinal cord. Now, please don't worry yourself unduly. Isolated episodes can occur like this and nothing more happens for years and years. We will just have to see. Still, I'm glad to hear you've picked up a bit over the last week or two.

You will see that the doctor is working hard at slipping in a little information and then negating this by qualification and reassurances. In fact, although this is an invented piece of transcript, it is based on experiences described to me by a young woman, the only difference being that her doctor actually refused to mention the term 'multiple sclerosis' to her, although in a confidential consultation with her mother he gave a positive diagnosis of the disease. Ironically, the family already had experience of it and the woman, together with her parents, had already decided that this was the nature of her illness.

The general effect of the doctor's attempt to shelter her was simply to create annoyance and mistrust.

The vital point derived from this example is that the doctor appears kindly and seems to be trying to shelter his patient. This was certainly the case, but there was another underlying motive – he was also looking after his own anxieties by avoiding contact with the potential distress of his patient. *He feared her distress and so gave a watered-down version of the diagnosis.*

It was just an isolated case? Elian and Dean (1985) interviewed 167 patients diagnosed as having multiple sclerosis. They found the following situation:

18% were ignorant of the nature of their illness
24% had been informed by a doctor other than the diagnosing consultant
19% had relied on guessing what it was themselves
6% had found out by accident (e.g. from a cleaner)

It was further discovered that although only 27% had been spontaneously informed by their consultant, 83% preferred to be properly informed.

When we are anxious we will avoid the sources of that anxiety if it is possible. Most of us find it difficult to provoke distress and fear in others: it makes us anxious and our natural tendency, therefore, is to avoid actually doing this, hence the great debate in medicine concerning 'whether to tell or not'. This is no real debate, in fact, and as Ley (1982a) stated, research clearly shows that the vast majority of people want full, honest medical information. For example, Reynolds *et al.* (1981) interviewed 67 people with advanced cancer. They were concerned to know that proportion wished to be kept informed. Their findings were:

Wanting information on the diagnosis: 91%
Wanting information on the symptoms: 92%
Wanting information on the treatment and side effects: 97%
Wanting information on the prognosis: 88%

The continuing resistance to this type of research finding and the still common belief that the truth will be destructive, goes back to the fact that we, the professionals, are the people with a problem as much as our patients. Many of us find it hard to endure their reactions to distressing information and so resort to the various evasive strategies of holding back information, 'filtering' information and giving placatory, reassuring statements which create false hopes. In short, one of the most common characteristics of those giving information in a hospital environment is that of being governed by an anxiety about creating anxiety.

INFORMATIONAL CARE IN PRACTICE

The atmosphere changes now. No longer will I be presenting theory; rather, I will be writing in the style of an instructor. What you will find, therefore, in this and the following chapters, is my understanding of psychological functioning and my views on the best way to go about psychological care. These views are based on first-hand experience in hospitals and involve a certain amount of innovation in practice. I will not be presenting proof and evidence in a formal manner but rather telling you in quite definite terms how *I* provide psychological care and how I think *you* should provide psychological care. Because of this change in style you must maintain your own critical perspective. Discuss the ideas and clarify what you find acceptable.

There are several other features to bear in mind. I will not be teaching the skills of psychological care in relation to any specific area of medicine – the basic principles apply to all the specialties. My own experience includes a considerable amount of work with people in renal failure and so several case examples are used from this branch of medicine, but there is no special significance in this. It is also important for you to realize that, in order to teach the complete approach to psychological care, I assume an ideal environment for the work, particularly in this chapter. That is, I assume you will have sufficient time, a manageable flow of relatively long-stay patients (as opposed to a fast-flowing tide of new faces) and colleagues who understand and value the work. I have not lost sight of the real world and the comparatively disadvantageous circumstances in which you may actually work. Nevertheless, for the purposes of clear teaching, it is easier to use the example of an idealized setting so that you have a good model with which to compare things.

Remember that, although I usually refer to nurses as the people conducting psychological care, the other professions in the hospital service are very much in my mind too.

There is no great mystique involved with the work. It looks after itself if certain vital principles are observed. These are:

1. An identified person is assigned to take basic responsibility for providing and maintaining the level of information a patient holds. There is no set level of information required; rather, the target adopted is to maintain reasonable levels with adequate understanding in relation to the individual's abilities. This does not imply that

one member of staff monopolizes the transfer of information, rather that their job is to check that the patient has been, and remains, well informed, and to make up any deficits.

2. The work of assessing a person's knowledge and expectations must be emphasized to the same degree as actually giving information – that is, prior to and after the communication of significant information, it becomes standard practice to check what a person knows, how accurate and complete this is, and what expectations they generate from this material. Since the objective is to maintain optimum levels of accurate information, it is necessary to *monitor* what people actually do with the information they are given. Simply to deliver information without linking this to prior levels of understanding and failing to check back on another occasion to see what and how much as been retained, is a particularly effective way of being ineffectual.

3. The task of giving information should be professionalized (but not, emphatically not, dehumanized). Like any other skill – venepuncture, for example – there is a right way and a wrong way to go about the task. Thus people involved in giving information should be trained in the role and approach it with a professional attitude. It is quite unacceptable that it be left as an uncoordinated, amateurish free-for-all, conducted by people who, although trained in their own field, are actually untrained in the skills of communication. The training is not hard and basically requires the adaptation of well known communication skills to the special needs of ill and injured people within the hospital environment.

4. Informational care depends heavily on a system of cooperation between the staff involved with any one patient. Unless this system of cooperation exists, consistent and high-quality information exchange will always break down. In other words, if, say, as a primary nurse you are responsible for the informational care of a group of patients, the medical staff must recognize that, as the medical decision-makers, they have a vital responsibility to keep *you* informed of their general thoughts, intentions, changes of plan and treatment strategies – that is, regularly updating you on what is happening. Wherever possible, this will be *in advance*, not in retrospect. The effort on the part of the medical team to inform other staff will form a highly significant contribution to the system. In recognizing this, the doctors will *work* at keeping you informed and you will not have to pursue them for information, or find yourself being treated condescendingly as if you were party to a considerable favour. All staff will work to contribute and make available their information to facilitate the programme of care. The task is not onerous – many other types of organization achieve this.

5. Informational care will be seen as part of required duties with an

appropriate level of priority. There will therefore be a proper allocation of time so that staff can meet the requirement.

In summary:

- Allocation of responsibility
- Monitoring information accuracy
- Professionalized information exchange
- Integration.

GIVING INFORMATIONAL CARE

May we work now on an exercise which draws these principles together? Assume that we have to design a programme of informational care suitable for patients newly admitted to a typical hospital unit. How should this be conducted? I will present a case based on my own work with people in kidney failure as the background to an extended example. We will assume that you work as a nurse in the unit.

We have been advised by the consultant nephrologist that one Carol Morris is likely to need dialysis treatment within about six months. The date is vague, however. The situation is as follows: Carol, a 31-year-old mother of two young children, complained two months previously to her GP of pain in her kidneys and blood in her urine. The doctor gave her antibiotics, took a urine sample and asked her to return in a week. She was not able to report much improvement on her second visit. A blood sample was taken. The blood analysis revealed levels of urea and creatinine which alarmed the doctor. Her kidneys appeared to be failing. He told Carol that she had a serious kidney condition and that he wanted her to see a specialist straight away. This was her wish too, since she was feeling pretty rough and was becoming worried. The nephrologist saw her three times in all and diagnosed a rapidly progressing glomerulonephritis. Appropriate drug therapy was given in an attempt to contain the disease and improve her blood condition. It was, however, just a holding strategy. The expectation was that the kidneys would continue to deteriorate and dialysis would be needed some time in the next six to nine months, the earlier date being more likely.

The consultant, as a contributor to the unit's scheme of informational care, conveyed this information to Carol in a gentle but non-evasive way. He asked her to begin domestic preparations so that she could reside in the unit for about eight weeks (assuming no complications) at a time to be decided according to the rate at which her kidneys deteriorated. He gave her a brief outline on the nature of dialysis and the various events to come, including her training for independent dialysis using the continuous ambulatory peritoneal dialysis (CAPD) method. The meeting ended with the doctor telling Carol that the nursing staff at the unit would be advised of her position and would make contact *in advance* of her admission. With that, he formally advised the sister-in-charge to expect Carol to join the CAPD training scheme within the next nine months.

This is where you come in on the story because the sister has just asked if you will accept the assignment to deal with Carol's psychological care. As your supervisor in these matters, I said yes before you could get a word in. Our attention here is solely on the informational care aspects of your work with Carol, although in reality you would offer emotional care and counselling as required.

We must begin by planning out the informational care programme. The first job is easy, sketching out the framework of contacts. These are best planned as different phases:

1. *Pre-admission contacts* – normally two sessions of about an hour's duration will be needed, one early on in Carol's waiting period and a second when she is getting near to admission (NB: There is a very great deal to explain in circumstances of kidney failure. With other types of illness and treatment 15 minutes may well suffice.)
2. *Admission contact* – this will occur as soon after admission as is possible for us and suitable for Carol (she may be too ill initially). The length of the meeting will vary with circumstances.
3. *Post-admission contacts* – here we must operate on an 'as and when required' basis, related to Carol's general progress, medical problems, informational input from other staff, etc. On average, we should allow 15 to 20 minutes once or twice a week.

The general objective of these meetings is not to monopolize information exchange. We expect all the medical and nursing staff to 'care by informing'. *Our job is to monitor the level of understanding and information and maintain it at adequate levels.* We need Carol and her husband to understand what has happened and what is going to happen, thus enabling them to follow the progress and problems through and collaborate with the staff. We want to insulate them from the destructive experiences brought about through inadequate information, thereby minimizing anxiety, confusion and anger. The tendencies towards information drift must also be opposed. Lastly, we must make sure that they are not vulnerable in that they could be traumatically surprised by complications and changes in plan of which they have no prior knowledge. Obviously, you cannot go through the book – this forewarning has to be limited to common problems. Everyone knows, for example, that Carol has a 10% chance or more of contracting peritonitis in the first three months and that this might require a period of emergency haemodialysis, so setting her training back. *She* should know this too, since advance information allows preparation (information should be a shared property).

The work in these various phases is basically the same, therefore we will take as the main illustration the pre-admission contact period. These particular meetings form the foundation of preventive informational care. In an hour or two you can do much to prevent months of worry and doubt. You begin by writing to Carol, inviting her to attend the unit with her husband during the interim period before admission. Your letter explains that they will be shown around the unit and meet with some of the staff and people training in dialysis. After that they will have a meeting with you to receive more information, and then be shown instructional videos on kidney failure and life with CAPD.

Your job in this first session is to check what they have retained from the consultations with the nephrologist and then set about consolidating and amplifying this knowledge as seems appropriate. You will carry in your mind the following objectives. First, the Morrises will be given a further explanation of the work kidneys do, why Carol's have failed and how peritoneal dialysis works to simulate kidney function. This will be kept basic but adequate, since they will be exposed to much new information on this visit. Simple reading material will be given for them to study in their own time. You will then explain and write down the broad outline of events which will take place during Carol's first week of treatment. The initial event will be the minor operation for the insertion of the peritoneal catheter. Levels of pain, location of the operation, type of anaesthetic and her feelings after the operation will be detailed. You will go on to say that shortly after the insertion of the catheter, Carol will receive 36 hours' continuous dialysis with 60 litres of dialysate fluid being passed through her abdomen during this time. The sensations produced by this treatment will be clearly described. You will continue by illustrating the events after this initial dialysis: how Carol will change to dialysing nightly for a week, with 20 litres of dialysate being passed through her abdomen during each eight to nine hour session, after which dialysis will be decreased to alternating nights. You will explain that, as well as improving the condition of the blood, this concentrated dialysis is also meant to create some stretching of the abdominal wall in order that two litres of dialysate fluid can be run into the abdomen without discomfort.

Lastly in this first meeting, you will give Carol and her husband brief details of the conversion to the bag system. They need to understand that there is much more to learn than may be covered in this first meeting, but you do not want to give them too much information at once. They will be learning steadily for three months or more. These two people have no background in medicine and they may need patient coaching with some of the ideas. It is vital that they be given time to formulate questions and express anxieties.

The IIFAC Scheme

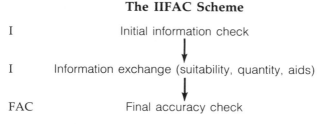

Figure 4.2: IIFAC – The basis of good information exchange

We have allowed about two hours for this visit, during which time they will be faced with a great deal to absorb. Thus, we must be mindful of the objectives of caring by informing and the need to 'professionalize' the work. We wish them to understand and retain meaningful, usable information, and must therefore use language which they can follow, progress at a pace which suits their capacity to learn, and avoid creating an atmosphere wherein they become inhibited and pretend to understand instead of feeling free to question when they do not. Above all, there must be an ever-present awareness on your part that 'something told does not mean something heard and understood'. To counter the various obstacles against effective information exchange, I suggest that you use an approach to communication which I will term *monitored information exchange*. It is very simple. Information is broken down into manageable packages and with each package you go through the following cycle: initial check/information exchange/final accuracy check. Use the mnemonic IIFAC to remember it by: Initial check, Information exchange and Final Accuracy Check. The activity during each element of the cycle is as follows:

- *Initial check* (I) – check what is already known or expected in relation to the information package being dealt with. Do not just ask patients if they have previously been told something – have them actually state the information back to you so that you can assess it for accuracy and completeness.
- *Information exchange* (I) – where there is some knowledge, correct and extend this as is necessary in order to achieve an adequate level of information. Where there is no knowledge, start at the beginning. Use diagrams and make simple notes for the patient as you go along. (*You* make the notes – being under some pressure, your patient may well make bad notes.) In long sessions *use a tape recorder* and give them the cassette to take away and play through at home, or on the ward for that matter.

- *Final Accuracy Check* (FAC) – once you have delivered a package of information and dealt with questions, *check again* – do not just ask your patients if they understood: have them repeat back the information and assess its accuracy. Coach them again in the elements which have been blocked, forgotten or misunderstood.

Now, perhaps we should eavesdrop on some typical moments in this work.

Case Example A

Carol and her husband have completed their viewing of the unit and you have settled down with them in the office for their 'pre-admission briefing'. In your letter of appointment you asked them to confirm their attendance, and say whether or not they possessed an audio tape player and would bring a cassette in order to record the briefing. They gave affirmation to both of these and brought with them a one-hour cassette which is running on the unit machine. You also have note-paper to hand for written material (ideally you will be able to give them a small file with preprinted dialysis literature which the unit will inevitably have) and a notebook so that everything may be kept together. 'And who will pay for this?' do I hear? Put it this way: if Carol survives ten years she will have run through many thousands of pounds in medical expenses. Clearly the unit's budget can stand the price of a few files and notepads.

You have made sure that they are both adequately relaxed and capable of giving attention to the content of the session. Do not press on regardless if they are not: there is no point in giving information if people are not in a state to receive it. Another time will have to be found for them. Assuming everything is favourable, give them the following orientation. All patients of the unit have a special relationship with one nurse who looks after their personal needs and acts as a counsellor. This person is also responsible for keeping them fully informed. Introduce yourself as *their* nurse–counsellor. Then go on to start the first session thus:

Nurse: I am going to go through the important aspects of kidney failure and give you some information on how dialysis treatment works and how you must be made ready for it. I will also be giving you a diary of the events occurring in your first week after admission here. I know that you've been told some of this before, but I don't know which aspects and whether you've been able to remember it all. What I'll do is split everything up into convenient parts and before we go through each one, I'll ask you what you've been told and what you remember of it. This makes it easier for me to start off at the right place and do a good job. Don't worry at all if you've forgotten things that Dr

Thomas told you or if you don't find them clear – it's going to take some time before you get it all straightened out and at this stage it would be ridiculous of anyone to expect you to have remembered much because it's all so unfamiliar.

Thirty minutes later the briefing is well under way. Carol and her husband are moderately at ease and seem to have coped with the basics of kidney function and dialysis. Now you will move on to the next unit of information, that is, the insertion of the abdominal catheter. As always throughout informational work, use the IIFAC cycle (initial check/information exchange/final accuracy check).

I (initial check)

Nurse: Right, so we've gone through how they decide when you need to start dialysis. You understand that eventually you'll have a date to come in here, but no-one knows when this will be because we can't say exactly how long your kidneys will take before they stop working completely. So, do you recall what will happen first when you come in?
Carol: Well, obviously I have to go onto those machines that we saw in the long-stay area.
Nurse: Do you need any preparation?
Carol: Dr Thomas said I had to have an operation.
Nurse: Yes, that's correct. What have you been told about the point of the operation? Do you have any details, like how big it is, where it will be done and what kind of anaesthetic will be used?
Carol: Oh dear, I think you were right when you said we'd forget things. I know the doctor explained some of it to me but that was three weeks ago. I have a plastic tube inserted into my stomach for the peritoneal machine to work. He said it would be a small operation, I think. I don't know much more – is it done in the main hospital?

I (information exchange)

Nurse: All right. You have the most important piece of information so let's go through the details now. I've brought along the plastic catheter for you to look at. You understand that the dialysis machine pumps fluid in and out of your body cavity – it does this through one of these tubes. Take a look at this diagram. Here, you see, the tube just lies in your body cavity against the intestines – it doesn't go into any organ at all – and the fluid is pumped in so that it surrounds the organs. The operation you will have is to place the tube in position in the abdomen and stitch the outer end into your skin.

First, you'll be given a drug to make you relax – a premedication, it's called. This will be an hour or so before the operation. Then you'll go into our procedures room, which is like a small operating theatre. I'll take you along for a look at it before you go. You don't leave the unit for this operation. Once you're settled, you'll be given a local anaesthetic. Normally this is the only part that actually hurts at all. You'll have four or five injections of the anaesthetic fluid under your skin near to your navel. The first one will sting, nothing too desperate, rather like a dental injection. You'll feel the fluid stretching your skin. After that, the skin stops feeling pain and the other injections will not sting so much. It's very important to remember that this injection just stops you feeling pain, it doesn't stop you feeling pressure and skin sensations and, of course, you'll stay awake for the whole of the operation. When the area is numb, the doctor will make a two- or three-inch cut in the skin and muscle – don't forget, you'll feel no pain but *will* feel his movements. He'll then feed the tube through the cut to meet the lining of your abdomen which is called the peritoneum. This is very tough tissue and to get the tube through, he'll ask you to tense your abdominal area. He'll then push down on the tube. It'll seem like a heavy push to you and there will be a feeling like something suddenly giving as it goes through. I'm told it's an odd experience but it doesn't hurt and no damage will be done.

Lastly, he'll continue to feed the tube through and then stitch your skin up around the dacron collar at its end. The wound will be cleaned up and you'll go back to your room for your first peritoneal dialysis. In all, it should take 20 to 30 minutes once he begins the anaesthetizing. Have you got any questions yet or is there anything you'd like me to go over again or explain more clearly?

Carol: Show me where he makes the incision.

Nurse: Probably just here, to the left and just below the navel.

Husband: She gets a bit nervous with injections – she might faint on you.

Nurse: The drug Carol will have before the operation should make her relaxed and happy. If she's still tense, though, she can ask for more. We'll check carefully. . .

FAC (final accuracy check)

Nurse: Right then, let me see if anything I told you was unclear or if it was too much to take in at once. Imagine that I'm one of your relatives. Explain to me what the operation is about and how it's to be done.

Carol: I can't do it as well as you.

Nurse: Don't look at it that way, as if it's an exam. I just want to check how clear *I* was to you and make sure that you've the right information to take away.

Carol: All right. I would tell her that I have to undergo a small operation to have a plastic tube called a catheter inserted in my abdomen.

This is to let fluid in and out. The operation starts with a local anaesthetic. . .

Nurse: What about the premed?

Carol: Oh yes, I have a relaxing drug first then a series of local anaesthetic injections in the skin to the left of my navel. These might hurt at first but they take effect quickly and I won't feel anything.

Nurse: Not quite – the injections just stop you feeling pain. You'll feel everything else.

Carol: Right, I remember. After that, an incision is made. . .

You must work away at this final check, teaching again any 'foggy patches'. Satisfy yourself on the quality of your information. *Be professional, care by informing properly and checking your own work.* Note that if you have given sufficient visual and auditory aids there is no special need for your patient to remember everything at this stage. In this particular case, Carol has notes and a tape recording. Remembering it all is not important as long as she plays the tape through to reacquaint herself with the material and glances through your notes. Failing to understand or getting it wrong *is* important, though, and this is what you must eradicate in the final accuracy check. Despite your efforts, by the next time you meet Carol, the forces of selective listening and recall, information drift and so on, may have blurred some of your information and you will almost certainly need to rework some of the material. Figure 4.3, taken from Nichols (1991), gives a full summary of the material to be covered for complete preparation. It serves as a model for any specialty.

Interlude

Let us take a moment between examples for a couple of short anecdotes which demonstrate the opposite of informational care, and show how thoroughly professional people are often bungling amateurs at the task of communication and information exchange. These are both events which occurred during the months that I have been writing this book, and whose accuracy I have checked.

Mrs V. (a nursing sister, as it happens) elected for minor surgery to remove a varicose vein in her leg. The surgeon came to see her before the operation, briefed her on what he planned to do and went away secure in the knowledge that 'she had been told'. Sadly, half an hour before his visit, the staff nurse had given Mrs V. her premedication drug. After the operation, Mrs W. asked the nurse, 'did Dr S. come and see me before the operation or was it a dream? I haven't the least idea what he said to me if he did come'. Had the surgeon checked on

Item	Tutorial content
Arrival at the procedure room and pre-op preparation	Location? Who will be there? Character of room? (Visit?) Sedation: options, how to arrange garments, position.
Anaesthetic: key information	Local anaesthetic used, gives pricking feeling then stings; stops all pain of operation, but pressure, pulling and puncturing tissues are felt vividly. Op takes about 30 mins.
Management skills for the client	Self-monitoring: tension scale, relaxation (unless bracing), breathing control, cognitive strategies, negotiation if distressed, understanding of the logic and status of the operation.
Insertion of the trocar	Explain trocar function, strong sensation followed by giving sensation (trocar cannot go in too far).
Catheter insertion	Little sensation until catheter in position near rectum, may be local pain from nerve ends if catheter presses on rectum, unlikely to be severe, signal if in difficulties.
Dialysate run into abdomen	May leak from wound at this stage, expect wet feeling, this is not bleeding.
Tunnelling of catheter	Inform why this is done, sensations of manipulation will be strong.
After the operation	Expect soreness and aches in the rectal area for up to a week – possibly pain in shoulder if fluid irritates diaphragm (explain referred pain). Initially when fluid runs out it will be blood-coloured. This is normal.
Support	Give general support, allow time for questions, check the accuracy of their understanding, establish their feeling state.

Figure 4.3: Peritoneal catheter insertion: psychological care preparation schedule (Remember: expectations – understanding – control – support)

her state to receive information and checked again after the information exchange, he would have gone away thinking, 'She has not been told – I left it too late.'

Mrs N. developed shingles on her face which spread to her left eye. She arranged to see an eye specialist privately, since the local hospital could not give immediate assistance. On meeting the specialist, he discovered her eye to be substantially damaged by the shingles, with raised pressure and iritis as complications. He said, 'I will admit you and see what I can do, but don't hold out too much hope'. While he talked at length on the condition of the eye, he gave no more information on the actual events to come in hospital. Then followed two days of near terror for Mrs N., who was highly anxious concerning any form of medical attention and was left alone to face the full range of horror fantasies concerning operations on the eye. On admission, her nurses knew little more than she about what would happen. They made no attempt to find out, either. One of them did say, however, that maybe she would be given an injection into the eye the next day. Mrs N. spent the night awake in an anxiety state. Nobody meant her any harm, of course. They were, to be frank, just clueless about how to care by informing. Incidentally, Mrs N. was 70 and had a history of heart damage. There was a real risk that the induced anxiety could have put her into heart failure.

Giving realistic information – not just the good news

I want to illustrate two aspects of informational care which merit special emphasis. First, there is the idea of *preparing people for likely complications*, and secondly, *your role as the person who finds things out on behalf of your patient*.

Carol has come back for her second pre-admission briefing with you. Part of your task today is making sure that she understands the common problems resulting from the insertion of the peritoneal catheter and subsequent dialysis. Her family will cope better if they have contingency plans and do not become drawn into inflexible beliefs that suggest a reliable timetable of events.

I (initial check)

Nurse: Have you any information to do with common problems after the operation and during the first few weeks of dialysis?
Carol: No, none at all. I didn't know that there was any, to be honest.

I (information exchange)

Nurse: Well, to be equally honest, it would be unrealistic to expect any side of medicine to be problem-free. We have our fair share of difficulties in renal medicine. I want to tell you about them so that if you do run into one or the other of the common problems you won't be surprised, or feel that we've let you down. I'll write them out as a list and tell you about each one. First, the end of the catheter may become obstructed, either because it has slid into a poor position and is blocked by the intestines, or because the end has become clogged with omentum (tissue which sometimes grows round foreign matter). This is in no way dangerous but will mean that the catheter has to be repositioned in a second similar operation. The chances of needing a second operation are about one in ten. Very occasionally there have to be three attempts before things are right. Sometimes there are difficulties with the other end of the catheter, where the dacron collar forms a joint with the skin. This can leak and the dialysate fluid seeps out during dialysis. Again, this usually leads to a repositioning operation. Also, about one in five of our people develop infections at the site – these will be treated by antibiotics.

Another very common problem is peritonitis. What happens here is that bacteria or fungal organisms manage to get inside the abdominal cavity and the lining (the peritoneum) becomes infected by them. Even with apparently fastidious sterile techniques this can still happen. We would love to be able to prevent it but at the moment it's not possible. If you develop peritonitis, you'll have a very high temperature, severe abdominal pains and will generally feel unwell. It's not pleasant, I'm afraid. It's treated by strong antibiotics run in with the dialysate fluid and you'll also be given painkillers. So you see, Carol, when you make your plans for going home after training, you must be flexible and bear in mind two things. Your chances of getting peritonitis during training are definite, but not high. If it occurs it will *delay* your training. Occasionally people with resistant forms of peritonitis have to convert to haemodialysis for a while. This interrupts your training and will delay your change to home dialysis by maybe six weeks or more. Fortunately this doesn't happen to many people. That's about it, I'm glad to say. Do you have any questions?

Having completed the information exchange, you will, of course, monitor your success in communicating these facts with the FAC (final accuracy check). The task, you can see, is quite simple. Instead of a conspiracy of silence or adoption of the myth, 'the less they know the less they worry', you draw people in on the event by sharing information in order that they can make advance preparations. They will worry, naturally. It is, after all, a worrying situation to be in, but it will be productive worry, preparing themselves emotionally and allowing imaginary rehearsals for the events should they ever occur. Whenever you can, do give advance information. With surgical cases, for example, tell people in advance of the type and severity of pain they will have to deal with. Do not try and protect them by hiding information. All you are doing is making them more vulnerable, but *do* make sure that the advance information is complete and includes an indication on how likely problems are dealt with.

The second aspect to be emphasized is the function I have termed 'acting as an agent on behalf of your patient'. Once again, the principle is exceptionally simple: your job is to keep your patient informed at an optimum level. If she asks something or it becomes clear that a piece of information is important and you do not have that information, take positive steps to obtain it. This is why goodwill on the part of medical colleagues is important.

For example, it is now three weeks after her admission and Carol has indeed contracted peritonitis. In times of crisis like this she will be frightened and will need regular short visits from you to keep a good check on what she knows and is expecting to happen. You have looked in for one of these brief visits:

Carol: The ward round was rushed this morning and I didn't get much chance for questions. How long will it be before I can go back onto peritoneal dialysis?
Nurse: I don't know at the moment. I'll ask Dr Thomas at the meeting this afternoon how he thinks the peritonitis is responding to treatment. I'll ask him to give me his estimate for the best possible and worst possible outcomes in your case.
(Later)
Nurse: Hello, Carol. I've just looked in for a second. Dr Thomas thinks that at the worst you'll have to stay on emergency haemodialysis for another week. Yesterday morning's specimen was quite encouraging, though, and his most optimistic guess is one more haemodialysis session then back to CAPD. So, somewhere between two days and a week. I've written that down for you to show your husband.

When you take on informational care work with your patients, you must work intelligently in relation to the adopted task, following a course with each individual which keeps them informed throughout the various stages of their illness. The work cannot be rigidly time-tabled or rule-bound to any extent – it must follow the flow of medical events. Maybe Carol will develop peritonitis, maybe she will not. A few weeks after changing to home dialysis she might be offered a transplant, and even if this is initially successful, it could fail at any time. Each new medical event needs information and, since it will bring with it a variety of outcomes, there be a need for preventive advance information. Your own patients, like Carol, will need to know of the likely procedures and complications confronting them, the physical experiences, social disruption and the most/least favourable estimates of outcome. It is, though, *your responsibility* to organize the interventions. You must think for your patients, bear the burden of decision and conduct your task with professional thoroughness at all times. Each person's needs will differ and you must be pragmatic and thoughtful. If you are good at your job, you will be making a major contribution towards your patients' wellbeing and they will be cared for in a more complete sense.

EDUCATIONAL CARE

Information which is highly standardized can often be delivered as a standard package, either verbally or in written form. Thus, as well as the more personalized, ongoing informational care, certain specialties will also need educational materials and programmes, the fields of diabetes and dialysis being obvious examples. I will not be dealing at length with this aspect but will settle for one or two comments and include some examples from developments at Exeter Renal Unit.

We have found it very valuable at the unit to keep a record of what has been taught to people on the dialysis training programme, who taught it and how well the trainee patient/partner got on. This came about as a result of criticisms voiced by subjects in the survey by Nichols and Springford (1984). Among other things, they complained of inconsistency and confusion in what was being taught by different nurses. At that particular time I was taking flying lessons, and noted with interest the way in which the instructors kept a full log of the content of each lesson and my performance therein. If I then had a different instructor he would read this log and know what needed to be repeated or done next. This notion was passed on to my colleague, Polly Woodhams, the sister in charge of the Renal Unit, and she developed a training log for the dialysis programme. Part of this is shown as Appendix 1.

Quite clearly, clarity and simplicity in written information is paramount. However, what really matters in educational material, from my point of view, is the extent to which it anticipates exactly what the patient and their partner will really benefit from knowing; that is, it prevents stress by giving them information that eliminates doubt and confusion. For example, as well as the personal informational care work prior to the surgical construction of a fistula for the purposes of haemodialysis, patients are given a written memory aid to keep with them at home. This, again, was developed by Polly Woodhams. It is simple, written in everyday language and anticipates experiences and possible problems. It outlines any action necessary. In other words, it shares knowledge on a stress-preventing basis. This little piece of educational care is shown in Figure 4.4.

Sometimes, standard information cannot be given to patients

because there is a high degree of individual difference in the details for treatment and rehabilitation. One way of tackling this is demonstrated in Appendix 2. We had run into difficulties trying to produce written material for people who were about to have a kidney transplant: there were too many variations to deal with. As an alternative we thought it might be useful to give people *standard questions* to ask in order to get back the details for their own case. The questions anticipate these doubts and worries. Patients are given the standard list of questions and asked to book time with their primary nurse to obtain the answers.

WORKING WITH PARTNERS

In some specialties partners are pressed into being the home-based caregiver, for example in cases of multiple sclerosis, stroke, severe chronic pain, etc. If you are to give complete care, these partners also need to benefit from your knowledge and experience. Again, the strategy of sharing knowledge in order to reduce the risk of difficulties should prevail. In Nichols (1987) I outline some of the psychological

Looking After Your Fistula

1. For the first week, the wound will be covered by a dressing and you may have the arm in a sling for a day or two while the wound heals.
2. There may be some pain initially, which usually responds to simple painkilling tablets and the use of the sling.
3. You should not wear any rings on the same hand till all swelling disappears.
4. Fingers should always remain warm and pink. If they become cold or blue, notify the kidney unit at once.
5. There should be a pulsating or buzzing sensation over the wound, which indicates that the fistula is working. If this stops, inform the kidney unit *immediately*, and be prepared to come to the unit.
6. The fistula arm may be used once it is pain-free, provided that you keep the wound dry and clean.
7. Remember, not all fistulae work. If they fail, this may mean another attempt to construct a fistula, usually at a different site.

Figure 4.4: An example of standardized educational care

issues linked to the role of caregiver. There are predictable mistakes that caregivers often make, with predictable, stressful consequences. These can be 'headed off' by sensitive informational care work. The following is an example of the sort of briefing which ought to take place before a patient is discharged home into the care of his or her partner or family caregiver:

Nurse: Because you feel horrified and enormously sad for your husband, you will probably experience a great need to do things for him. It will seem hard to make any demands on him and most likely you will want to do everything for him, tolerate his mood changes uncomplainingly, and sacrifice something of yourself and your own life as a gesture. You will probably feel guilty that you are well and mobile and can continue life normally and, because of this guilt, elect to give up many of your activities in order to be with your husband. There is danger in this for you, though.

Should he be an invalid for a very long time, if you become locked into this pattern then two things might happen. First, you may play a hand in turning your husband into a severely dependent person who will have lost the ability to reciprocate care and effort, and who may drift into being a manipulating, demanding person with a very narrow focus of interest concerned primarily with his own needs. Secondly, you will have narrowed your own life down so that it is very stressed and you feel dreadfully trapped, exploited and a 'beast of burden'. You will greatly resent your husband's behaviour and demands but feel too guilty to demand change. Things will mount up and the strain on you will increase and could bring very great distress.

From the beginning, then, you must be aware of the need for self-care and be aware of the importance of maintaining your own identity, interests and activities. Although your husband is ill and will be an invalid, you must set up your pattern of living so that he strives for a degree of independence from your constant attention. Before discharge you should discuss this together, perhaps with my help, so that you both agree about the general objective. He needs to understand that in de-stressing your own situation by practising self-care and maintaining your own identity you are not being callous, but preserving your ability to go on giving care for a long period. You both need to remind one another about the risks of drifting into an excessive invalid or excessive caregiving pattern.

THE ETHOS OF INFORMATIONAL AND EDUCATIONAL CARE

As you will by now have gathered, one of the main points of informational care is to reduce the risk of stress and distress in illness and injury by sharing knowledge. What if people do not want to know? A small proportion of people do get on better if they can maintain a passive position: 'Just do what you have to, doctor and leave me out of it'. This is unusual though. Most people want good, reliable information.

Having said this, always check how people are responding to the information you give and encourage them to share their reactions. Later in the book I use the term 'advisory counselling', which is synonymous with informational care. As a name, it does convey the notion of combining the informational care approach with that of emotional care and basic counselling. These skills are dealt with in the following chapters.

There is one last point to mention: do consider setting up an information 'hot-line' – in other words, an easy means of access to information for people who are outpatients or discharged. Maintain the background of support and informational care for your ex-patients if you possibly can. It is very cheap to do and can save a great deal of time and money.

CHAPTER 5

Emotional Care and Monitoring Psychological State

In this chapter our attention is on the emotional aspects of illness. I will not be listing differing types of reaction in relation to different illnesses or injuries, though – this material is very well covered in books such as Broome (1989), Lacey and Burns (1989) and Kaptein *et al.* (1990). My concern is elsewhere. First, I think that you should devote some reading and thought to the origin and significance of emotional reactions in illness. Linked to this there is an equally important issue which needs your attention, namely, how do you react to your own emotions and how do you react to the emotions of other people? Although it may seem something of a chore, it is important to go through this material before you launch into helping people by means of emotional care. The first part of this chapter looks at these issues.

Once we have established an understanding on emotional reactions in illness, this dictates an attitude towards what should be done in order to provide suitable care. The second part of the chapter therefore concerns an approach for giving emotional care. As a final subsection, I put together some thoughts for you on how to monitor psychological state – the central task of psychological care.

UNDERSTANDING EMOTIONAL REACTIONS TO ILLNESS AND INJURY

If people are emotionally active in circumstances which make them want to hide their emotions or suppress them because of feelings of shame and embarrassment, then they are effectively in a non-caring or even hostile environment. With seriously ill or injured people, there is a high likelihood of greatly increased emotional reactions. These people will usually be in the midst of a traumatic experience, which seems socially and physically threatening, is often alien in character,

96

and involves separation from the home and supportive network of family and friends.

All of the professions involved in hospital treatment have a role in which emotional care is relevant and necessary, whether it is a doctor confirming to a patient that he is developing cancer or kidney failure, a speech therapist beginning work with a stroke victim, a physio-therapist assisting someone with severe spinal injury, an occupational therapist giving attention to an amputee or a nurse admitting a woman prior to a mastectomy. These professionals will all fall short of the tar-get of genuine care, unless they either contribute to basic emotional care themselves or make sure that it is provided by someone else in the team. What, then, are the key elements to emotional care? Is it truly understood, let alone practised, in the typical hospital setting?

NURSES' CONCEPTS OF EMOTIONAL CARE

I will begin by reflecting on the position of some newly trained nurses whom I take to be representative of the new psychological awareness in the nursing profession. The event was a tutorial session a few months ago in which I found myself engaged in something of a heated confrontation. One of the nurses was offended because I had gone through some of the material from Chapters 2 and 3 with them, lamenting the absence of proper psychological care in hospitals, 'You talk', she said, 'as if we have not had any training in psychological care. Half of our work at training school was on the psychological side of things.' I felt a little awkward at this because I did not wish to belit-tle her experience and training nor to antagonize the very people whose interest and help I was seeking; added to which it gave me the uncomfortable feeling that I might be getting out of date. So we chatted on, circling around the complaint for a while. Shortly it became rele-vant to explore what she had in her mind when she talked of giving psychological care, or to be more specific, emotional care, since we had turned to that as the subject in hand. The issue was how should a nurse respond to someone in her care who had become deeply dis-tressed and was clearly entertaining suicidal thoughts. The outspoken nurse gave her version thus:

Nurse: The important thing to remember is that you must listen to people who are distressed and allow them to talk about their problems, even if it is while you are doing some other task. You must not ignore their emotions or try and stifle them.
Psychologist: What is the point of encouraging this kind of conversation?
Nurse: The point is that it allows people to express their feelings.

When they do that, the nurse can see what their problem is about and maybe help them with it.

Psychologist: So what objective do you have in your mind with this approach?

Nurse: Well, obviously if people are very upset or anxious you want to do something about it, you can't just ignore it. Your job as a nurse is to look after them and deal with problems. Many people need to talk with someone and that is part of our job. We have to help them ovecome their distressed feelings and, if they are suicidal, help them see a point to life.

I went away from that exchange thinking that this nurse had indeed received training which pointed her well and truly in the direction of emotional care. Her role concept included a considerable component of psychological concern. But I also felt that her training had stopped short of a full understanding and that, as it had been left, she would not be as effective as she might be in the work. Furthermore, she would actually be rather vulnerable herself in such work, since her training had not included any personal preparation.

Basically, the nurse was saying that the emotional comfort of people in hospital is an important objective for nurses to work towards and that they must therefore be attentive to the emotional state of the people under their care. The main response by the nurse to emotional distress is that of listening in order to allow feelings to be expressed. During these interactions, the nurse will be vigilant to discover a person's problems and thus ways in which she can help. She will search for ways to respond which will directly alleviate the distressed state, or alter a person's outlook. The general approach in this work appears to be 'as and when required', fitting it in round the routines of nursing. Notice that the underlying concept is really that of an *informal treatment* (in the broadest sense) which depends heavily on the performance of the nurse. She must use her abilities to appraise the difficulties and attempt some resolution to bring about relief to the distressed person. There is nothing wrong in that, you might feel; it sounds like they are doing a good job. Well, we should take a closer look before deciding one way or the other.

Some unhelpful assumptions

First, let us examine some of the *assumptions* concerning emotional care which are manifest in the statement of approach conveyed through this conversation. Put briefly, these are:

1. An emotional reaction is regarded as an adverse state, something that the nurse must work to diminish or limit; in other words, there is the feel of the illness/treatment concept.

2. Emotional reactions are usually provoked by 'problems' and thus the means of achieving emotional calm in a distressed person is by first identifying the key problems and then coming up with something that helps – often this is taken to mean finding something helpful to say.
3. Emotional care is implemented only when a person is seen to be in distress; it is thus an unscheduled activity limited to 'casualties' and not a specific task routinely undertaken with all seriously ill or injured people.

I wonder what your view of these statements is and whether or not you feel that they represent an accurate picture. My own judgment is that the concepts of emotional functioning and emotional care advanced by the nurse were far too limiting. First, there was little recognition of *normal* emotional functioning. In times of high stress and threatened or actual losses in life, it is *normal and usual* for people to react with strong emotions. Such reactions are part of a process and have a significant function. However, with the approach described, such normal, functional, emotional reactions were basically construed as abnormal. Consequently, the orientation adopted towards emotional reaction was of something necessarily needing treatment, something to be attacked and 'cured' like infections. In fact, this can actually be the opposite of helpful – damaging even – since the attitude denies 'permission' for the normal emotional process and may encourage emotional suppression which blocks important *processes* (the point will be expanded below).

A second adverse feature was the implication that emotional care should be directed to people who show overt signs of need, that is, they have become openly distressed or actually break down. A broader, more realistic view is that all seriously ill or injured people will inevitably need emotional care, not because they are necessarily distressed but in order to help them be more comfortable and to facilitate the natural emotional processes which attend such major life crises. As a parallel to this, of course, those involved in emotional care will be available to assist people who have become overwhelmed and disabled by very strong reactions or actual psychological disturbance. In other words, *there are two types of emotion to be held in mind*, the normal responses which are part of functional emotional processes, and emotional disturbances which have their basis in some psychopathology. Where one ends and the other begins is rarely clear, but one thing is certain: many instances of obvious emotional responding observed in hospitals are not abnormal and do not need 'treating' in the sense of eliminating a disease.

I find a worrisome third aspect buried in this conversation, to do with the effect of the last point on nurses or people involved in emotional care. With the 'illness–treatment' theme influencing one's approach, the nurse becomes burdened with the need to do or say something in order to reduce a patient's state of emotional activity. Now this is a heavy burden to bear and certainly one which I would not welcome for myself. It seems to lie behind an anxious statement which I have heard so many young nurses make: 'I did not know what to say, I felt I might say something wrong and make her worse'. The problem is that the felt obligation to do or say something introduces a tension, since the nurse's performance is judged by whether or not emotional activity subsides. If she cannot find a way of shifting her patient into a less emotional state, she appears to have failed and feels inadequate and guilty. I do assure you that eliminating emotional reaction is *not* the primary target of emotional care. On the contrary, it is concerned with providing an interpersonal atmosphere which facilitates emotional processes by giving the opportunity for their expression. Thus, in some cases, *emotional care involves helping a person into an emotional response*. So you see that it is a great handicap if the basic concept is one in which the continuation of an emotional reaction is seen as some kind of failure on the part of the nurse. It may be the opposite – a sign, as we will see shortly, of her effectiveness.

We have reached the point where some conclusion has to be made as a result of examing the assumptions revealed in this conversation with the nurse. My view is this: the nurse was oriented in the right direction. She recognized the importance of emotional care and saw it as a significant component of her job. She realized that it required involvement on her part and that she had to work verbally in a rather intimate relationship. However, she worked with the idea that emotional reactions are something to be 'dealt with' and diminished by means of discovering the problems which are presumed to act as the cause. In other words, she was including emotional activity in her general medical illness scheme of things. This, I believe, is a significant mistake which will reduce her ability in emotional care and cause her considerable personal difficulty.

So, now to the business of putting forward the alternative ideas. From now on this chapter will be set out as a short 'teach-in', giving the basic elements to prepare you for emotional care work.

PERSONAL PREPARATION

Your own attitudes to emotion

In the normal course of our education we are taught little about emotional functioning, either at home or at school. There are some fortunate exceptions, but most of us are launched on the world with little to guide us other than the stereotyped views from our native culture as expressed within our family subculture. Although there is no convenient way of assessing the precise outcome of this situation, what is obvious is that the level of understanding on matters to do with emotional functioning varies greatly from person to person. Very many people are quite ill at ease with the experience of emotion, either finding great difficulty in recognizing their own emotional life or feeling greatly perturbed by the emotional life of others.

In the former case there will be a defensive style, repressing personal emotion and denying awareness of it to conscious experience. So, for example, a man may deny that he is anxious in a particular situation and believe that to be the case, whereas the language of his body and behaviour states very clearly that he *is* anxious. Such a characteristic leads an individual to struggle very hard to hold back emotion, and if this bid fails there is a sense of shame and failure. In the latter case, face-to-face contact with emotional expression in others gives a feeling of agitated discomfort and so the need is to escape it or, if that is not possible, to stem the flow of emotion in the other by one means or another. Sometimes people are uncomfortable with one sort of emotion but not others. For example, a woman may find it easy to deal with depressed feelings in her friends, but want to rush away from their anger.

In considerable contrast, it is possible to find people who are fully in touch with, and accepting of, their own emotional life. They have the facility of expressing this to others without inhibition. More than that, they do not find emotional expression in other people to be threatening and may even have a 'feel' for what is going on inside others. Thus, our lesson in emotional care starts with an unsurprising assertion. *We all have our own characteristic patterns of reactions to our own emotions, ranging from inhibited, shameful and blocking through to open, allowing and accepting. Similarly, we all have our own characteristic patterns of reactions to emotional expression by other people, ranging from threatened, denying, rejecting and suppressing to at ease, approaching and encouraging.*

The differences between us will, in part, be related to experiences in our childhood. One person in a recent training group recalled having been punished and shamed in childhood for emotional expressiveness, and taught to strive for emotional inertness. Such a style was modelled and rewarded by his parents and key figures in his schooling. Another member described how, as a child, she had to deal with the traumatic exposure to her mother's frequent severe depressions, which eventually led to a successful suicide bid. Both these people found that their adult personalities were influenced by a powerful need to hold back their own emotions, and they experienced considerable discomfort with any significant show of feeling by others. As the work of the training group progressed and they both relaxed a little, they were able to take stock and identify that for years the whole business of emotion and personal feeling had been a difficult struggle. Both, in their own ways, had actively fought against any (in their eyes) 'weakness' in letting emotion through. In effect, they had blocked off an important part of their lives as people, stunting development as mature individuals.

Personal questions to be asked

Where is this taking us? Both these people were in medically related professions and both wanted to take on some activities to do with psychological care. However, they were still hampered *themselves* by inhibitions and fears to do with emotion. (Indeed, part of their desire to get involved with this kind of work was probably the fact that they had gone through some very damaging experiences in childhood and, as adults, still felt a need for healing care which they expressed by turning in concern to the care of others.) Because of this, without further personal development they could never be very effective in the work of emotional care since these difficulties would intrude. In particular, their behaviour in the more demanding areas of emotional care would be influenced by *their own anxieties and needs, rather than those of the patient.*

In contrast to some of the mechanistic roles in medicine, in emotional care your own personal development is of considerable significance. Simply learning procedures and having an enthusiasm to get involved is insufficient. It is important that people intending to take on this work have themselves developed to a point where there is reasonable freedom from personal difficulties and inhibitions to do with the expression of human emotion. Thus, for you, the very first steps in training involve your development as a person. It is necessary for you to assess your position when it comes to dealing with emotion. How capable are you of identifying your own emotions and allowing expression of these without anxiety and shame? Can you express emotion without a sense of being weak such that an apology is required? How capable are you of communicating your emotions directly to others, as opposed to acting them out while verbally denying them, or even attempting to hide them completely? I do not mean this in a trivial sense, nor is the implication that we should all be uninhibited and give vent to emotions in any situation and with any person. I am talking of a developed capacity to accept rather than deny feeling, and a capacity for self-disclosure and sharing with appropriate people, in appropriate situations, without tenseness. Clearly this has to be developed as a situation-specific skill, the opposite skill being necessary at times. For example, the *inhibition* of emotional expression is important during complex surgery, important planning committees or emergency situations.

In the same way, you must also ask the question, 'How do I respond to the emotions of other people – am I at ease with them or do they make me feel tense? Do I cast around for some means of stopping them?' This effort made towards self-knowledge will prove of considerable value. In the short term, it will allow a perspective on one's state of readiness for work of this type, and also throw into relief targets for necessary personal development. In the long term, for many people, the very act of thinking and talking in this way and reflecting on one's properties as a person in relation to certain ideals actually begins to produce slow change and development of a positive type.

I will not claim that self-help of this nature is easy. Most of the people who function as counsellors or psychological therapists have been assisted in the endeavour by formal training courses, which include much work of this type and make it so much easier. Nevertheless, I have to be honest with you. In any other activity, 'the workman is as good as his tools', the point being that in psychological care work *you* are the tool and your 'cutting edge' is partly determined by your progress in the kind of personal development that we have been discussing.

Having raised the issue, I must sadly leave you in the lurch with it, since it is way beyond the scope of this book to encompass the topic in depth. Use what resources you have. Study your behaviour in relation to emotional functioning. Involve people with whom you have close relationships in giving you feedback on your most characteristic ways of dealing with emotion. If you have the chance of using time in a discussion group to take up this theme, then exploit the opportunity. I will, before moving on though, offer an aid. If your thoughts turn to this subject in any depth and you feel you have some work to do towards personal preparation, what is the ideal? What should you aim for? Figure 5.1 is my version of the ideal to use as a basis for further thought and discussion.

● **Reactions to his/her own emotional responses**

Attitude Emotion and the flow of personal feeling are valued and respected as an essential part of human behaviour.

Understanding There is recognition that certain experiences are bound to evoke powerful emotional reactions and that, in most cases, these are signs of a normal process to do with preparedness, adjustment and change. It is understood that the reflexive denial and repression of emotional response is an abnormality.

Awareness The person has achieved development to the point where there is an awareness of the flow of personal feeling with the ability to identify and 'own' these feelings without needing to deny or block them.

Expression There is an ability to express emotion and be emotional with 'appropriate others' without anxiety or shame. The ability is experienced as normal, mature and advantageous. There is also recognition that certain circumstances require the temporary suppression of emotion where it would obstruct other important activities,
Self-knowledge This person has some idea of his/her 'trouble spots' in relation to personal emotion. That is, there will be awareness of which emotions are easy to express and accept and which are difficult and what type of situation or people create inhibition.

● **Reactions to the emotional response of other people**

Attitude and understanding The positive attitude towards personal emotions will be extended to encompass the emotional expressions of other people. Emotion is valued as a significant and inherent part of human functioning. It is seen as a normal component of the overall reaction to illness or injury.
Absence of negative reactions: when in face-to-face contact with the emotional reactions of others, there is an ability to accept the situation:

- without horror and an anxious need to escape
- without a need to encourage the other person to suppress his reaction and shift him to an emotionally neutral state in order to meet a personal need for safety and comfort
- without a sense of hurry to resolve the issue involved and produce emotional calm based on the belief that active emotional responding is something that has to be stemmed and thus needs 'treating'
- without a feeling of being trapped or paralysed by the other person's emotion
- without a feeling of guilt that one is personally responsible but powerless to do anything
- without a need to increase interpersonal distance for fear that one's own emotions will be stirred and revealed

Positive reactions: there will be a sense of supporting and sharing in an experience which involves the patients' need to discharge emotion without any 'curative' response from the listener, together with the recognition that the patients' reaction may be an aspect of complex emotional processes which could continue for some time. There is thus a relaxed acceptance of the present state, with a concern for immediate comfort rather than a drive for the urgent suppression of the reaction.

There will be an ability to be close and empathize with the feelings involved, to communicate this involvement together with the knowledge that feelings can be shared in safety, with freedom from comments that would evoke defensive feelings.
Self-knowledge This person will have an awareness of the different effects that exposure to various emotional reactions has on him/her, some probably being easier to deal with for the individual than others. It will be accepted that exposure to the emotions of another can be troubling at times and the use of support and discussion on a regular basis will be felt as comfortable and advantageous.

Figure 5.1: Some characteristics of a person thoroughly suited to the task of emotional care

To keep this all in perspective, remember that we are talking of ideals here. I cannot say that I have met too many people who are quite so

well-rounded as this – which, to impart a confidence, is to my satisfaction, since people without any hang-ups at all always seem a hint
insufferable to me. Nevertheless, most of the people working in this
field have struggled some way along the path towards these ideals and
I hope that you too will see the need and take up the challenge.

UNDERSTANDING EMOTION AND PERSONAL FEELING

The basis of personal feeling

It would be foolish to get involved in the work of emotional care without a reasonable understanding of emotional functioning. This section
therefore serves as an orientation to the topic. It is a rather hotly
debated area with some fierce disagreements, and I have to warn you
that it is my view you are getting and that not all psychologists would
accept it.

Much of our behaviour is determined by what we see and how we
react to what we see. In fact, we are in a constant state of reaction to
the world about us and also to our inner world of thought and fantasy.
This flow of reaction is something which involves our whole body. Our
reactions are, at the physical level, a constant shifting of body state to
various patterns appropriate to the perceptions of the moment. It is
this sensing of the body state which forms the basis of what we call
feelings. The concept of feeling is rather broader than that of emotion,
although the two words are close in meaning and are often used inter-
changeably. It is common for people to confuse the constant, ever-
present flow of personal feeling with major emotional reactions. For
example, on various occasions in group therapy sessions, I have asked
members what their particular feeling was at a specific moment in conversation. Some have said, 'I'm not feeling anything'. What they
actually meant was, 'I'm not anxious, angry, tearful or depressed' – in
other words, they have no obvious major emotion. The reality is that
under normal circumstances it is impossible to be without feeling, since
the word refers to the experience of one's body state and its meaningful relationship to the events of the moment. It is, however, frequently
the case that we are not immediately aware of our feelings because our
attention is elsewhere. Also, not everybody understands how to identify feeling and it takes a little guidance in the means of getting in
touch. Basically, it involves sensing the overall state that your body is
in – reading the message of the body, we might say.

Gendlin (1978) has developed this idea and introduced a technique
called focusing, which sharpens people's ability to identify the 'felt
sense' of their body. His basic point is that if we require to know
exactly what we are feeling we have to learn ways of inquiring within.

Our body state *is* our feeling; we thus have to search out the nature of our body state at any one time to identify feeling. If, therefore, the members of my group had stopped momentarily and 'read out the feeling message' of their overall body states, they would have been able to discriminate the various sorts of feeling typically generated in group sessions. These would include interested and alert, or tense and on guard with a sense of something difficult about to happen, relaxed and uninvolved, on edge with a protective concern, bubbly, at ease, agitated with something to say which is difficult to get out, and so on.

The point is that being alive and being human inevitably involves a constantly changing flow of feelings as our bodies, thoughts and overall conscious experience take in the succession of stimuli to which we are sensitive. Of course, the complete experience of personal feelings involves more than just physical response and changed body state. As writers in existential psychology suggest, feeling is a synthesis of other functions which can involve changes in the quality of the experience of the world, but it is beyond our range to develop this point further here. Sometimes feelings may be present on a long-term basis, related perhaps to certain circumstances which prevail for a lengthy period. An example of this would be the experience of threat to one's sense of wholeness as a person if cancer was identified in the testes or breast.

So, in summary, as we take in a constant flow of perceptions we react totally, with our whole body and our whole experience. Sensing the consequent body state is the basis to feeling and emotion.

The distinction between emotion and feeling is vague and not, I think, one which we should divert to investigate. It is probably easiest if we adopt the convention of regarding emotion as a term used to imply strong feelings; that is, there is a physiological impact on body state beyond the usual and we become aware of changes in our physiology, general behaviour, verbal expressions and thinking. There may also be new behaviour which is not necessarily under voluntary control, like crying and angry outbursts. In other words, while in an emotional state, daily behaviour is more obviously dominated by global shifts in body state which we label anxiety, depression, euphoria, grief, anger, etc.

I want to stress the point that the concept of 'feelings' is often used loosely and disparagingly in western culture, the inference being that they are an indecent sideshow within us which is rather embarrassing or, for men particularly, something to be grown out of. A variant of this is the aseptic atmosphere of the hospital, wherein feelings are often greeted like bacteria. Thus, anxiety inhibitors and antidepressants are handed out with the same urgent sense of getting rid of something threatening as are antibiotics. Such attitudes betray a gross misunderstanding and conceptual distortion. Feelings are a product of the core processes of reaction which direct our behaviour. We behave through our perceptions and consequent feeling reactions. They are an ever-present, central feature of living. Our normal functioning is such that (if I may use a metaphor to make the point) we are 'designed' to have feelings as a fundamental part of our system of responding. If we wished to build a computer simulation of human functioning, a significant portion of the programming would be in the provision of feelings.

Conclusions

If you are going to offer emotional care you must be at ease with the idea and experience of human feeling and the ways in which it is expressed. Above all, you must realize that in the majority of cases you will encounter in the general hospital setting, the feeling reactions of others are *normal*. Do not, therefore, be frightened by them and do not become involved in efforts to stifle them or suppress them with drugs without very careful thought as to the appropriateness in the individual cases.

Illustrations of emotional processes

From your training in whatever profession you have been drawn to, you will have noticed that human physiology is staggeringly complex and elegantly economical. Each function interlocks with the others to give a functional harmony. In terms of current biological assumptions, we have evolved in this way by a remorseless process, selecting out the most effective changes. Few features can be demonstrated that are redundant, without function, or inefficient. In this context, our emotional life has an enigmatic quality. At first sight, emotional reactions are cumbersome obstacles to efficient function and would be better swept away. After all, we could argue for a moment, they do not actually do anything of real use for us. Or do they?

I have described above the view that what we call feelings are, in part, the sensing of body state. The various patterns of body state, ranging through the relaxed-resting state to high levels of tension and vigilance, or attraction and sexual arousal, etc., are in reality states of *preparation and adaptation* to the needs of perceived circumstances. The obvious point is that personal feelings reveal a continuous process whereby the combination of a person's physical and psychological resources can be directed and energized to provide the most appropriate and most effective response.

Consider a person reflecting on forthcoming exams, who realizes that time is short, the ground to be covered is great and the threat of failure is real. He responds with the feeling of nervous, tense urgency. His focus of attention narrows more to work, his sense of urgency fuels a far greater capacity to work, study, stay awake and keep going than normal. Other activities are displaced and seem less important because of the nervous energy. These are unpleasant feelings but they are *functional, part of an adaptive process* which serves to optimize the person's efficiency in a situation of perceived threat. Without them, his behaviour would remain unchanged and the exams would come and go with predictable outcome.

In the same way the emotional reactions which you will observe in your career in the health care professions, are often processes which have a function and are to do with a person's preparation for a taxing event or adaptation to a stressing change. *Because these processes are functional, the essential attitude towards them should be that of giving assistance which will aid their completion.* Take very careful note of this point, because it is central to a full understanding of emotional reactions. The states of apparent emotional upheaval which attend life crises such as illness or the death of a relative should not be seen as if *they* were illnesses. They are changes in a person's whole state which indicate a process of change and preparation.

To avoid introducing any confusion, I should make two qualifications here in order to accommodate the idea of abnormal reactions. First, while it is normal behaviour to react to what we see, many people experience excessive difficulty because they see threat where there is none, or expect loss when it will never happen. That is, *the problem is not how a person is feeling but what they are seeing.* As I so often hear myself saying in seminars, 'Given the way she sees the situation she *should* be anxious. It would be abnormal if she were not, the real problem is the way she sees it all'. Unless people have a physical disorder which creates an anxious state, say thyroid trouble or other hormonal disturbances, where people react with excessive emotional power, the safest assumption must be that the presence of such strong feeling is a normal response to what they are seeing in the situation – but their perception may be inaccurate and distorted. Secondly, a proportion of people enter the experience of illness already overly sensitized to certain elements of personal threat by prior experience, and thus their emotional reaction is amplified by factors originating from the past. This is likely to be the case with so-called neurotic or anxious personalities. With these two qualifications in mind, I will leave the topic of abnormal reactions until later on.

Your basic ideas on the nature of emotion are extremely important. They will determine the stance you take towards the people you work with. I have been stressing the notion of valuing personal feeling as a normal and important aspect of human functioning, arguing that the idea of emotional reactions as some state of disorder or illness which must be treated is quite wrong for the majority of cases in a general hospital. Instead, the reactions are best seen as processes which have a function. Our next step is to come down to earth a little and make sense of all these through a couple of case examples. These will attempt to convey the way in which anxiety and the grief/depressive reactions can be accounted for within the terms of this conceptualization.

Case 1: Productive anxiety

A youngish woman, Paula by name and 34 years old, was employed as a medical receptionist. She was divorced and due to remarry within three months when, to her great distress, her GP advised an urgent consultation with a surgeon because she almost certainly had a well-advanced cancer in her right breast. The GP's fears were confirmed. The surgeon, a considerate man, spent some time with Paula and talked through the implications. He could see no way out of the problem other than a mastectomy. He could not be certain whether he could limit this to a simple mastectomy or not. If the cancer was extensive then, in his view, a more disfiguring radical mastectomy would be the only safe option (this was some years ago). He appreciated her situation and offered the reassurance that he would minimize surgery to what was absolutely necessary. A date for admission was offered, with the operation scheduled to take place two weeks later.

During these two weeks Paula was in a state of considerable anxiety. She found herself distracted by a procession of tense, worrying thoughts. The normal routines of her day were difficult to concentrate on and social interaction suddenly became an ordeal. At night she was restless and lay awake for many hours, with her heart thumping and an alert tension denying her sleep. She spent considerable time contacting people that she knew had experienced a mastectomy, and she also made appointments with several consultants in alternative medicine to sound them out on ways of reversing cancer other than surgery. In the end she felt that the actual threat to life, since the cancer appeared to be advanced, did not give these approaches sufficient time. The risks seemed too great. On the day of her admission to the hospital, Paula was in control but still gripped by a powerful feeling of anxiety. She anxiously questioned the anaesthetist (being aware of the risks of general anaesthesia) and the surgeon when they called in to see her, stressing again how fearful she was of the outcome of the surgery and pressing the surgeon to cause as little change as possible. Her anxiety conveyed itself to the nursing staff too, who were concerned and offered reassurance.

How should we regard the anxiety that gripped Paula during these times and kept her awake late into the night before her operation? First, we must recognize that as a normally adjusted, average human, she *should* have been anxious. Like all normal people, she responded with the characteristic changes which we call anxiety, when she perceived threat. What threat was she in touch with? There were several elements. In the first place there was the risk of continuing illness and death within a year or two, after suffering the agonies of treatment and the illness itself. Secondly, the surgery would destroy (for a while at least) her sense of being a complete person. She would be disfigured to a greater or lesser degree, and in her fantasy of the future would loathe the remains of her breast, feeling that she would always want to hide it and apologize for it. Both of these were direct physical threats, but the latter brought with it profound psychosocial threats. Paula had used her body as a way of presenting herself to the world. She had a good shape and was proud of it. Her initial approaches in developing relationships with men were dependent on her physical attraction, and she valued an active sex life both for its own sake and as a means of securing relationships. Her self-image was thus under threat and her known safe route to securing relationships looked as if it was to be closed off. Thirdly, and worst of all, her impending marriage also seemed under threat. The relationship had, to a certain extent, been built around Paula's physical attractiveness and the importance that she had in her partner's eyes as a sexual partner. Now, she agonized, this would no longer be possible. The most frightening fantasy was of revealing the wound to her boyfriend. The marriage plans might well founder, maybe he would pull out, maybe she should pull out. In this thought there was buried a last frightening implication. Perhaps she would end up on her own, stripped of her impact as a person (in her judgement) and with no secure relationships. These were Paula's perceptions. For two weeks the thoughts and images ran endlessly through her consciousness.

It would be ridiculous to say to a person in Paula's position, 'Don't be anxious'. She is anxious for a good reason. She realizes that the situation she faces threatens her both physically and socially. She has responded as she is 'designed' to respond, and needs understanding, support and companionship with her anxiety.

But take a closer look at the outcome of her anxiety. I want you to see that, although it is uncomfortable and she would dearly wish it to go away, *it is adaptive and does have a function*. Her anxiety is, among other things, a state of raised vigilance and increased energy to tackle the threat. It has led to her to strive to master the situation by rapidly finding out about the effects of mastectomy, seeking various alternatives to the operation and, within limits, influence her surgeon's approach. In other words, she has adopted a confrontational stance, which is the positive, adaptive outcome of the emotional reaction. While this has been going on she has also been involved in what some writers call 'the work of worrying'. She has created in fantasy the various outcomes and experiences that could well present themselves to her in reality during the months to come. She will now not be overwhelmed by surprise if any of these actually become reality. She is braced, and has to some extent rehearsed the experiences in advance. *In other words, the anxious worrying has been a sort of preparation. It has been painful but it has had a function. It is in this sense, therefore, that we should talk of her anxiety as a functional emotional process.*

Case 2: The work of grief

I will preface this case description with a fragment of theory. People have the capacity to become attached to other people – we call this bonding. It is a complex emotional and perceptual event that most of us are acquainted with through personal experience. When such bonds are broken through some separating event, a powerful emotional response takes place which is termed grief. The feelings involved range through despair, anguish, anger, intense sadness and even sensations of physical pain. With these feelings there is usually a flood of thought, memories and images to do with the lost person. During grieving, attention is focused on what has been lost to the exclusion of other interests, but as the months go by, this process seems to lead to an erosion of the emotional bonding. The images of the lost person no longer have such a powerful capacity to trigger emotion and other people or aspects of life begin to acquire more significance again. Janis and Levanthal (1965) describe this as the work of grieving. Their belief is that when a person is heavily bonded to another and that bond is severed, it is not possible for the bereaved person to make new bonds immediately because the old ones are still active and have a blocking effect. In grieving, a process occurs which progressively weakens the blocking effect of the old bonds. The apparent turmoil of thought and memory centred on the lost person functions to erode the power of the emotional attachment. The repetitiveness of so-called reflective grief exhausts the response. With the completion of this process, the person is again free to make new attachments.

Rachman (1980) talks of a similar idea which he terms 'emotional processing'. Whenever we experience psychological trauma, such as an incident with a profoundly shocking or frightening impact, or the loss of someone to whom we are attached, it is a normal characteristic, Rachman observes, for the event to intrude in our thoughts with great frequency and to trigger the associated emotions over and over again. (Some of you may have experienced the 'I can't get it out of my thoughts' effect after an accident, for example.) After a period of this unsettling activity, the impact of the event lessens in that it no longer has the power to produce the emotional response. The emotional processing is complete. When, for one reason or another, this period of emotional processing is blocked, atypical patterns of extended grief result. There may even be episodes of emotional disturbance, with phobic or obsessional features.

With these thoughts in mind, the following case example should make more sense. The case involves another woman, Sue, who went into renal failure at the age of 38. At the time she was a nurse in charge of a children's unit. Sue was happily married but without children of her own since early on she had decided that her career was of central importance to her. She had never regretted the decision and had progressed steadily in her field to become well respected and highly skilled. The kidney failure was unexpected, following a short but severe viral infection. She could not believe it at first, but as she recovered from the panic and physical agonies of severe uraemia, the awful truth bore down on her. The nurses caring for her reported that after a short spell of being rather gracious and kindly, she became angry, often snapping at the nurses for no apparent reason. Her mood changed again a day or two later and she became withdrawn and tearful, not in a hysterical or overt way, but spending long periods alone in her room weeping, turning away company and responding little to the attempts by the doctors, nurses or relatives to comfort her. She ate little and was not much interested in caring for herself. In dialysis sessions she adopted the approach of stoical endurance, keeping her eyes shut much of the time rather than learning about the techniques and beginning her training towards self-sufficiency. She was clearly very down and the senior registrar handling her case thought she was clinically depressed and wanted her to take antidepressants. Some of the staff began to be offended by her rebuffs and entered her room only when it was necessary. So what was going on?

If we remain loyal to the idea that her reaction was part of a normal emotional process which would make sense if we knew what she was seeing and thinking in this situation, then our thoughts must turn to the notion that this was a pattern of behaviour rather similar to the grief reaction. Who was dead or departed though? The answer was clear; in Sue's inner world *part of her had died*, although she would not describe it quite like that herself. Her existence was centred on her role as a nurse, where she dealt with very dependent young people and their anxious parents. This included a vision of the future, with her career extending until retirement age. Much of her sense of worth and strategy of living was locked up in this 'core role'. Now, as a realist who understood the basic problems of living by dialysis and the gamble of renal transplantation, she was well aware that her career had been cut dead. A most important, central part of her life was gone, the very basis of her self-image and self-worth. Her feeling was of anger, protest and a despairing loss. She had begun to grieve for this part of herself. Thus the slow emotional process that would take many months to complete was under way. The daily experience of the dialysis unit compounded the loss. Each hour she had to relate to people still in possession of the role she had loved so much. This triggered resentment which she knew was unreasonable, and the reversal of roles led to feelings of being humiliated and diminished. It was as if a part of her had been amputated.

From this case study there are two lessons for us. First, that grieving is a response which can occur in relation to *any* major loss. We can be bonded to aspects of our physical, social or psychological selves, to key roles or even objectives in the future. If these bonds are powerful and stable, their unexpected severance will be traumatic and probably trigger the grieving reaction. Secondly (as with Sue), such reactions do have a function. Through this process, with its turmoil of thought and feeling, comes the eventual weakening of the bonds to the lost object of attachment and thus the freedom to develop a new life. The aim with people who react in this way should not be to 'knock the depression out' or to 'get her over it as soon as soon as possible' but to help her into and through the process, to facilitate its completion.

THE PRACTICE OF EMOTIONAL CARE

MAKING PEOPLE COMFORTABLE

In the previous section, I have advanced the view that emotional reactions in people facing the trauma of serious illness or injury a) are to be expected, b) should in most cases be conceived as normal behaviour, and c) should be valued as processes which enable adaptation to threat or transition through major life changes involving loss of role or body parts. It has been recognized that the occurrence of such reactions is primarily determined by the way in which people perceive their situations. Some will experience severe threat or loss, others will actively deny contact with such perceptions (usually a short-term defence which collapses) and a third group will perceive the situation in alternative, less threatening ways, and so appear fairly self-contained. Much will depend on a person's position in life and whether 'core roles' are threatened (it is a useful exercise to ask yourself how *you* would react at present if you were involved in an accident that led, say, to the loss of an arm). It must also be remembered that the general atmosphere in hospitals creates a situation where very many people are highly active emotionally, but struggle desperately to hide this from staff and relatives.

The reason that so much space has been allocated to the development of this theme is that *the work of emotional care is based on a basic premise, namely, we are not treating emotional illness but rather facilitating emotional processes and supporting people through the period of time when such processes are ongoing.* At this point, however, there could well be some confusion. Am I saying that we should leave people to bear the full impact of these sometimes painful emotional experiences because they are important processes? By no means – emotional care has the same target as, say, basic nursing care. That is, to make people comfortable and bring them to a condition which is most likely to promote rapid healing and a return to health. In these terms there is nothing wrong in assisting people with some kind of sedation or sleeping aid if they seek it. The impact of strong emotion can be exhausting and alarming in itself. Clearly, any resources that genuinely improve a person's condition and make him more comfortable should be exploited. However, it is important to retain the perspective that *assistance with drugs is in order to make people more comfortable and not as a treatment to combat emotion because it is being misconstrued as an illness.* This approach would not only reveal a staggering ignorance of the phenomena involved, but would compound the atmosphere of denial and have a blocking effect on the emotional processes involved. It would be a case of medicine making things worse, not better.

THE EMOTIONS OF ILLNESS

What can you expect to meet if you get involved in the work of emotional care? There is little point in my constructing a detailed and tedious list of emotional reactions related to illness. It would be unrealistic anyway since, as a life experience, illness and involvement with the medical and medically related professions can be painful, harrowing, frustrating, depriving, frightening, severely threatening, depressing, humiliating, intimidating, boring, annoying, intimate, evocative of profound relief and gratitude, safe, relaxing, nurturant with great human warmth, comic, inspiring and much more. In other words, the whole range of human feelings will be encountered. Most commonly you will be dealing with fragile people working hard to contain feelings of anxiety, anger, grief and depression, who may also show warm feelings of trust, affection, gratitude and dependency. In the majority of cases there will be no mystery about why people are feeling as they do, assuming, that is, you develop contact and through careful listening begin to see their world through their eyes. In many cases you will understand quite clearly because you would feel something similar if you took their place. Perhaps it will be helpful to use another case example here to show that sometimes the character of a person's reactions can be surprising, but it does make sense when their position is made clear.

Eddie was another dialysis trainee, 43 years old and a draughtsman by trade. He was about three months into his training and had reached the point where he was receiving instruction in the art of needling – that is, placing two cannulae into his fistula prior to a haemodialysis session. The trouble was that when Eddie was in the unit everybody knew it. He was angry in a subdued way all the time, but would suddenly flare up into terrible tempers, openly shouting at the nurses. Occasionally objects were thrown. He seemed genuinely angry with the staff, but for no obvious reason. He received the same treatment as everybody else. The nurses found his behaviour hurtful and annoying and saw it as being unreasonable.

The psychologist was involved in this case and after several sessions was able to explain to the nurses what was happening. Briefly, Eddie had been the son of a harsh, critical man who endlessly undermined Eddie's sense of worth by belittling his achievements and driving him on to do better by sneering at his efforts. He had emerged into adulthood as a man who was phobic of failure. He instantly abandoned anything at which he could not do well, and drove himself to his limits in everything that he did. He had taken on his father's critical attitude. The handicap induced by kidney failure is severe loss of energy and a certain degree of intellectual slowing. This had led Eddie to be increasingly critical of himself, increasingly impatient of all his new limitations. He turned his despising condemnation onto himself. Presenting this weakened self at the haemodialysis training unit was an agony. When he had to tackle subtle and complex skills such as venepuncture, his needs were to master them instantly. When he could not do so an uncontrollable anger surged through him, for when he looked at himself he could only see failure. Although this anger was meant for himself, he could not aggress against himself effectively so it spilled over in his interactions with the nurses.

BASIC STEPS IN EMOTIONAL CARE

Now at last we can get down to the issue of what is actually done. To illustrate the elements of emotional care I will develop an extended example and 'talk you through it' as if you had to do the work personally. What is to come could apply equally to a doctor, physiotherapist, speech or occupational therapist, but for convenience it will be written using the image of a nurse as the central figure. The illustration will be an idealization in that I will assume a development in this particular ward to the point where the nurses offer psychological care to all the people passing through it and, in the case of the more seriously ill who are making a longer stay, have an allocation of time and a suitable place for emotional care work.

Your patient is John Rayner. He is 42 years old. Two days ago he sustained a moderate myocardial infarction. His condition has now stabilized without evident disrhythmia and he will be resident in your ward for about two weeks. John works as a self-employed plumber in a style typical of the so-called coronary-prone personality, that is, building up long hours with little rest, taking few holidays and driven by a restless need to keep on striving towards some private objective of achievement and perfection. There are two children in his family, together with Ruth, his wife, who runs the office end of the business. You will find him a little tense, wary of what is happening to him and rather close to tears at times.

Laying the foundation

John does not know you as a person. He needs to feel secure with you and to achieve this, you must spend a little time with him, time during which you are not fussing with one or another of a dozen duties but when you sit on his bed and look at him and talk with him. The content is not vital but what is important is that he can sense what kind of a person you are and he can feel that you have the capacity to relate to him without nervousness on an open, honest basis. He must sense your caring intentions and discover you to be someone who does not put him on his guard. With this in mind, you should make several brief visits, simply to find out how he is doing and to exchange words with him about whatever seems a sensible topic. On one such visit you should let him know that you will be talking with him at greater length soon on how he is feeling personally as a result of his coronary.

Initiating emotional care

Your entry into emotional care work with John must come as a gentle invitation, with plenty of scope for him to take his time, delay his response or even refuse. You *offer* care, never force it. At the same time, note that you take the initiative and do not wait for 'something to come up' to precipitate your action. Some people, however, will beat you to the offer because they have an urgent need to talk out some of their feelings and they begin before you have a chance to issue an invitation, but John is more defensive. In casual ward conversation he is adopting a denying strategy, saying that he is alright and is already planning how to sort out a couple of incomplete jobs. At the same time, the message of his manner is that he is unsure and has taken a heavy blow which has shattered his confidence.

The invitation will be your version of the following:

Nurse: 'Part of my work is helping people with the personal and emotional side of their illness. Many people coming into the ward find it stressful and have anxieties, and often times of depression. I do not know whether this applies to you, John, but at this point in your treatment I would normally put aside half an hour to meet with you in private to check how you are getting on and how this has affected you personally. Is this something you would like to take part in?

If he is comfortable with the idea, arrange a meeting within the next day or so to do just that.

What you are doing here is giving John permission to have a personal side to his illness and validating it by showing that it merits separate attention, but dealing with it as a normal part of the care in the ward. Part of the reassurance necessary at this phase is to communicate the idea of normality, that strong feeling reactions are to be expected and are part of the normal pattern of illness such as coronary heart disease. The more you can make this just a part of the routine and relax about it yourself, the better. Observe John's reaction to your invitation carefully. If he seems bothered about it, rather than arranging your first session check back with him later, saying that you felt he was a little unsure about the suggestion of talking over the personal side of things and would he rather leave it for a while.

Beginning the first session

We will assume that John gets on with you and feels positive to the thought of someone with whom he can talk through his reactions to the heart attack. You have organized a time and the first 'session' is imminent. Incidentally, a word about time and setting: since we are talking of ideals, I should say that the least optimum conditions for this kind of work is perched on a bed, in uniform and in an open ward. The optimum conditions (in my view) are to make use of an interview room, office or individual bedroom, to be out of uniform and to have an agreement not to be interrupted. We have to accept reality, though, and if people are in bed, in plaster with traction, or linked to monitors or dialysis machines, such conditions will be unobtainable. But give thought to making your patient as socially comfortable as you can.

Just before beginning, let us pause a moment and think about you. Why are you doing this? What is your motive and in what frame of mind are you meeting John? These are important questions and we should establish this as a ground rule: never lose sight of yourself and your own needs in this kind of work. Monitor your state because there may be times when it would be best to leave the work to somebody else. A meeting is about to take place in which John will have the opportunity of reflecting on his feelings and the circumstances that prevail upon him. He may be very closed up about it, in which case it will be a fairly desultory session. He may only be able to describe some of the thoughts and feelings he has experienced, in a flat, held-in way, but it is also a possibility that in talking of his experiences, emotions which have been held back will begin to well up. *You must expect his emotions and be at peace with them.* To use an analogy, surgery cannot be undertaken without contact with blood and, in the same way, it is not possible to be involved in emotional care without face-to-face contact with the emotional experiences of others. If, for example, John should break down and shed some tears and this makes you want to say, 'don't cry', or feel guilty as if something has gone wrong and it is your fault, *do not go any further* – you are not ready for it yet. Your own needs will start to predominate and your tension will block the very events which need to be facilitated. Added to which, you will, frankly, be something of a fake because a situation is being created which you, rather than John, cannot handle.

Assuming that this moment of self-inquiry reveals nothing to make you hesitate, let's get you to meet with John Rayner now – he is expecting you. If you have the use of a room, take him to it or, better still, meet him there. You should sit near him, looking at him in a relaxed manner, ideally out of uniform, not behind a desk and without pen and notepad. Hopefully you will have already established the reciprocal use of first names. If the session has to be on the ward, then do everything you can to create the atmosphere of two equal people meeting in some sort of privacy.

Task number one is to lead him slowly to the targets of the encounter, so be very clear what these are. You know that there is a high likelihood that he is experiencing considerable emotional upheaval as he appraises the significance of his heart attack. Your intention is to relieve the isolation of this emotional processing and offer a situation wherein he can express his feelings, live them in the presence of another (which may not be possible with family members and certainly is not possible in the busy routine of ward life) and experience care through tension-free acceptance. He will probably find this a new situation and be unsure of his ground, needing to approach it in easy steps. Your opening remarks, therefore, are important because they will carry the guidelines he will be searching for. Avoid patronizing put-downs such as, 'It's time we had our little talk', or officious professional-to-patient openings like, 'Now, John, I would like to ask you a few questions'. I would not want to suggest any sort of script or a standard opening – you must develop your own style with a view to leading him in the right direction, relaxing both himself and yourself and giving it the feel of a normal part of the ward work. However, here is a typical opening exchange which does have a gentle, directive quality. (Bear in mind that John comes across as being rather tense and wary and will probably not prove an easy talker to start off with.)

Nurse: Well, John, I'd like to check on how you've found these last few days since your coronary.

John: I've been glad to be here. I got a bit wound up the day it happened, didn't know what had hit me – you do mean me to talk about the personal side and not my chest pains, don't you?

Nurse: I'd like you to talk about whatever is on your mind, but you're quite right, this isn't really for dealing with the medical side of things. I was wondering what it's been doing to you in terms of how you've been thinking and feeling since you came in here.

John: Shock, that's what's in my mind. I can't believe it – just can't believe it. And worried – you don't know the half of it.

This type of beginning gives John a sense of direction and allows him to choose his own pace. He can start by dealing with past experiences and past feelings, which allows a little distancing and also enables him to test out your reactions. It will be quite useful to get him to talk out in full his reactions to the last few days (rather like an abreaction) as an exercise to get both of you used to working together and dealing with the emotional aspects. Later on, after his early disclosures, one or two prompts may help if he becomes blocked. For example:

Nurse: If, in your imagination, you could tell someone who is shortly going to have a heart attack about the difficult side of it, the things that have really troubled you, what would you say?

Or,

Nurse: I've never had a heart attack although I've nursed many people that have, so I see it from a different angle. From your experiences, what are the aspects that have a lot of personal impact that I might not know about?

This kind of conversation may well be an important learning experience for John. He will either flourish and develop his capacity for this type of communication or shrink back to become defensive and closed off. Thus, your job in this first encounter is to ensure that events foster this learning. It is the way you handle the session and your reaction to what he says which will determine his progress. *Your key role is that of giving supportive validation towards feeling-based communication; in other words, he receives confirmation that these particular types of self-disclosure are valid and exactly what the session is about.* Your primary means of achieving this is by listening with undivided attention, reflecting back what he is saying from time to time to show that you understand and accept it, together with giving occasional encouragement and assistance if he gets blocked. Beyond that, you have no brief at present, since we are confined to purely emotional care and not counselling. Any urge you may have to 'cure' needs to be resisted – your objective is to *allow* feelings, not obstruct them.

Later stages of the first session

Assume that John has taken a quarter of an hour or so recalling his experiences and feelings of the last few days. He seems to have settled to the task and is talking easily. He is fairly matter-of-fact, though guarded. As he talks of his feelings he clearly has no real contact with them in the sense that he is not giving himself the time or the opportunity to sense these feelings and let them stir him now. He is holding them at bay. In formal psychotherapy it would be part of the therapist's task to direct such a client in ways which would develop greater contact with his feelings and free him from the defensive denial that was taking place. Here, however, this is not the case. You are not involved as a psychological therapist. The objective in emotional care is not to activate people into greater emotional responsiveness, it is *to care for them on the level at which they are functioning*. In other words, try not to become exasperated with him and hold back any need to prod him or stir things up. You must remember he is not in a strong state and will be much better without additional sources of upheaval. Never forget, therefore, that you are offering him an invitation to talk with you – he has no obligation to do so – otherwise the meeting could be threatening and counterproductive. The chances are, though, that if your work with him maintains the character described below, he will feel increasingly able to make contact with his feeling reactions in your presence.

As the initial session proceeds, it may be helpful to bring John closer to the here-and-now, to his present state of feeling. Again, a gentle invitation such as:

Nurse: So how are things for you today, what is your feeling at the moment?

And a little later on,

Nurse: If you can't get to sleep tonight and are lying awake thinking of what has happened and what is going to happen, what will your thoughts be and how will you be feeling?

I have mentioned several times in this chapter that your general approach in this encounter is of great significance. It is through the medium of your reactions that people such as John learn a new attitude and a new ability with feeling-based communications. By no means all of your patients will need this kind of initiation. Some will be thoroughly at ease with this type of communication and will not need you to guide them, although they will need to feel they can trust you. In my own experience, though, the proportion of patients like John is quite high, so perhaps we should press on to specify in more detail the elements of emotional care in order that you have something to guide you (see Figure 5.2).

Aim: To assist normal emotional processes

Skills:
Making the situation safe for the patient and giving 'permission' for emotional expression
Leading the patient to get 'in touch' with feeling reactions
Helping with and encouraging the *full* expression of feeling
Communicating back understanding and relaxed acceptance
Giving support by showing that the patient's emotions are respected and valued

Figure 5.2: Emotional care in illness

THE CORE CONTENT OF EMOTIONAL CARE

Pause now and spend a moment or two reflecting on Figure 5.2. This sets out the basic steps to be taken when you are giving emotional care. These will be illustrated by an extended example in the sections to follow.

Making the situation feel safe

Emotional care depends on safety. That is, your patients feel safe with you, by which I mean they sense that they will not be attacked, embarrassed, humiliated, judged inadequate or devalued. This atmosphere of safety will come from the character and tone of your reactions to the disclosures they make. The overall message conveyed in your replies must be that the disclosure of personal feeling, the worries, regrets, anger, sadnesses, black thoughts and so on are appropriate within the context of the session, and that the situation harbours no threat. Part of the sense of safety will come from the realization that you respect the emotional upheaval provoked by illness as a normal event, which makes you neither tense, embarrassed nor despising.

People will often begin a series of meetings like this in a wary state. It is a little foreign and they are wondering what you will think of them, but on the whole, they will not feel the need to be defensive or shy away in embarrassment unless you introduce such an atmosphere. So consider what you say in terms of whether it makes for safety or threat. Never, for example, directly challenge, contradict or devalue a person's experiences and the feelings associated with them, since that will drive him into a defensive position. Even kindly meant challenges may have the opposite effect to that intended. For example:

John: My wife is such a worrier, sometimes I feel more bothered about her than I do about the heart trouble itself.
Ineffective Nurse: It's silly to be worrying about things like that; your

job is to get well and you won't do this by getting bothered about other people and things you have no control over. She'll be alright, I'm sure. **Comment**: Basically this is a rejecting communication which begins by construing John's feeling of concern for his wife as 'silly'. It does not teach him that feelings are accepted and valued – it teaches him to be wary because revelations of inner feelings may result in statements from the nurse which are belittling. In other words, the situation is made unsafe to John. In contrast:

Effective Nurse: Well, let's expand on that for a while because it's obviously very important to you. When you say you feel very bothered about her, what are you actually referring to? Do you mean you feel nervous, angry, protective or what?
Comment: This response carries the message that the disclosure is of importance as it stands, worth spending time on, worth elaborating. The interest by the nurse and her readiness to see such experiences as acceptable make the situation appear safe to John.

By taking up the things a patient says, acknowledging them and encouraging an elaboration, you are declaring them valid. This is the necessary source of safety. With a prevailing atmosphere of this type, wary people like John will reach a position where they feel more secure. Their experience is that 'I am free to talk of my feelings, that is what is wanted. She understands and accepts how I feel, I sense her support and sympathy. I do not feel devalued or humiliated, it is easy to talk with her'. In this light you can see why so many of the communications from medical and nursing staff in, say, a ward round situation, are grotesque *devaluations* of personal feeling. I quote from a recent event:

Consultant: How are we this morning? Nurse tells me you have been a bit upset?
Patient: Yes; I've been feeling a bit depressed for the last two days. I keep wanting to cry.
Consultant: Absolutely no reason for you to be depressed, my dear, everything is going well, it's all healing up nicely. Just a bit of post-operation blues, I expect. You'll have to try and get things like that out of your head. I'll get nurse to give you some pills to shift it.

Giving permission for emotions and emotional expression

Have you noticed in your work, or general living for that matter, that when people become emotional they will usually apologize. A mother, on hearing that her child was deaf, broke down and cried in the presence of her GP – and then apologized. A man I met a few weeks ago who had gone into sudden renal failure was very emotional and when talking about the effect this would have on the way his wife regarded him, burst into tears – and then apologized to me. It's natural enough, of course. In our society a show of emotion is considered as embarrassing, something which should happen in private. As we have seen, though, a significant proportion of your patients will be in a state of emotional reaction. For them the difficulty is that in the typical hospital subculture, with its emphasis on control, the atmosphere of aseptic routines, the growing technology and above all, the wide social distance maintained between professionals and patients, the sense of the inappropriateness of emotional reaction is amplified; there is little place for human feeling. Put another way, in the average hospital setting there is no natural permission within the subculture for this expression of feeling. For you, this presents a tide to swim against because emotional care work requires that the opposite conditions prevail. A clear sense of *positive permission* for the expression of human feeling is vital.

Without doubt, this is a difficult and complex objective for professionals in a hospital setting. It presents various potential problems, not the least of which will be in staff relations. For example, it will be difficult not to feel hostile when a patient with whom you have established an atmosphere fostering permission for emotional expression is treated roughly by an insensitive colleague *because* they have shown emotion. (The risk of interprofessional division as a consequence of this work is obvious and will have to be monitored with great care, since it would be to no-one's advantage if, say, the nursing profession changed with great rapidity in the direction of psychological care while the medical profession lagged behind. A divisive tension could be created since the traditional behaviour of the medical profession could not be allowed to damage and retard progress of this type.)

How, then, is 'permission' given? Again, the important factor is the character of your reactions and communications in the presence of your patient's emotion. This is why I earlier placed such stress on personal preparation. You cannot create a permission-giving atmosphere if you do not feel permission for your own emotional life, or are ill at ease with that of others. Let us return to your encounter with John Rayner to find some concrete examples. Your first interview with him has gone well enough. He is relaxed, happy to talk, clearly getting something out of it but still keeping the issue of his feelings at arm's length. You are happy to work with him at this level, trying to guide him gently in his first experiences of emotional care and using the flow of conversation as a way of making him feel safe and supported. Attention has turned to his feelings of the day and John has mentioned for the first time that he feels very down at times. So let us eavesdrop on your future skilled self and see how it is done.

John: I do have some awful thoughts sometimes, like last night and when I woke up this morning. I haven't told anyone and it would really upset my wife. I expect you'll think it's stupid. (He is giving you a warning – there is something he needs to reveal but in doing so becomes vulnerable.)

Nurse: Take your time, John. Just say what you feel comfortable saying and then I'll be honest with you and tell you how I feel about it.

John: I find myself thinking ... gosh, it's so stupid ... I find myself thinking that now I've got heart disease the best part of my life is over. I don't mean I want to do myself in, but yesterday I thought maybe it's best if I have another coronary and that finishes it. I'll never keep the business going like I need to, and I was top of the squash ladder, really strong for my age and, I hope you don't mind me saying it, pretty good in bed. It all seems to be gone now. I keep remembering my Dad in his wheelchair – I don't want to be like that. (At this point tears trickle down John's face and he cannot continue talking.)

Nurse: She says nothing, puts her hand on John's hand and simply gives him a tissue. She does not fuss or shuffle around in tension but waits a little while in silence still looking at him in a relaxed way. *She is at ease with his emotion. She cares about it but it is not her fault so she does not feel guilty – it belongs to the situation that John is in.*

John: I'm sorry, I didn't mean to make a fuss like this.

Nurse: Are you embarrassed?

John: Yes, you must think I'm a complete fool.

Nurse: I can see that you aren't used to sharing your emotions with other people, John. You seem so condemning of yourself, using words like 'stupid' and 'fool'. Is that how you actually see yourself at the moment?

John: Well, perhaps not, I know what you mean. I don't really mean it quite like that, I got a bit flustered.

Nurse: You were saying that you felt finished and would be happy for it all to end.

John: That's right. Not all the time, you know, but sometimes I get low, can't seem to shake it off. Can you understand?

Nurse: Yes, I can. It feels like a terribly sad experience that you're going through. (There's a silence for a minute or so – John is lost in thought.)

Nurse: What are you thinking?

John: Just about what the doctor said. Then I was wondering what you thought of a grown man crying.

Nurse: Alright, I said I would give you my views, so here they are. You have had a severe shock and things are going to change a lot for you. It's been frightening and the future looks frightening too. So it's bound to stir up some intense feelings including, as you've found, wishing yourself dead. It will probably be months or even longer before you feel emotionally strong again. That's how it is for many of the

people who have heart attacks. I'm pleased that you've been able to share this side of your illness with me. I don't suppose it is easy to tell your wife. (Pause) How are you feeling at the moment?
John: A bit choked up to be honest.
Nurse: Would you like to leave it there for today or go on and tell me a little more about the sad experience when you woke up this morning?
John: Well, I don't know really, have you got the time? It's a relief to talk about it.

You can see what is happening here. John is, in effect, asking questions and you are answering them. It is all about 'what do you think of me now that I have told you my depressed thoughts and shown you my emotions?' It is a critical moment. You could well have ruined things if you had become anxious at John's distress and tried to rush in with placatory platitudes in order to stem the tears. It did not happen that way, though, and the situation was used to good effect, giving him time and then showing him the way towards a positive attitude to his own emotion. *You introduced the element of permission.* Then you gave the responsibility of deciding whether or not to continue to John. He clearly felt safe, he clearly sensed the permission and he opted to continue. Some of the later contacts with him will similarly involve depressed feelings, tears and anger. He will again need your calmness and your reaffirmation of permission to have and express such emotion.

Facilitating emotional expression

The means

We are pursuing the case of a man who does not find the actual process of introspection and verbal disclosure of personal feeling easy. Apart from these acquired inhibitions from earlier years, John has a limited (I should say undeveloped) skill in working out how he is reacting – in Gendlin's (1978) terms he has poor contact with the 'felt sense'. As we have noted, people vary greatly in their expressive ability. Some will not need help at all. Many will struggle though, and you cannot leave them to flounder. After all, the main point of these encounters is to give an opportunity for the expression of feeling. The skill of facilitating the expression of feeling is something that psychological therapists spend many years acquiring, and cannot be picked up by means of a few quick tips. Like any craft, you must spend time and more time developing a feel for the material for use and slowly elaborate your knowledge and repertoire of abilities. Thus I will try and illustrate the notion of facilitation and lodge it in your mind as an asset to strive for – through discussion with more experienced people and plenty of practice.

Several incidents during the contacts with John had in common the feature of a rushed and impoverished expression of feeling on his part – he seemed to be glossing over important issues. In these instances, assistance into further expression of feeling would obviously be worthwhile, as long as he remained comfortable with it. An example of this is illustrated in the next portion of transcript. Let's assume that you are not a beginner but are well trained in this work and have considerable experience. This is probably how you would handle the following situation:

John: (Talking of the ward round of yesterday morning) When the doctor said I would have to find another sport, that I couldn't go on with competitive squash, it really got to me. I was in quite a stew for an hour or so. Funny, isn't it, that it seemed to bother me so much, but it's only a game, I suppose. (Pauses) Anyway, then the wife came up later and we had a look at a few invoices . . .

Nurse: John, hold it a minute there, because you've mentioned feeling really bothered but I'm not sure what you were actually thinking and feeling. You've rushed through it. Go back to that bad moment you had and let's go through it again.

John: Well, it was afterwards, really, they had gone on to Bob in the next bed. I suppose it just came home a bit. My heart turned over – you know.

Nurse: Alright, try and bring back what you were picturing in your mind and the actual feelings it stirred up.

John: This is going to start me off again.

Nurse: If you're not comfortable going through it then leave it for now.

John: No, I do feel better when I get things off my chest.

Nurse: What was in your thoughts at that time?

John: Going back into the club, I think. I've been playing squash there for five years. I'm doing well – was doing well – in the squash league and I play for the first team.

Nurse: What did you imagine, I mean, what did you actually visualize that upset you?

John: Going in and having them see me like this. Well, they won't see that much difference but they'll know about me, and all I will be able to do is sit and watch – a has-been. That's what got to me, turning up like a cripple.

Nurse: And this makes you feel . . .

John: Angry. Really wild, like I could smash something.

Nurse: Can you take it a little further, John, pause for a moment and picture that situation again? You're angry at something or someone. Do you know what?

John: It's this feeling of being out of it, a write-off. I have to be at the top of things – can't stand being second best. It was the same with the

business. I don't know – I can feel it now, like needing to shout and punch something – punch myself I suppose.
Nurse: You feel angry because your body is letting you down, do you mean?
John: Not exactly. In here you get the message that it's almost your fault that you've had a heart attack and that if you'd done things differently you'd still be fine. They only tell you after it's happened though. No, I feel as if I'm to blame, really. I've knocked myself out of everything that matters.

You see how by catching things at the right moment and then getting him to go back and put a microscope on a particular incident this led him into a greater awareness of what was happening at that time, and helped him identify the feelings involved and express them. Notice also that you do not challenge these feelings or comment on them. You work at helping him express them and elaborate his contact with them. The more he makes contact with his anger and works his way through it, the sooner he will be free from it. You are helping the process develop.

This skill is heavily dependent on noticing that a person is clearly feeling a great deal but that this is partially blocked from expression. Your patient must be gently led back to discover the source of feeling in more detail, perhaps feel it then and there in your presence. But again, note very carefully, this is not about pushing someone into emotional activation for its own sake. You take him as far as *his* limits allow, no more. If he is pressed, a tension will grow and you will have made a bad mistake.

The reason

A short reminder on why you should put emphasis on facilitating emotional reactions. They often signify important ongoing psychological processes of adaptive preparation and adaptive change. The processes can usually be aided by direct and frequent expression of the feelings involved to another person and, when there is blocking, assistance in the expression of the feelings. This promotes the 'working through' of the process. An example of a rather more advanced form of this work is a specific form of therapy known as guided mourning. Mawson *et al.* (1981) described how people locked into a state of morbid grief which had persisted for twelve months or more were assisted by therapy sessions in which the therapist encouraged them to face those thoughts, memories, photographs and possessions of their lost partners most likely to trigger the powerful grieving feeling. This was done over and over again in the course of several therapy sessions. It inevitably produced a great flood of emotion. However, in comparison to a control group that did not have these facilitating experiences, the people accepting this therapy were measurably less disturbed by grief two weeks later. Guided mourning serves as a rather more dramatic illustration of the value of facilitating rather than inhibiting emotional processes. It is a psychological therapy, though, and not part of emotional care, so I would not suggest you adopt such an approach.

In your work of emotional care, one of the major objectives is to create a situation which encourages and supports emotional expression so that a person may settle more rapidly into a stable adjustment to the *consequences* of illness or injury. But again, I will plead caution. The facilitation of emotional expression is not just stirring people into emotion. That in itself is aimless, punitive and counterproductive, so go very cautiously with this aspect of emotional care, or you may do emotional damage.

Communicating empathy and acceptance – sharing personal feeling

These elements of emotional care merit separate attention.

Empathy

A person with good empathy accurately identifies what another person is feeling. Sometimes this is achieved without actually being told, because there is an ability to read non-verbal behaviour and sense the sort of impact a situation is having on a person. For you, presumably at a beginning level, it is a matter of listening very carefully to the statements of the patient and trying to project yourself into his experience. It means forgetting the need to perform as a counsellor and say the right thing, and relaxing into the work of picking up what the patient is seeing and thinking and then identifying the feeling – trying to get inside his world. If you can do this, you will, in many cases, echo his feelings within yourself, almost like resonating in sympathy. Letting your patient know that you do have empathy is important. It bridges the gap, producing a closeness and the necessary feelings of safety. You can do this from time to time by repeating back a recent statement, together with a little elaboration. Following the last words of John in the previous section, one might have said 'Yes, I understand, I can pick up an awful feeling of bottled-in rage – frustrating because it's difficult to really vent anger on yourself and get rid of it like you would if you were cross with another person'.

I will give you another illustration. Hopefully you will cope with my momentarily jumping to an entirely different case. This is of a session with a woman who had developed multiple sclerosis. She is white-faced and shaky as she talks of the future.

Woman: It's not knowing how long it will take or how far it will go. I

could be incontinent and barely mobile within a couple of years . . .
(she cannot continue for a while – she sobs bitterly and the psychologist holds her hand) . . . the children, how will I protect my children,
they will have to watch me get ill, and weaker, and die. That's awful.
What a burden for them.

Psychologist: (Near to tears himself, but not fighting it since this was a
moment of intense empathy and closeness; they were sharing the
emotion of the situation.) I can sense how painful your need is as a
mother to protect your children from this distress. Putting myself in
your place just now – it makes my throat ache too – so much sadness
and fright for them to bear and such a need in you to protect them.

Returning empathy is rather like being a mirror. You take in and sometimes take on the emotions of the moment and reveal this to your
patient.

Acceptance

There is little more to say on this since it falls within the material
covered in the earlier section on making your patient feel safe. Your
position is of one who values and respects the reactions of the individual. In emotional care, whether these reactions are based on correct or
false perceptions (provided this can actually be decided) is not a central
issue. The important thing is that, given the way your patient is experiencing the situation, his reactions are accepted by you and given
value. This should be communicated frequently in your exchanges.
However, I am not saying that if a person is responding to a perception
which is an obvious distortion of reality you should leave him that
way. If you remember, we are being disciplined in this chapter and are
dealing purely with emotional care. The business of leading people to
alternative perceptions comes in the work of counselling, which has
been split, rather artificially perhaps, from emotional care for the purposes of clear teaching.

Sharing personal feeling

Many medical schools teach that the ideal conduct for a doctor is of
concerned detachment. A lengthy process of indoctrination is fostered
to produce young doctors who have the ability to remain emotionally
switched off and uninvolved. This atmosphere can spill over to the
other professions to a certain extent, so that a whole department or
ward can appear resolutely detached and preoccupied with stifling
personal feeling. Where professions do experience feeling, it is common for them to mask this feeling from the population of hospital
patients (although again we should note the wind of change in the
philosophy of nursing care and the fact that the detached, feelingless

nurse is synonymous with a bad nurse in the new climate of nursing schools and nursing literature).

In the specific context of emotional care work, it would be a bizarre posture to adopt if you set out to hide your own feelings and remain stonily detached. At the same time, over-involvement such that you become caught up in your patient's situation to a degree which disturbs you is also unacceptable. Somewhere between the extremes of personal detachment and over-involvement there is a middle, optimal approach. Obviously this will differ in character from the so-called medical manner of relating, the most obvious difference being that one does exchange views and, on occasions, share thoughts, experiences and feelings. There does need to be restraint, however, since the object of meeting with a patient for emotional care is for him to express *his* feelings and thoughts, not to spend time listening to yours. Nevertheless, a little self-disclosure on your part prevents you being construed as a neutral professional (which fosters inibition) and builds a sense of mutual trust. Also, by occasionally sharing your feelings about the issue being dealt with, either verbally or by actually showing the emotion, you reduce the asymmetry that typifies a relationship between a 'professional and his patient'. In so doing, you make possible a genuine trusting relationship which can be used to achieve the aims of emotional care.

Let us be clear about what is being suggested here. Certainly the work of emotional care is professional work, and you should never lose sight of the fact that you are engaged in professional duties during the session. The relationship which develops with your patient needs to be of a genuine, human quality, but at the same time under control and limited. This is not in any way equivalent to developing an open friendship. It is possible to have a sense of human closeness and remain within the limits of your role, pursuing the targets of good emotional care. This contained relationship will be to your advantage when you are engaged with the same patient in the other areas of nursing or professional work which form the main proportion of your working day.

Thus, when it feels appropriate and when it complements the aspects of emotional care which have been dealt with above, be free in mentioning your own reactions, perhaps disclosing what you feel when you project yourself into the patient's position, or what you feel in the here-and-now, listening to him. There may be times when you identify very strongly with your patient's emotions and find yourself very moved by them, near to tears perhaps. In most cases it will be productive to be open and just simply share the emotion rather than desperately fighting it off or steering the subject onto neutral ground for your own safety, not the least reason being that you should not ask your patient to be more open in emotional expression when you are still stuck with powerful inhibitions yourself.

Support

Support is really a product rather than an activity. If there is a consistent and readily available provision of emotional care as just described, then it will inevitably be supportive. The awareness by a patient that his experience and feelings are known and understood by another person, the availability of that person to spend time with him in the immediate future so that the patient may continue to talk through difficulties, discharge feelings and experience acceptance with sensitive caring, provides the basis of support. Notice that it is not a particularly active role. Being supportive at the emotional level does not mean taking over a person's problems and solving them, or adopting some kind of psychotherapeutic approach in order to give treatment and diminish stress. It is primarily that you offer your time and are capable of spending this time with the patient in the ways shown here – that is, absorbing what he says, understanding, empathizing and gently assisting him with the task of confronting and expressing feeling. In so doing, you guarantee that your patient is not isolated with his feelings and thoughts – you remove the stress which comes from being alone with heavy emotional burdens.

Let me just expand the point in relation to the care of the dying. As you can see, emotional care with dying people cannot in any way hope to alter the basic situation. Death is inevitable, there are no long-term issues of adaptation and rehabilitation. In these terms there is therefore little to actually be done. It is, however, of extreme value to provide a caring, supportive companionship throughout the period leading to death. The availability of someone with whom it is possible to share *all* types of thought and *all* types of feeling, with whom one can grieve or protest, or just take the nurturing experience of feeling closeness and concern, is the basis of support for dying people.

The need to do or say something

I want to emphasize the last point in a way which I hope you will find reassuring. Nurses have often expressed the fear: 'I might say something wrong' or 'I won't know what to say'. Similarly, they have talked to me of feeling uncomfortable in emotional care work because they did not say much and did even less. Please remember, therefore, the following phrase – pin it up on your wall where you will keep seeing it:

IN EMOTIONAL CARE THE PROCESS IS AS IMPORTANT AS THE CONTENT

In other words, the *experience of being listened to* by a skilled nurse affects a person as much as what she says. You will be offering a valuable and relatively rare event in the lives of many people. Someone who listens, absorbs and shares and does not rush in with advice and crude attempts to cheer them up. Perhaps for the first time in their lives, they will have openly shared emotion in complete safety. The interpersonal process of doing this calms, frees and lifts them. Hence, most nurses can recall events in which a patient has suddenly 'poured it all out' while they have said very little. Later, that patient usually says: 'Thanks for listening to me yesterday, I felt a lot better after it'.

Ending a session

We must not forget that you have been left in the middle of a session with John Rayner. You have many other things to do and have nearly used up the 30 minutes allocated to the first meeting. How should you end?

It is quite a good idea to establish the length of a session at its start. That way, you will not be found in the middle of an important exchange surreptitiously looking at your watch and worrying about the time. Be firm and be definite. I usually give an estimate of time and later signal the end of a session in advance by saying something like, 'We will have to finish in five minutes. Is there anything else you would like to mention in the time we have left?'

On most occasions, finishing will present no problems. Just do it easily and naturally. If it has been a relaxed and fairly inactive meeting you can simply bid one another goodbye, ideally reaching an agreement on when you will next meet. On occasions, though, it will not have been a relaxed event and your patient may have been through some distressing or disturbing material with you, expressing much emotion. In this instance use your last five minutes to bring him back into the here-and-now and effect a sense of completion if possible. Let's return to you and John for a moment to illustrate this. You set aside 30 minutes for the first meeting and time is up. In the latter part of the session, John slipped out from behind his defensive screen and talked of his sense of loss as he identified the changes that would occur following his coronary. It was probably the first time in his life that he had systematically talked of his feelings in this way. It was not easy and clearly he was very emotional at times. An appropriate way to end would be like this:

Nurse: We must finish in a moment, John. I have to do some observations. How are you feeling?

John: Well, I'm sorry to have taken up your time like this...

Nurse: It's part of our work, we believe that it's important.

John: It's still kind of you to take such an interest. I appreciate it.

Nurse: So how are you feeling then – you'll be back with the others in the ward soon. Is it going to be alright?

John: I'm feeling alright now – sort of relieved. I think I'll just stay on my own for a while, though.

Nurse: Good. I'll probably have 20 minutes or so with you at the end of the week, but if you need to talk anything through before then you will let me know, won't you?

Deciding the pattern of contact – are all patients the same?

The first meeting with John Rayner is now over, the work of providing him with emotional care has begun. Tomorrow you will be asked to provide care for an older woman admitted three days ago with pericarditis. Should you deal with them both in an identical way in a fixed pattern of contacts or will there be differences?

The obvious fact is that people coming into a hospital differ in every possible way. Their length of stay, severity of illness, social background and back-up, personality and the actual nature of their psychological responses to the situation are just some of the variables. In one sense, every seriously ill or injured person will need your emotional care. Thus, ideally, it should be offered to all patients. Realistically, though the extent to which this is a major commitment for you will vary in relation to each person's needs at the time (and your own availability). Some people will remain genuinely stable and self-contained throughout their stay, and your work need be little more than occasional brief meetings to enquire how they are getting on at a personal level and, in so doing, reassuring them that the concern you have for them persists. However, during the course of an illness there can be changes in circumstance which destroy confidence and so you must be prepared to handle their altered needs should the atmosphere change.

On the other hand, a sizeable proportion of the seriously ill are bound to be in great emotional upheaval. We know this from the research reported in Chapter 2. In these cases, early contact with frequent meetings are the ideal, particularly when 'crises' occur. For example, a woman taken into a kidney unit had spent eight weeks training to self-sufficiency in continuous ambulatory peritoneal dialysis. Her first three weeks had been an appalling time for her, what with the shock of unexpected kidney failure and the tremendous disruption to her life. However, she had some good care and made real progress in coming to terms with her future. By the seventh week she was considered competent with her dialysis technique and was looking forward to going back to her family. In fact, to be honest, she was desperate to return home. Disaster struck, though, in the form of a persistent fungal peritonitis. This did not respond well to antibiotics and she had to transfer into the haemodialysis unit for a period while attempts to contain the infection were pursued. It looked as though she could not go home for another two or three weeks at least, and might have to abandon CAPD and start afresh with the six-month haemodialysis training programme. In this case, several of the staff, including myself, joined to make very full and necessary provision of emotional care. There were informal contacts with nurses each day and I met her on a scheduled basis once or twice a week. We rode this crisis out with her and were able to respond similarly when a transplant attempt failed some two years later.

Then, of course, there is *your* situation to consider. The pattern of working followed by nurses allows frequent unscheduled contact, perhaps dropping in to see a person briefly once a day, with occasional longer sessions. In contrast, a speech therapist, say, will often work on an outpatient basis with weekly scheduled meetings. Basically, you have to work within the confines of your role. The most important thing is to be flexible and *'read' the needs of your patient*, altering the pattern of your contacts accordingly. The same applies to where you meet. All my examples so far are idealized. They talk of 'sessions', implying periods of uninterrupted work in the privacy of a separate room. You may not have this facility, in which case, improvization and flexibility are the essential qualities needed. The main thing is to find a way to offer the core elements of emotional care in good time and with sufficient frequency to meet the needs of the individual case, but staying within the limits of your environment and work pattern. There are no rules; you must be the judge.

Formal versus informal structuring

This is a point about which I have some strong feelings myself. The debate goes rather like this:

Nurse: I don't like this idea of making appointments to see people as you suggest. I think you can talk with people much better if you do it informally. I find that people talk to me a lot when I'm giving them a bath.
Second Nurse: It's easier when you're helping them with something like dressing – they chatter away and tell you their problems.
A Dozen Other Nurses at a Dozen Other Training Sessions: Yes, it's much easier to talk when you are bathing them or doing something. Making it formal means it would be harder.
Psychologist: You are disappointing me. You haven't really under-

stood some of the basic principles. Can't you see that all you are doing is expressing your own anxiety about coping with the work and then building defences and escape routes? It's the old, trusty, nurses' defence against responsibility – the flight into fragmentation of roles and task-oriented nursing.

If you are bathing someone then your attention is divided. There will be distractions and interruptions to do with this task and you will not be able to look at your patient, or they you, and you will not be able to think about what is happening. This is *downgrading* emotional care to a casual, non-professional, superficial and unimportant event. Such encounters in the bathtub would never guarantee that emotional care work was conducted consistently with all patients, and would never give a setting where you could work systematically at making things safe, giving permission, elaborating the expression of feeling, empathizing and so on. Lastly, it would lead to chaos. Who would be working with whom? Who would assess the emotional needs and progress of an individual patient?

No. Emphatically no. This is not the way to do it. Emotional care is a subtle, skilful, professional activity. It does not need people who are so insecure about the work that they must build in major defences of this type. In the bathroom consultation the nurse is dressed, the patient naked – there is marked social asymmetry. The nurse can deflect the conversation whenever she feels pressed by using some distraction to do with the bathing, or ending the bath. She can hide her own reactions. Worst of all, she can jolly along and trivialize the whole event. By combining tasks, the nurse reduces her accountability in the situation so that she is not really seen to be engaged in specific psychological tasks at all. Would other extensions of professional activity be attempted in such a defensive way – venepuncture, for example?

Now, what I will confirm is that social settings such as bath times do create a special caring, rather regressed atmosphere. The nurse is literally much more like a mother. These times should be used as a complement to the structured psychological care work. They are important additions, *but never substitutes*. When you arrange a session of emotional care work it must have your full attention and its value must be confirmed by giving the work its own time. So, if your concept of emotional care is such that you see a chat about problems during bathtime as sufficient, you have failed to absorb the key ideas and, sadly, I would not see you as competent in emotional care.

Having said this, I do realize that emotional care work can be a new and rather intimidating venture. That is why you need support, training and a place where you can work through your own anxieties to find confidence.

Relatives

In certain areas of medicine, research shows that many immediate relatives are clearly emotionally disturbed by events. The ideal, of course, would be to extend emotional care to them too. Perhaps 12% of my working time at the kidney unit is spent with relatives. The obvious problem, though, is the availability of time. This is an issue for discussion and practical compromise, I guess. It is pointless over-extending staff, as the quality of their work will fade as they tire.

Beyond these comments, I think that I must declare the issue of whether to extend care to certain relatives and how these are selected as beyond the brief of this book, but it is something to keep in mind and debate in your ward or department. The approach to the work is exactly the same as that undertaken with patients and does not need separate treatment. In Nichols (1987), I outline the general approach to psychological care for partners and other caregivers. If you have a special interest in this aspect of care, you may find that material helpful.

YOUR OWN REACTIONS, OBJECTIVITY, FEEDBACK AND SUPPORT FOR YOURSELF

On occasions, one or other of the nurses that I work with will say something like, 'Can I talk with you about John Rayner (or whoever) for a few minutes; I'm struggling a little with him at the moment'. I find these extremely reassuring requests because they carry a message: namely, that the nurses *are able to notice when they are over-extended*, either because they are trying to achieve an objective with a particular patient but have lost direction and feel powerless to achieve this, or because they have become troubled at an emotional level themselves in relation to a case. *This capacity to keep a watch on oneself is important and you must work hard to develop it.* I'll expand this point with a few notes on the various aspects involved.

Losing objectivity

Inevitably some people will prove very difficult for you to work with. From time to time, you may feel yourself having considerable problems, perhaps resenting something about your patient and feeling a growing anger during the contacts. Once in a while, you are likely to identify intensely with a particular patient and thus be drawn into their perception. Then you too are vulnerable to the extent of being paralysed by their despair and sense of defeat. It happens to us all and it can be very uncomfortable. Similarly, most of us in this work have discovered how easy it can be to lose objectivity (or at least neutrality), and edge into accepting the patient's beliefs concerning relationships and verbal transactions, without checking the alternative perspectives with the other people involved. While working specifically in emotional care (not counselling) the effort towards acceptance of a person's feelings is not, you will remember, to be confused with attributing the status of fact to what they are seeing and saying. In accepting and valuing a person's reactions you do not assume the accuracy of their perception. This is very important indeed where other members of the family are involved, or indeed, other members of staff.

Recently, I had a couple of meetings with a woman who had gone into kidney failure. She became very distressed during a weekend visit home because she felt her family did not need her and were glad to have her away in hospital. Her conviction was a powerful force and I had to work hard to retain a neutral view and keep myself mindful that 'this is how she sees it now; when she is stronger she may see it differently, the family may see it differently'. As it turned out, she did change her perception quite markedly within a couple of weeks. Meanwhile, I had met her husband to check his view of things and discovered that he could not understand why she had changed, but possibly they had run around her too much and left her with no feeling of function in the home. It was very helpful for me to have access to his view to help bolster my own neutrality. She felt rejected by the family, they did not feel rejecting to her. Thus, I was able to accept her feelings as reasonable in relation to her perception, but I did not challenge this perception directly in order to retain a good level of safety and support. Our conversations did, however, lead her to reflect and check through the issue herself, with a positive outcome.

A side effect of losing neutrality and being 'sucked into' your patient's view of things is that you may unwittingly become the victim of manipulation. Your patient may not realize his or her own motive, so it is not necessarily a hostile or reprehensible tendency. Nevertheless, it will cause you difficulties in professional relationships if you appear to be drawn into your patients' beliefs.

Two types of 'professional reflex' will insulate you from these danger areas. You need to develop them. First, wherever possible, diplomatically check alternative views of a situation with whoever else is involved. This is not to obtain the 'correct' version, but to establish the alternatives in order to maintain neutrality. The very act of doing this will help you resist crossing the threshold into absorbing your patient's views as a statement of reality, and will endlessly teach you that one person's perception of a situation can be enormously different from another's. In this type of work, there is little point in chasing after the accurate perception, which is often mirage-like anyway. What is important, though, is working to understand and, where productive, communicate the alternative perceptions to each party.

Patient: If you want the truth, the staff at this place get my back up.
Nurse: Why are you especially angry at the staff today – has something gone wrong?
Patient: I'm pretty fed up with lying here all day long and being ignored, that's all. It's like you're invisible when you're moved to one of these side rooms.
Second nurse (when asked about the attention he had received): Well, we have been quite busy with a couple of admissions but I've popped in twice and I know Jan has been in at least once.

Furnished with this information the first nurse can maintain the neutrality of her position. Quite possibly some other issue is disturbing the patient and the anger is being displaced on to a convenient issue. Then again, he might, without explanation, have suddenly seen less of the staff because of being moved. The important thing is that he is angry: that needs to be worked with.

Secondly, *regular case discussions and feedback* are essential. A psychological therapist who does not discipline himself to discuss his work regularly with a colleague is doing shoddy work. This applies similarly with counsellors or those giving psychological care. Without the feedback of another experienced person, there is no good way of discovering that your self-monitoring is accurate. In one's analysis of a case, it is easy to allow personal needs to influence the handling of it without awareness of this happening. One can, for example, lose sight of one's level of involvement and any tendency towards being manipulated that may have crept in. It would be wrong, however, to see discussions with other professionals in terms of having *mistakes* pointed out. That would put us all on the defensive, and this is a much more positive exercise than that. You seek the view of another on the way you are dealing with a case in order to extend your perception and glimpse possibilities which would not otherwise have been available.

Good, constructive feedback from a colleague is invaluable in helping you assess what is happening to both you and your patient, and in determining the future direction to follow. It is unprofessional to work without such feedback, although once you have a good level of experience it is not necessary to do this with all cases. Arbitrarily, I will commit myself and say that a minimum of one out of ten cases should be discussed in depth. In the beginning stages, though, when supervision is necessary, each case should be discussed, although to be realistic, not always in great depth. Probably the most effective way of doing this is for a group of people working at psychological care to meet once a month to share case experiences and comments. Another task for you, therefore, is to ensure you have someone to do this with. If necessary, phone up your local clinical psychologist – you could do worse.

Support for you

Once you do have a setting in which you can talk through some of your case work with another person who is engaged in similar duties, there also exists the opportunity of support for you. You will need it. At times there will be some rather powerful feelings within you as a direct consequence of the emotional care work. Occasionally a case will pull you down, make you feel inadequate and ineffective. Sometimes you will feel that you have handled it badly and have a restless feeling of irritation at yourself, or a patient will make you feel angry and resentful. Again, this is an experience and a need common to all people who work in the psychological field. Thus, it is a professional *responsibility* to ensure support for yourself. Chapter 7 takes up this theme.

MONITORING PSYCHOLOGICAL STATE

You will remember from Chapter 3 that the whole of the psychological care scheme is built on the basic routine task of monitoring and recording the psychological state of your patients. From this information, you will be able to judge needs in terms of emotional care, counselling, informational care and so on.

What is required of you in this task? Basically, you need to make regular observations on how your patients are doing psychologically. From this you can establish what their main needs seem to be. It is a simple but vital role which, as far as inpatients are concerned, can only effectively be taken on by nurses because they are the people with reliable daily contact. In outpatient settings or community care, whoever has the contact ought to provide the psychological observations.

How should it be done? In general, keep it simple and keep it short, otherwise it will become a tiresome chore and there will be a strong temptation to forget it. At the same time, such observations have to be kept meaningful and of value. One option is to use brief psychological record cards which are filled in at reasonable intervals, maybe once a week or what ever time interval suits ward life. These can be available during any case discussion or handover briefings, otherwise being kept with the patient's notes or nursing records. As, say, a primary nurse, you will, of course, always be trying to keep the psychological state of your patients in mind. The routine of using the record cards regularly will assist you in this. One of the points of the record cards is to introduce a moment into each week when you focus attention on the overall impression you have of your patient's psychological state, and then answer the question 'What action needs to be taken?' Figure 5.3 gives one version of a psychological record card.

PSYCHOLOGICAL REPORT

PATIENT _ _ _ _ _ _ _ _ _ DATE _ _ _ _ _ NURSE _ _ _ _ _ _ _ _ _

PREDOMINANT MOOD STATE: anxious, tense, frightened, tearful, low, depressed, withdrawn, bewildered, restless, angry, aggrieved? Relaxed, cheerful, strong, good morale? Other?

Comments:

. . . .
. . . .
. . . .

ANY SPECIAL WORRIES, PSYCHOLOGICAL PROBLEMS OR PSYCHOLOGICAL NEEDS?

. . . .
. . . .
. . . .

HOW WELL INFORMED?

. . . .
. . . .
. . . .

WHAT ACTION DO I NEED TO TAKE (IF ANY)?

. . . .
. . . .
. . . .

Figure 5.3: Periodic record of psychological care

The best way to gather the information you need is to approach your patients in the open, safe, supportive style of emotional care and just spend a little time with them every now and again, judging their general state. For example:

Nurse: Hi, Fran. I've just looked in for five minutes to see how things are for you at the moment. How have your last couple of days and nights been?

Sense the atmosphere Fran carries with her. Is she psychologically comfortable or uncomfortable? Is she worried and tense or relaxed? Visibly anxious, tearful or depressed? Preoccupied with a problem – if so, what? Angry – if so, why? Different from last time – if so, how? All that you are doing really is being a little more systematic about noticing the things you would be generally aware of anyway. Obviously, if you encounter anything which demands action on your part in terms of additional psychological care work, then you will take that action.

Otherwise, you are just monitoring, that is, keeping yourself informed on how your patients are in a more systematic way.

Referring for therapy

Your contact with a patient through the process of monitoring psychological state and giving emotional care will enable you to assess the severity of any psychological difficulty. Sometimes it will seem that a patient's needs go beyond psychological *care* and that he or she really needs psychological *therapy*. In other words, you have to call in the assistance of a trained psychological therapist. Usually, this will be a clinical psychologist (note that they might use the title health psychologist in a general hospital setting) or, possibly, a social worker or another health care professional who has undertaken special training. This situation is dealt with at length in the latter part of Chapter 6.

CONCLUDING COMMENTS

In some ways, this chapter has had an artificial air about it. It has dealt solely with emotional care and the examples used stop short at emotional care. In reality, other elements of psychological care may be required too. I excluded these from the examples above for the purpose of clear teaching. The most likely situation is that, in giving emotional care, other than finding a need for further information work, it will seem appropriate to extend your emotional care with a patient into a simple form of counselling. This is the substance of the first half of Chapter 6.

Counselling and Therapy

In building up the elements of a scheme for psychological care we have covered monitoring psychological state, informational/educational care and emotional care. In carrying out each of these, you may find yourself in a situation which requires the fourth major element of this scheme, namely, counselling. Counselling is an approach to care which lies somewhere between the relatively non-intervening style of emotional care and the in-depth, highly interventionist style of psychological therapy. No-one, of course, expects you to become involved with your patients at a level which approaches psychological therapy. It would not be appropriate unless you have had extensive training. However, competent health care professionals giving psychological care will, ideally, have basic counselling skills and will see that psychological care is a blend of informational and emotional care, both of which are supplemented when necessary by basic counselling.

It is worth noting that, in urging the development of counselling skills throughout the entire health care field, Davis and Fallowfield (1991) also promote the notion of *basic* counselling skills. Their view is that *all* health care professionals should receive some counselling training, if only to promote improved and caring communication between staff and patients. They do not suggest that all health care professionals should act as counsellors: rather, that the style of interaction acquired in counselling training is very beneficial for improved communication. In their view, counselling in any depth will usually be conducted by someone in a more specialized role who has had more advanced training. In my approach, I suppose you could say that I split the difference. Staff giving psychological care should know what counselling is and be able to offer it at a basic level. At the same time, they should not function at the level of therapists or professional counsellors, but be aware of a cut-off point at which care stops and therapy begins. At this point the correct move in psychological care is to refer the case to a psychological therapist or professional counsellor.

In this chapter I will try to convey the basis of counselling and then indicate the boundary between counselling as part of psychological care and more intensive counselling or psychological therapy.

142

TWO MODES OF COUNSELLING

We have at the outset to deal with a problem of ambiguity to do with the term counselling. As used in relation to psychological care, counselling refers to a way of assisting people with difficulties which do not lend themselves to instant solution, especially through passing on information or giving advice. In other words, the focus of concern is on personal dilemmas such as emotional conflicts and relationship struggles to which there are no immediate clear answers or dependable codes of correct or incorrect behaviour. However, it is not unusual to hear of legal counselling, careers counselling, sexual counselling and so on. These, in contrast, are clearly forms of counselling which are all very much concerned with giving information and advice, and generally being fairly directive. At first sight this can appear contradictory.

I find it helpful to describe counselling as having two modes: advisory and personal. In psychological care it is not unusual to switch back and forwards between these two modes during the course of a session, but we must be aware of this switch because they require very different styles of interaction.

Advisory counselling

informational counselling
advice
shaping attitude
helping behaviour change

counsellor ⟶ client

Personal counselling

experience
feeling
perception
motive

counsellor ⟵ client

Figure 6.1: Modes of counselling in medicine

If you will refer to Figure 6.1 for a moment, you will see the main differences between the two approaches. Perhaps the most important piece of information in this figure is the direction of the two arrows, which indicate the direction of the main flow of communication. Thus, in advisory counselling, much of the flow of communication is from the counsellor to the patient. To some extent, we can say that it is the communication which the counsellor needs to exchange with the patient. This is effectively another name for informational care, as mentioned in Chapter 4. In medicine, health care professionals often do need to give information and advice which will help adjustment and coping. Sometimes they have to promote attitudes and behaviour change. Think, for example, of a case of a young woman who becomes diabetic shortly before marrying. Such work is best conducted as a blend of the two counselling styles, with periodic attention to the reactions of the people involved. These reactions must be checked, and, if necessary, explored. To do this effectively, it is necessary to shift into the other mode of counselling, that is, personal counselling.

Personal counselling draws on the same style of interaction as emotional care and is best seen as an extension of emotional care. Often, it will be in the context of giving emotional care that you will expand what you are doing with a patient to make it a personal counselling session. In personal counselling, the counsellor does not arrive at a session with anything specific to say, as would be the case in advisory counselling. Rather, the counsellor arrives knowing only that he or she has to provide a safe interpersonal environment in order that the clients or patients may explore the feelings, perceptions and motives linked to whatever issues concern them. In personal counselling, the primary role of the counsellor is to facilitate this in-depth exploration of personal experience. What makes it different from emotional care is that the process goes on to include checking the accuracy of perceptions, increasing awareness of motive and, if relevant, to work on targets for change and problem solving.

A BRIEFING ON PERSONAL COUNSELLING

A counsellor and client (NB: I will use the term 'client' in this section – it is the convention in counselling) engage directly in conversations centred on the issues which the client finds problematic. Examples of these would be the woman who finds herself embittered with self-blame when, after years of assistance from a gynaecologist, she still fails to become pregnant, or the man who knows he should make the effort to maintain social contact after a stroke has affected his speech, but wants to hide away. With such difficulties, the target in counselling is to enable clients to achieve a new understanding of themselves and to see new perspectives in the situations they face. In other words, there will be personal education. At the same time, the client will experience being truly listened to, feeling truly understood and will benefit from a supportive relationship.

In my hospital work, it is a not infrequent experience to hear staff of one profession or another saying something like, 'that person needs counselling'. A little investigatory probing reveals that the concept in their head is usually in the order of 'letting them talk about their problems and giving them handy bits of advice'. Such notions reveal a serious ignorance of the subtle skills and targets of counselling, I fear. The counselling conversation is not an ordinary, everyday conversation. It has special features designed to remove certain aspects of everyday conversation and to emphasize others which may not normally be present. This is why some basic training in counselling skills is important since, even with the best will in the world, sitting down to 'do counselling' simply on the basis of trying to be helpful will often lead to a sterile outcome. Thus, we should begin by being clear on what counselling is *not* about, by listing a few common erroneous notions:

1. That counselling is *directly* concerned with making people less emotional, or even stemming emotion.
2. That counselling involves giving direct advice to clients or attempting to solve their problems for them.
3. That counselling involves challenging a client's feelings and perceptions in order to impose one's own values and perceptions, these having the feel of being more realistic or accurate.
4. That counselling is an activity which may be instigated in order to satisfy *our* need to make people feel and function better (this is a felt misconception rather than one which is consciously thought).

In fact, if you regard these not just as misconceptions but also hold them as taboos in counselling, you will avoid some of the more serious errors too – which is a rather more significant achievement.

The targets in counselling

Taking things a step further, while you are studiously refraining from giving out advice or persuading people to see things your way, you will, of course, be engaged in the positive acts of counselling. Egan (1990) has set out a useful, three-stage scheme to explain what these are. The stages unfold in the following way:

Stage 1 – exploring and clarifying the problem situation

People turn to counsellors when things have gone badly and they are confused and distressed. Quite often, though, they will not be truly clear about what exactly is disturbing them, but are only able to report the consequences, such as agitation and depression. Thus the special working relationship formed in counselling is focused progressively on encouraging in-depth 'self-exploration', so expanding the client's contact with his personal feelings and perceptual habits. This in turn leads to a clarification of the nature of the difficulty.

Stage 2 – setting goals based on dynamic understanding

This is perhaps the phase of counselling which might be described as educational. The client is drawn into piecing together the discoveries from Stage 1 and generating a clearer picture of himself and others in the problem situation. This process includes what is called the 'dynamics' of the situation, that is, the psychological forces (motives, needs, fears, blocks, etc.) which have emerged from the discussion. In other words, a deeper understanding is achieved, including perhaps recognition of issues which previously have been blocked from conscious awareness. Again, it must be stressed that the client is led to make these insights himself: he is not lectured at or persuaded into acceptance. *Counselling brings out what is already within.* Egan's style is very much action-oriented and so the end-point of this stage is the use of acquired personal knowledge to declare targets or goals for change and resolution.

Stage 3 – facilitating action

The targets declared by people will vary enormously. For some they will be highly concrete, such as making headway with the business of social rehabilitation after a long, disabling illness. For others, the targets will be less concrete, say, achieving acceptance after the loss of a body part or the beginning of an illness which narrows life down. Whatever the nature, the counselling relationship is used to help the individual into change. Reappraisal, confronting awkward issues, taking initiatives, seeking ways out of an impasse, and testing out the reality of feared situations become the final focal point of attention.

From this you can gain the general feel of counselling. It is not in-depth therapy. Diagnosis of personality or psychodynamic features plays no real part. It is a limited, supportive activity aimed at developing a person's understanding and placing him or her in a position where it is possible to decide upon and initiate constructive change. The counsellor is active in creating the special relationship and atmosphere of the sessions, but his or her input is subtle, *drawing the client towards greater personal insight.* The effect is intended to be that of a catalyst.

No doubt you will be curious about the special style of conversing and the special atmosphere of which I have spoken. These are the product of what normally goes under the heading 'counselling skills'. Once more, I will draw up a list with brief explanations to illustrate these. Some of them will be familiar, since they are identical to those needed in emotional care.

Counselling skills

In any reasonable training course you will be taught and encouraged to rehearse the following skills (these are illustrated in the extended example given later).

1. *Provision of the working interpersonal relationship* – as in the other elements of care, the all-important foundation stone of effective counselling is the manner in which the counsellor relates to and interacts with the client. The atmosphere needs to be non-anxious, non-threatening, without the sense of being forced. This means, of course, that the counsellor must genuinely be relaxed in the situation and free from personal tension and threat, since these will inevitably be transmitted to the client if they are present. The relaxed stance with clients will stem, in part, from the counsellor remaining mindful that her role is not that of providing instant solutions, but is more to do with fostering a relationship which serves as a 'growth medium'. In other words, the style of relating by the counsellor communicates caring support and gives 'permission' for the client (in fact, positively encourages) to search out and express a whole range of inner feelings and experiences. This enables discoveries to be made which lead to personal insight and, later, personal change.

2. *Listening skills* – through practice and guidance, a trainee counsellor learns a particular style of listening, described as giving full and free attention. It simply involves following very intently what the client is saying while constantly asking oneself, 'What is this person trying to say with his words, his facial expression, his posture, the areas he chooses to talk of freely and the things he is clearly avoiding?' One is *listening to hear, understand and emphasize* and not, initially at least, to make a reply. However, by the use of gaze, posture and occasional remarks, the client remains very aware of the counsellor's attention.

3. *Probing* – while listening in this intent manner, the counsellor may notice areas of vagueness or avoidance in the client's communication. Normally it will be appropriate to lead the client to say more on these topics. This is called elaboration and the counsellor will facilitate this by gentle, probing questions.

4. *Reflecting/communicating understanding* – the counselling conversation is a joint product put together by the close collaboration of the two (or more) people involved. A constant requirement of the counsellor is to communicate back her understanding and to check the accuracy of this by means of the client's reactions. As opposed to commenting upon or evaluating the client's experience, the

counsellor 'reflects' back what has been said, that is, gives a brief repeat version in her own words to show understanding, together with other supporting comments which also indicate that attention and understanding are being maintained.

5. *Empathizing* – as was explained in Chapter 5, to have empathy means to truly comprehend and identify with another person's experiences. If you are in empathy with, say, the feelings of a woman who has to lose a breast, it means that you know her feelings, you can project yourself into her place and, on the basis of what she has said to you, make contact with what it is like to be her. That is, you sense the thoughts and feelings which assail her. Empathy does not come from prior knowledge – that would be false empathy. True empathy comes from exploring with the client the exact nature of her experiences. As you listen intently, it becomes possible to sense her feelings because you have allowed yourself full exposure to her description of the feelings, perceptions and expectations related to the loss of a breast. To some extent, the ability to empathize depends on the level of 'in-touchness' a person has with her own feelings of life. Obviously, if one is 'switched off' to feeling, then the skill of empathy will not be available. Again, though, this is a skill which develops with guidance and practice.

6. *Challenging skills* – here I borrow Egan's (1990) term. Whereas the early stages of counselling see little by way of active intervention on the part of the counsellor, as trust develops and the client becomes both accepting and experienced in the counselling 'encounter', so then the counsellor may adopt rather stronger facilitating techniques. Among these are:

   • *Confrontation*: when the counsellor detects evasiveness, inconsistencies, clear-cut blocking or denial, game-playing, the maintenance of a facade etc., she will confront the client with her observations, suggesting to the client what she believes is happening. Obviously, the skill is to learn how to do this so that it is helpful and leads the client on to productive self-discovery (as opposed to being destructive of rapport, so setting back the working relationship).

   • *Communicating intuitive empathy*: when an experienced counsellor has gained and absorbed a full account of a person's difficulty, she may discover herself echoing the feelings of her client (empathizing) to a degree which seems to go beyond what has actually been said. She will sense that the client is feeling something that he is unable to express verbally, perhaps because he is denying the feelings. At appropriate times, the counsellor will suggest to the client that such feelings apply to him. If the client has matured in the work, he will examine the suggestions honestly, seeking to see if they fit, which may then lead to a further advance in insight.

- *Sharing and self-disclosure*: occasions occur in counselling when the client is assisted if the counsellor discloses her own feelings and experiences to the client. For example, the counsellor may reveal how she felt in a particular situation, perhaps describing her feelings after a death has been experienced. The point of such disclosure would be to augment levels of support or further the growth of insight.
- *Focusing on the here-and-now*: a second form of self-disclosure by the counsellor is the communication of her thoughts and feelings concerning the quality of the relationship that has developed between the client and herself. She focuses attention on the 'here-and-now' aspects of the work, drawing attention to the significant patterns which may have emerged. This may be relevant as a means of giving feedback to the client on his characteristic styles of relating and interacting, assuming that the pattern of relating in the counselling session reflects behaviour elsewhere which is causing difficulties.
- *Information sharing*: a client may be entrenched in a way of viewing a situation, a 'perceptual and emotional set', as we say. On occasions, it is helpful to gently feed in factual information which encourages new views and new thinking.

COUNSELLING IN PRACTICE

There is something rather lifeless about such lists and brief descriptions as these, so I will try to bring it all to life for you by examples of typical transactions during a counselling session.

Case study

Nan Smith (short for Nancy) has been in my office for 30 minutes or so. I have been asked to see her by the ward sister. Her husband, Leslie, aged 62 years, is dying from cancer of the liver. As yet, he has not been informed of this, primarily because Nan has insisted that he must not know. At present, the open talk by staff with Leslie refers only to liver disorders. The request to see Nan came as a result of events occurring during the evening visit the day before. Nan had travelled in for visiting as usual but Leslie had been withdrawn and incommunicative. He lay turned away from her and apart from a few angry remarks, barely spoke. He had been like this with the nurses as well, a complete change from his stoical, cheery self. To make matters worse, he was virtually refusing to take liquid, thus becoming marginally dehydrated. Not surprisingly, Nan was deeply hurt and showed as much to the nurses. They asked if she would like to see the unit psychologist and she felt that she would. Now, here we are halfway into our first meeting.

She is talking easily and openly, although in rather short statements and so I have adopted the strategy of keeping the flow going by using facilitating questions. We have covered the background to the incident yesterday, which basically involved her describing events during the last few months and expressing her sadness that things should end like this for them. Leslie may have only a few more weeks to live and after a long, happy marriage suddenly, for no accountable reason, he is angry and rejecting towards her:

Nan: You see, I don't know what's best. Maybe he'd rather I didn't come. It's as if I've done something wrong but I just can't think what. Like yesterday, I tried to chat to him for a while and cheer him up a little but it's very hard when he just stays silent. He's very poorly, of course, but he's been worse before and never behaved like this. What do you think I should do?

Counsellor: I don't know at the moment, Nan. It's really something for you to decide when we've talked it all through. Can I ask you to give me an idea of how this has affected you? (*A question to lead her to an expression of personal feeling while avoiding getting drawn into giving instant advice.*)

Nan: I've felt very upset by it. I couldn't sleep last night, I got a bit panicky. All of us have been trying to give him company and take him out of himself a bit. You see, the family isn't used to rows or bad feeling. We're very close and at a time like this – we all know it's cancer but he doesn't – we just don't want him to get upset and start brooding because he'll think of his brother who died five years ago with cancer and then get frightened. We don't want him frightened and upset.

Counsellor: You want to protect him up to the end, but this bad atmosphere stops you? (*Reflecting back.*)

Nan: Yes, that's it, and I worry that the children will blame me if he gets upset or depressed. What we all want is for him to have an easy time, not get in a state like his brother did – but now something's gone wrong and I feel it's my fault. (*In tears, I help her deal with them and give her time.*)

Counsellor: I understand your confusion, Nan, you feel you've done something wrong but don't know what. Let's take it a step further. What are your memories of the visit the day before yesterday? (*A direct question to help develop the description of events.*)

Nan: Nothing out of the ordinary, really. He was quiet. I did most of the talking. He seemed a bit depressed at one point – I remember he said he'd never see our daughter again – she's in Australia, you know.

Counsellor: How did you reply?

Nan: I told him he was being silly again and that he would be better soon and home in a few days. It was then that he first turned away from me. He didn't say anything or do anything, just turned away (*pauses again, near to tears*) and he wouldn't talk any more, except to say it was time for me to go.

Counsellor: What were your feelings at that moment?

Nan: Well, I felt dreadful. It isn't like him. We've had our differences like anyone else but we've always faced up to one another and said what we think – I couldn't cope with him going silent like that.

Counsellor: Try and enlarge on what you mean when you say you felt dreadful. (*Probing.*)

Nan: I suppose I felt worried in case it was my fault – guilty, you might say, and to be honest, I felt a bit cross. I didn't deserve to be treated like that. I've been putting so much effort into looking after him and keeping him cheerful. Yes, I felt cross, which is terrible because the poor soul's so ill and I know he doesn't mean any harm. But it wasn't as if I'd been sharp with him or said anything offensive. I was just cheering him up, letting him know that we were all waiting for him to come home. They have to keep up hope, you know, but I couldn't cope with him silent and turned away. That did hurt me. Its been a hard time for me too.

Counsellor: You felt he'd turned on you unfairly without good reason, especially after the things you've been through recently. (*Reflecting, showing understanding.*)

Nan: Yes, and now I just don't know what to do.

Counsellor: Do you have any idea at all what he might have been thinking or feeling? (*Encouraging her to explore.*)

Nan: Well, I've been through it over and over again – oh, I don't know, really. He hates being in hospital, away from his home. Both his father and brother died of cancer and in a way, I think he's been expecting it. He's been under a lot of strain worrying.

Counsellor: It isn't just him that worries, is it? (*Probing.*)

Nan: No, I've probably fretted about it more than him over the last few years – it's something we never talk about but it's always there, if you know what I mean. It's been hanging over my family since his brother died. They were twins, you see. His brother had a rough time of it too. I've worried for us all. I had to see the doctor myself about nerves last month because of this.

Counsellor: Nan, I can see that you've carried a great deal of anxiety about Leslie and the risk of him dying of cancer. It feels as if you've been really frightened during the last few years so that it has affected the way you've talked, or rather, not talked, to Leslie about it all, and what you've asked others to say to him. Maybe *your* anxiety has led to a long silence which Leslie now finds difficult. (*Intuitive empathy – a 'challenge' to her to consider a new perspective to do with her own anxiety.*)

Nan: (after a long pause) He was badly upset by his father's death and then his brother's a few years later. We just never talked about cancer again. I was thinking that it runs in the family and that he'd be next. It used to make me feel sick. I didn't want him to know I was thinking this way. I mean, he might have been thinking the same but we just sort of never mentioned it. When he got ill a year ago I went to see our doctor on my own to ask him outright – I couldn't bear not knowing one way or the other. The doctor said he wasn't sure but quite likely it could be cancer. I don't know how I got through that week, I felt awful. I had to pretend I had a migraine. But I decided to do my best to get him by as long as possible without knowing it was cancer, that's why I asked the doctors not to tell him.

Counsellor: Why was this so important to you? (*Probing.*)

Nan: I just thought he would panic, sort of go under, I suppose. I didn't really know if he would, though. It just felt important. The children – well, I call them children but they're all married now – agreed that it was best, too.

Counsellor: It's as if by keeping it back from Leslie you could keep your own panic under control, live as if it were not happening. (*A challenge with a gentle, confronting interpretation of events.*)

Nan: Well, it was him I was thinking of, not myself. But I suppose you're right, really. I found it easier to cope with, just keeping it to myself. We could go on making plans for the future and keep life going. I didn't know what would happen if he found out – he might have just given up.

Counsellor: How sure are you that he doesn't know, or at least strongly suspect? (*A question to encourage exploration.*)

Nan: He'd have told me, though, wouldn't he? Perhaps not . . . he might be keeping his thoughts from me in the same way, I suppose. Do you think he knows then?

Counsellor: I haven't met your husband, Nan, I truly don't know. But my own feeling about the situation that has arisen leads me to think that at least he strongly suspects he has cancer. I want to ask you to do something. Imagine for a moment what Leslie must feel like if he does know. His doctors and nurses are evasive and just talk about waiting for tests. They'll not be straightforward with him since you've asked them not to be. You and the family seem oblivious and are chattering away about getting him home again soon, as if you believe everything is normal. Sometimes he tries to tell you what he thinks, like he'll never see your daughter in Australia again, but everyone rushes to stop him saying things like that and changes the subject. How do you think he feels; put yourself in his place for a moment. (*This is a combination of disclosure, giving my own reactions and a challenging exercise to expand Nan's thinking about the elements of the situation.*)

Nan: Oh dear, it's all so confusing. How would I feel? Well, if I really suspected that I had cancer, I'd be very frightened but at the same time I'd resent being treated as if I wasn't an adult and couldn't discuss it. I think I'd get cross and say something.

Counsellor: Would it feel lonely? (*A lead to expand the exploration.*)

Nan: Well, yes, I suppose so. It would be important to be able to talk about it to at least one or two people, share your fears, as it were... what would be more difficult... would be not trusting your family and doctors. Suspecting they were keeping something from you but at the same time talking about it behind your back. I can see now what you've been leading up to. You think that Leslie is behaving this way because no-one will actually tell him he's got cancer when he knows he has all the time – and we make it worse by being cheery and pretending nothing's wrong. (*Nan has now achieved the key insight.*)

Counsellor: I think you could be right, Nan. You see, people who are seriously ill and dying usually need several things. They need to know what's going to happen and when, so that they can prepare themselves and order their affairs according to their wishes – saying goodbye to people, for example. They also need stable companionship and the opportunity to draw on the support of close relationships. Without these they are very isolated and there can be a terrible feeling of being cut off. Dying is a phase of life we all have to deal with, and it's much more comfortable if it's shared and dealt with in a way which suits the dying person's own wishes. Leslie isn't being allowed these. He's surrounded by family and staff but is really quite alone because no-one will talk to him. He may have a great need to share this phase of his life with you, his close companion. (*Again this is a challenge to consider an alternative perspective. There is some information-giving as part of the challenge.*)

Nan: How should I alter things?

Counsellor: You know Leslie well, I don't know him at all, so that's for you to decide. But we can talk about some of the different ways of going about it if you wish.

This transcript is a near-verbatim record of a counselling session I was engaged in a year ago. Nan talked some more and resolved the problem of how to change the situation herself. I do not know exactly what she said but she did phone to say that she broached the subject in a simple, open way. Leslie didn't speak initially, instead he drank a whole glass of orange juice (if you remember, he was refusing fluids). Later, they talked long and hard, with many tears, but, Nan reported, they became very close and both drew a great deal from the remaining six months which they had together. Leslie died in psychological peace.

BASIC COUNSELLING SKILLS

As described in Chapter 5, emotional care is a form of care which does not call for much intervention. While it is not a passive approach, the objective is simply to allow patients to express feeling in a safe, supportive atmosphere, in order that they are not isolated with their troubles and can make progress with the emotional tasks created by illness and injury. Often, though, in giving emotional care you will feel that you should take things a little further and help your client into taking some action which will ease some source of stress for them. For example, Marion was a partner training as a dialysis helper. She took to it easily and was becoming quite proficient. She and her husband Peter were within a month or so of completing their training and beginning with dialysis at home. Sally, the primary nurse assigned to this couple, needed to see Marion to pass on some information about dates for the conversion to home dialysis. In the course of their meeting, Marion seemed rather distracted and harassed. As a result, Sally, judging that there were difficulties, suggested that they go into an empty side room to talk for ten minutes. The following conversation took place (this is reconstructed from notes made by Sally immediately after the conversation):

Nurse: Marion, can we talk for a minute? I felt that something was wrong talking to you just now, and I feel that I need to check how you are. How have you been since we last spoke?
Marion: I'm sorry Sally, I'm just tired and feeling a bit overburdened at the moment. I was on night shift at an old people's home last night and I'm feeling a bit light-headed.
Nurse: Have you been to bed at all?
Marion: No, I haven't actually. If I did I'd be asleep all day.
Nurse: I thought you had a part-time day job?
Marion: Yes, I do. That's for three days a week and I've started three nights at the home – we need the cash really.
Nurse: Two jobs, the children, Peter and dialysis training all together – what does it do to you? How are you feeling physically and emotionally?
Marion: I don't let myself feel anything. If I stopped and thought how tired I am I would collapse in a heap. I have to keep going somehow, for all of them . . . (long pause, followed by a statement in a quiet, broken voice) . . . I'm doing my best, but I don't know how long I can keep going like this. I put on a bright cheery face but I do feel . . . so . . . weighed down. I can't see any hope or any way out unless Peter gets a transplant.

Sally spends some time in straightforward emotional care, helping Marion express her feeling of burden and her fear that she will not be able to carry those burdens. Now, though, Sally feels that she has uncovered a situation which is putting Marion at risk: it is a self-imposed work stress problem. Resisting a perfectly human urge to wade in with kindly, reproving advice on the need to care for herself and take things more easily, she adopts a basic counselling stance with Marion. In other words, she leads Marion into a brief exploration of the thoughts, feelings and motives linked to the issue. She then helps for-mulate the first steps for action (in this case, seeing the psychologist). Sally opts to use gentle, probing questions to widen Marion's aware-ness of the feelings that drive her behaviour:

Nurse: Marion, can we just explore a couple of points so that I under-stand better? You are putting yourself under a fantastically heavy load. Why are you pushing yourself quite so hard; what is the feeling behind it?

Marion: (pauses) I don't want things to change more than is absolutely necessary. I think that I'm trying to keep things together and not let things change. I don't want Peter's kidney failure to harm the family.

Nurse: Do you see that as a risk?

Marion: Very much. It's the children . . . I don't want to be saying we can't do things or can't afford them now. I want to keep life as near as it was before.

Nurse: It feels so important to you – you are driving yourself to exhaustion trying to achieve it?

Marion: Well – not deliberately, I'm hoping I'll get used to it. I've man-aged so far, it's only this week that I have felt so shattered.

Nurse: Have you discussed it with the family, sort of had a family conference, or is it something which has come just from you?

Marion: No . . . not really, I suppose I haven't. It has just slowly built up I don't want to alarm the kids, there is 'O' levels coming up and so on. I . . . I want to keep everything as normal as I can for them. Peter is still in shock really, he doesn't need any more blows, and I don't think that the children should have to carry burdens.

Nurse: It feels like you are saying that it is so important not to let things change that you will work yourself to a standstill, make yourself ill even? It makes me worry about you.

Marion: mmmm . . . well, I can't see any other way.

Nurse: Are the other members of the family so bothered about change as you, do you think?

Marion: I don't know, maybe not. The children seem to have got used to the dialysis. Nick doesn't seem to bother much now, Sammy always asks her father how he is . . . but probably not . . . I suppose it's me who bothers most – just trying to keep it all together.

Nurse: Perhaps you are the one who is most frightened of things changing?

Marion: (long pause) Yes, I suppose I'm the one in a stew really. But I'm the only one who can see the long-term consequences.

The session went on for a few more minutes and ended thus:

Nurse: I think I can understand why you are doing so much and getting so stressed Marion, and I'm glad you can see that the real risk is to your own health. If that goes, the family will be in more difficulties. I wonder how you would feel about having some more help with it all. We have a unit counsellor – he is a health psychologist – who often helps partners in adjusting to the new demands of home dialysis and so on. Would you like me to arrange for you to meet him for a good long look at it all?

A meeting was arranged for later that week. As you can see, Sally went beyond emotional care but did not get involved at a great depth. She enabled Marion to take a look at the situation, identify that there was a problem and realize that her own need to prevent change was part of the problem. Sally stopped at that point and called in additional help (she did not hand the case over but engaged additional help). *This was a good example of basic counselling*. It got things started and identified aspects of the problem to be worked on. Equally importantly, Sally's intervention enabled Marion to move to the point where *she* could see that she had to work on her own reactions, otherwise she would go under.

As a general principle, it is best to consider basic counselling as something you move towards during emotional care work. Incidentally, do not take this as a rule – it is just the way it usually works out. Thus, the foundations to basic counselling are the same as in emotional care. The main difference is the progression into a more probing, exploring style, with a final 'what's to be done about it' phase. Let me impress one thing upon you, though: *it is a terrible error in counselling to believe that you have to solve your patients' problems personally, or that you have to say something very clever which somehow makes everything all right. With such targets, counselling becomes an awful burden.* Your role is to help people to see their problems more clearly, and then help them explore options for problem solving. Figure 6.2 sets out a summarized version of the steps in combined emotional care and basic counselling.

STEPS IN BASIC COUNSELLING

- Make the situation *safe* – style of greeting, manner, posture, freedom from observation/intrusion etc
- Give 'space and permission' for your patient to talk freely at his/her own pace
- Initially *emphasize listening*, using only short guiding questions or helping statements
- Encourage the *full expression of feeling* – if this is not naturally forthcoming gently encourage it at appropiate intervals. Allow time for tears or anger when they occur – don't fuss should there be strong feelings.
- Show your understanding and empathy by periodically 'reflecting back' the expressed feelings and experiences.
- *Avoid 'wading in' with instant advice*
- Eventually share your own feelings and reactions – giving your reactions to what you have heard and experienced while listening. Be brief; it is your patient's time.
- If it is appropriate, lead her/him into *setting objectives* for change or ways of dealing with a difficult situation. Help build up a list of options but remember, it is not your problem to solve.

Figure 6.2: Basic supportive counselling

PITFALLS

With the emphasis on training and skills, it must appear all too easy to go wrong in counselling work – to 'put two large feet in it' and end up turning things into a dreadful mess. This is not really very likely. Certainly, caution is important and the development of professionalism is essential, but there is no need for anxiety. I will say with confidence that most of you, as nurses and members of the therapist professions, will find basic counselling techniques within your scope – provided you can get off to a good start by finding a clear and supportive teacher. You must accept one thing, though. As in any skill, you will probably be clumsy at first and make mistakes. You must budget for making these and not be made tense by an unrealistic need to be powerful and faultless as a counsellor from the outset. Here, for example, are some of the typical bits of 'clumsiness' and errors made by a new or badly trained counsellor:

- Directing the conversation in a controlling manner, with rapid questions
- Not allowing the client time for thought
- Interrupting
- Not allowing silences – the counsellor talks to fill a silence
- Fussing nervously over tears
- Being compulsively reassuring

- Rushing in with advice
- Searching for specific problems rather than being feeling-centred
- Attempting to 'force' insights.

Those of us already involved in counselling have all made such errors and you will too.

In the long term, though, you will acquire a style of your own and, with proper case discussion and feedback, will mature away from such things. Then comes the vulnerable phase which, I fear, lasts for ever. Once we 'go solo' as counsellors and involve ourselves in regular case work there are still pitfalls. These are more to do with the emotional orientation that can develop between counsellors and their clients. We need another whole book to cope with this topic and so, once more, I must console myself by just sketching out the framework of ideas. The basic concept is to do with patterns developing in a counsellor's work which obstruct effective progress, and possibly make life uncomfortable for the counsellor. For example:

1. The counsellor becomes identified with her client and his problems to such a degree that she feels a strong personal commitment and urgency to do something to sort things out herself.
2. The counsellor becomes drawn into the client's limited view of a situation and becomes weighed down by the same helpless feelings as the client. There will be a sense of being trapped in an impasse, yet with the client leaning heavily and making powerful pleas for help.
3. The counsellor becomes so committed to resolving problems and 'saving' clients that she fails to see that certain clients have a 'vested interest' in their problem, and *need* it to deal with other issues in life. A hopeless struggle ensues which will end in the counsellor giving up the case in despair (a case for early referral, probably).
4. The counsellor unwittingly solicits dependency in her clients because it makes her feel powerful. Later, she becomes bogged down by cases that never seem to go away.
5. The counsellor becomes possessive towards a client and clings on to a case. Sometimes this sets up feelings of bitter resentment if other colleagues are involved, or leads to efforts to keep other people out of the case, thereby blocking the natural progression of events such as referring on to a psychological therapist. This may occur if the counsellor becomes bonded to the client in an overly powerful way, unconsciously linking him or her to another figure in life. Sometimes this possessiveness occurs when the counsellor

has a commitment which goes beyond the actual case – demonstrating prowess to colleagues or defending professional territory, perhaps.

It is the likelihood of such patterns developing that makes the importance of regular case discussion, together with genuine receptivity to feedback from colleagues, such an important aspect of professionalism in this work. Without it, you may fail to see gross distortions in the conduct of particular cases.

Counselling and post-traumatic stress reaction

Brief mention must be made of how you should deal with post-traumatic stress reaction. If you have patients being admitted who have undergone an unpredictable and traumatizing event, for example a road or air crash, an industrial accident or a house fire, you may identify during the ensuing days the features of post-traumatic stress. Your patients will report frequently reliving the event, like a video replaying. They will feel emotionally unsettled, apprehensive, possibly tearful and despairing. They may seem very withdrawn, irritable or confused, and may report feeling remote from normal everyday life. Initially, the best way of helping is to offer frequent opportunities to talk through and describe the event (repetition is very helpful). A supportive atmosphere is important and it can be helpful to give them a briefing on the reactions they are going through. If people are told to expect weeks, possibly months, of being affected by this reaction and that it is both normal and predictable, it has a reassuring effect. Under normal circumstances, the reaction will fade after a few weeks, but if it remains strong you should arrange a referral to a psychologist. For further reading, see *Nursing Times*, April 3rd 1991.

Training and further reading

There is no point in pretending that counselling skills can be acquired through a few quick lectures or just reading. Counselling is a subtle skill which is fashioned by experience, case supervision and attendance at a well-run training course. 'Great, but where can we get all that?' I hear you say. Basically, you have to take the initiative and seek it out.

I suggest two approaches as a start. First, find out (from an administrator) if you have a department of clinical or health psychology in your hospital. If not, find out the address of the nearest district department of clinical psychology. Get in contact with them and begin negotiating. Even if they cannot provide training themselves they ought to be able to direct you to sources of training. Secondly, for nurses, find out whether the continuing education programme in your locality includes counselling training. If not, try pressurizing the tutor into arranging a course. If both these lines fail, then write to the British Association of Counselling, 1 Regent Place, Rugby CV21 2PJ, who will give you up-to-date information on the counselling training activities in your part of the country.

In the meantime there are some excellent books which will help prepare you for training. You will find Egan (1990), and Tschudin (1991) helpful texts. Nelson-Jones (1988) is a full exposition with very useful illustrations and training exercises to work on. You may find it helpful to consider counselling and psychological care in relation to various specialties in medicine, in which case Davies and Fallowfield (1991) and Lacey and Burns (1989) give a wide selection of articles representing a good number of specialties.

REFERRING FOR THERAPY

Once you have taken an interest in the psychological aspects of illness and have begun to develop your work to include psychological care, then you will inevitably become more psychologically minded, noticing more of the psychological scenery. In itself, this will be a most valuable asset to the people you care for, but in the context of a fully functioning scheme of psychological care this ability provides the basis for monitoring the psychological state of your patients and being able to detect levels of distress or actual psychological disturbances which merit referral to a specialist in psychological therapy.

We are not talking here of you becoming a psychodiagnostician, attempting to identify the nature of a particular disturbance (phobic, depressive, psychotic etc.). Rather, the requirement is that you acquire the simple practical ability to recognize that a person's state has changed to a point where psychological care will probably prove to be insufficient. This could be on the occasion of your first contact, or at some point during your conduct of psychological care with a particular case.

Closely related to this is the issue of deciding how to manage referring a case – both from the point of view of your patient and how you manage the business yourself. The objective of psychological care is to minimize psychological distress and lead people through the harsh experiences of serious illness. A therapeutic relationship is formed which will, ideally, be a *lasting* resource. At the same time, it is unhelpful to 'cling' to a case when there is really a need for more specialized help. Letting go can be difficult, though. In addition to these issues there comes the not inconsiderable problem of how and where will you find more specialized help.

Who needs specialized help?

Although wanting to avoid seeming vague, I have to say that it is very difficult to list hard and fast criteria for dividing your patients into two groups, one of which would be described as 'in psychological difficulties and definitely needing referral to a psychological therapist.' The division is very much confused by various factors, for example the level of experience of the staff involved. A nurse with a good number of years' experience in psychological care will deal quite effectively with a certain case, whereas someone relatively new to the work will feel overwhelmed and need to refer the case on, both for her own comfort and to guarantee its effective management. Similarly, one unit or ward may have time and capacity for plenty of psychological work and will absorb some relatively demanding cases, while another will only be able to cope with basic preventive work and will need to refer cases other than those which can be dealt with by basic procedures. In short, the point at which referral is made is, to a degree, a matter of local adjustment.

A small proportion of general hospital patients will not generate any ambiguity, however. They will be people who have totally lost emotional control or who are clearly disabled psychologically, interpreting events in a bizarre way or clearly experiencing intense disturbances of psychological function, such as delusions, hallucinations or gross levels of emotional reaction. Such cases would normally lead to an automatic referral to the psychiatric service anyway, whether or not there had been developments in psychological care.

Another larger group will prove more difficult to reach a decision on. People in this group will not appear as grossly disturbed, but nevertheless will cause concern and leave you feeling that they are functioning very badly in some aspects of life. There will be a sense that they are afflicted by problems which do not appear to trouble the majority of your patients. Such cases will generate a feeling in you that the patient's reaction seems atypically severe; it may be hard to empathize with it. In addition, you might notice that your patient's long-standing behavioural and emotional patterns (the elements of personality) make him ill-suited to the stressing experience he is going through, and that he has entered a period of crisis in which he is becoming increasingly unable to cope – 'going under,' in fact. In other words, there will be something of a dilemma centred around sorting out whether this is just a case which needs a little more effort, or one for which early referral for therapy would be best.

Probably the best way to convey this to you is with several extremely brief outlines of cases which were referred to me by nurses because they felt the person's problems were at a level where psychological therapy was needed. In all these cases I felt they were correct in so thinking.

1. Most dialysis 'partners' are nervous when they are first trained to place cannulae in the fistula (the vein–artery anastomosis constructed for haemodialysis) of a person preparing for dialysis. Hilary was more than nervous. As the time approached to put her husband's cannulae in, her hands became very shaky, her face lost colour, there were signs of perspiration and she became physically very tense. She tried her best on three consecutive training sessions but had to give up each time. On the last attempt, she became so agitated that a nurse had to take her to the visitors' room and sit with her for a while because she was so distraught. In the following week she missed two sessions at the unit, later explaining that she had felt so anxious about coming that she was physically sick as she was getting ready to leave. She had, of course, developed a phobic reaction, for which she needed appropriate psychological therapy.

2. Beth had been seeing a speech therapist following a two-month period of aphonia. The speech therapist was competent in psychological care and blended this with the speech therapy. After two or three sessions, the therapist felt that Beth seemed very withdrawn and depressed, not in a tearful way but in a passive, helpless fashion. Her judgement was that the needs of her patient went beyond the care which she could offer in her weekly sessions and so she referred Beth to see me. Her depression turned out to be linked in with the aphonia. Both seemed to originate from the death of Beth's mother two years earlier, which had been a tremendous blow since it left her socially isolated. Her difficulty was best described as an atypical grief reaction and justified some five sessions of psychotherapy, which produced definite improvements.

3. Mark courageously decided to continue with his degree in architecture despite needing to dialyse three times a week. He remained remarkably well in physical terms but, as the unit sister who was making home visits reported, he was progressively becoming more irritable, fatigued, unkind to his wife and morosely withdrawn. He confessed to the sister on one visit that he felt near to 'cracking up.' There had been times at college when he had wanted physically to smash his work, and after such occasions he felt very low and tearful. She discussed with him whether it was best for him to meet the unit psychologist or for them to deal with it themselves. The sister privately felt that it might be a bit too much for her, since it would probably require several sessions in quick succession, and she did not have the time for that. It turned out that Mark preferred to work on the problem away from home and with a comparative stranger, anyway. Thus the home sister asked me to help him with this particular difficulty. We met for three separate sessions and discovered that Mark had reduced himself to a state of tense, angry fatigue in his endeavours to prove himself equal to the other

students. He was slower in his work now and, because of the prevailing uraemia, compensated by arriving earlier at college, working through lunch and forcing himself to work in the evenings when he should have been resting. He was repeating a long-standing pattern, namely a competitive need to achieve high levels of performance in comparison with his peers. Now, in kidney failure, this level of striving was unrealistic, and he was daily suffering frustrations and defeats as his energy proved insufficient and the distractions of dialysis interfered with his attempts to compete. He was clearly on the edge of exhaustion and near to a depressive reaction. We worked at understanding the origins of these needs and helping him to adjust to more realistic personal targets.

4. Maureen did not complain of psychological tension or discomfort but complained of feeling sick. She was at her worst when the drug trolley came round and her various prescriptions had to be swallowed. At these times, she spoke of severe nausea and several times a week actually was sick while attempting to swallow drugs. The sister in charge of her ward felt that the whole situation was rapidly getting out of hand and could clearly lead to serious difficulties. It seemed to her just the kind of thing that psychologists were invented for, and so it was not long before I had put in my first visit to meet Maureen. The difficulty, it transpired, was that she had always avoided medicines and drugs. She had been a health-food enthusiast and had not used any drugs at all throughout her adult life. Her reaction to drugs was, 'I know it's irrational, but it's like swallowing poison'. It also emerged that, as a child, she had been forced to take a daily 'medicine' – cod liver oil. She so hated this and became so tense that she was often sick after the daily ritual. She grew into adulthood with an aversion to medicine and turned to health foods as a defence against needing to take medicines. What appeared to be happening now was that the 'parental-like' authority of the nurses, urging her to swallow drugs (although she recognized that her life might depend on some of them) was producing the same emotional conflict and associated solution as in her childhood, namely to comply by attempting to swallow but defy by then being sick. It was an appropriate referral and therapy took two lines, dealing first with the basic conflict and secondly training in the management of tension so that swallowing could be completed without inducing vomiting. Sadly, Maureen died from other causes a week or so after we had begun working together.

As you may see, there is no obvious single behavioural or psychological feature which made these four cases 'a suitable case for referral'. At a general level, we could argue that in all of them there was an obvious risk of further deterioration and, to contain this risk, an informed psychological investigation together with necessary therapy was needed. It was also clear that the person initially handling each of these cases sensed something rather different about them in comparison to the more usual pattern. The severity of the anxiety reaction, the persistence of the depression, the degree to which efficiency in living was being affected and the power of the psychosomatic feature all suggested that these were patients requiring help with significant psychological difficulties, rather than people for whom good preventive care would suffice. Here, I think, is the key point. The approach to psychological care which I have been teaching is not to be confused with psychological therapy. The whole point is to anticipate difficulties and work in a preventive fashion, so minimizing the impact that these have. The counselling component of psychological care does extend the work to aiding patients in the resolution of difficulties in life, and there will never be a sharp divide on where counselling stops and therapy begins. It must be a considered judgement in relation to a patient's difficulties, in which you ask:

1. Does this look and feel like the kind of difficulty which falls within the range of basic counselling and emotional care, or does it require help beyond that level?
2. Is it within my personal capabilities and experience to handle it effectively?
3. Can I find sufficient time?

According to your answers, you will work on with a case or commit yourself to making a referral.

To whom do you refer?

Clinical or health psychologists

If your hospital does not already have clinical psychologists on the staff or (if it is very forward-looking) a department of health psychology run by clinical psychologists, then I suggest that you should contact the nearest Department of Clinical Psychology (your district administrator will give you the address) and build direct links with the psychologists there. They will almost certainly welcome your approach and will be able to handle a limited number of referrals. They will possibly consider working directly with you in the unit or ward (as I do), depending on how busy they are. They will almost certainly help out with training and advice on individual cases.

Social workers

So, too, you should approach the social work department. They will be a most valuable source in linking in with and discussing your work, and will probably be able to give direct assistance with a small number of cases. I frankly do not know the proportion of social workers who are competent in psychological therapy. It is not, to be honest, a profession which usually provides two or three years' intensive training in psychological therapy, as happens with clinical psychologists. Nevertheless, many social workers do take a keen interest in case work and have developed themselves to a good level of competence.

Professional and voluntary counsellors

Once more, depending on the area in which you work, there will be a varying provision of counselling services. There are usually various voluntary and sometimes professionally run organizations. It would be inappropriate to equate the services made available by such organizations with that of, say, a department of clinical psychology. They offer counselling skills, but not psychological therapy. However, if you are dealing with a person who needs continuity of care after discharge or who will benefit from intensive counselling which you cannot provide, then it is worth making inquiries as to what is available in your area.

In many places you will find people functioning as counsellors in the hospital service itself, often on a voluntary basis. Usually they will have had a reasonable training in counselling skills and work with considerable enthusiasm and sympathy for psychological care. They may need orienting to your specialty but will often be pleased to assist with a few patients. For example, from hearsay alone, I know of people in my own locality functioning as either voluntary or professional counsellors in an infertility clinic, a contraceptive clinic, a women's clinic, the hospice service, an alcoholism counselling service, and so on. Basically, if you want the assistance of counsellors and are prepared to look, there are a good number around. One resource they will have which you probably will not is the time to work with cases in depth. This does not, of course, mean packing your patients off to anyone who claims to be a counsellor. It is necessary to build up a relationship with a few, to acquaint yourself with their ability and learn to trust each other in working together. As always, it remains important to recognize limits and maintain professionalism, even when using voluntary counsellors.

Overall, by far the best bet is to review the options with the rest of the team and then attempt to establish regular links with a few people. Unless, of course, you already have someone on the staff who functions in the capacity of a psychological therapist.

What if you are defeated? What if no-one can be found who will assist with an individual case? Then you are pushed back into relying on your own resources. Offer what you can give and remember that *you can only offer so much*. You will always find someone to discuss the case and advise you – psychologist, psychiatrist or social worker. Telephone them; you will rarely be turned away.

Psychiatrists

The average general hospital will usually have an established procedure for coping with grossly disturbed people. Typically, this involves a nurse drawing the plight of her patient to the attention of relevant doctors, who will then call in one of the local psychiatrists. To tap into this procedure may not, however, necessarily be a very favourable move as far as the furtherance of good psychological care is concerned, with the exception, that is, of instances where a person has deteriorated into psychotic disturbance or gross and unmanageable levels of emotional reaction. The problem is, if I may make a few generalizations, that the conventional 'psychiatric event' will involve a diagnostic assessment and the virtually inevitable prescription of emotion-inhibiting drugs, with little else to follow. Not all psychiatrists function in this way, of course, but sadly it is quite prevalent. In terms of the aims of psychological care, the standard psychiatric approach is unacceptable for two reasons.

First, the type of difficulties which we have been discussing basically require treatment by psychological means in order to produce psychological change and activate psychological processes. The pharmacological approach has no central relevance since, although drugs may bring sedation and temporary relief, the actual problems ultimately have to be dealt with directly, as most of them do not conveniently disappear of their own accord. The situation would otherwise be analogous to that of treating toothache by painkillers alone. We know this would not prove effective. The cavity must be discovered, cleaned and filled. With patients who are in difficulties but not grossly disturbed, the same idea applies. Of course, people should be made comfortable if they so wish, and appropriate drugs made available to them for that purpose, *provided* there is full and honest discussion on what these drugs can achieve.

The second reason why the standard psychiatric approach is unacceptable is to do with its obvious implications – the whole message and value of your psychological care work will be undermined by a drug-oriented psychiatric consultation. *The point of drug therapy is to block and suppress emotion, treating it as an illness. This, I trust you will know by now, is not a valued objective in psychological care.* What I am arguing against, therefore, is a referral which leads to nothing other than drug therapy. At this point I must stress that I am not against the involvement of psychiatrists *per se* – quite the opposite. We need the help and support of psychologically minded psychiatrists very much.

Incidentally, if you find someone called a *liaison psychiatrist* you are in luck. They, like health psychologists, specialize in the care of the ill and injured.

The system for making a referral

Who does what when a referral is required? Is it the primary nurse, the sister in charge, the registrar or the consultant that should make the actual referral? As we look at this issue it is useful to discriminate between two types of referral. These are a) external referrals, where they are made to a specialist outside the membership of the unit or ward team, for example a psychologist; and b) internal referrals, where the referral is made to someone who is part of the team, for example the medical social worker.

If you have slotted into a scheme of psychological care there will be a procedure already. If not, then it is up to you to make a move and negotiate on the business of referral procedure with your colleagues. The situation concerning external referrals will probably be the most awkward to resolve. Let us say that you are a nurse and have been in close contact with a patient through your work of psychological care. You will now know him better than your colleagues because you will have spent more time with him than anyone else. Here is a dilemma. *Quite often the doctors will be the least well informed on the true psychological status of your patient.* Yet, as we have seen, the medical profession works hard to retain sole preserve over the decision-making and administrative power required to effect referrals. This is a power which is guarded jealously for a variety of reasons and it creates a difficulty for us. Put succinctly, the people most likely to know when a referral is necessary (those giving psychological care) do not normally have the power of referral, and those who have the power of referral are the least likely to know when a referral is necessary. Clearly this is inefficient and against the interests of people using the hospital service. There is thus a diplomatic task to be undertaken, since our aim is to create a system which minimizes psychological neglect. As initial awareness of the need for referral will probably be yours, you must negotiate a procedure wherein you are at least free to *initiate* the moves leading to a referral, which, if local circumstances require, may then be activated by the collective decision of the team or the sole act of the consultant in charge of the case.

A consultant does hold responsibility for what happens to the patient – he 'carries the can' if things should go wrong. This burden must be respected and it would be unreasonable to expect a consultant to delegate this basic responsibility except in exceptional circumstances. It is also clear that part of a consultant's function involves centralizing decision-making and so heading off clinical anarchy. We would therefore *expect* a consultant to be involved in a referral. However, it would similarly be unreasonable on the part of a medical consultant if he attempted to dominate the business of referring people who had been receiving psychological care from other staff who were more developed and informed in the work than he. We could not condone the obstruction or neglect of a necessary referral because a consultant was unable to recognize the need, or was possessed of personal whims antagonistic to psychological care which were based on prejudices rather than scientific analysis.

Overall, the best plan is to work out the issue directly and honestly with your senior nurse and consultant. Ideally, you will negotiate a compromise which recognizes your position as the member of staff most likely to be the best informed (assuming you have been working with a patient for a while) and accepts the consultant's position of overall responsibility. It should also be recognized that you must liaise with the person receiving the referral in order to brief him or her on the case. A system for joint consultation between yourself and the rest of the team, and action based on mutual agreement, is obviously the ideal.

Managing a referral from the patient's point of view

Nurse: I would like you to see our psychologist.
Patient: (inner voice) A psychologist, this is terrible. They think I'm going mad. To face this on top of everything else . . . I don't want to see him.

Does it mean abandonment and that you think they are not worth your time? Does it mean that you think they are going under or already regard them as 'mental'? Does it provoke fear, resentment, unhappiness or what?

Referral must be explained well and thoroughly talked through. Ideally, it will be a joint decision reached by yourself and the patient. You will explain your position, showing why you need someone to take over the case. You will be very clear on who the person actually is that your patient is expected to see, what they do and, most importantly, the significance of seeing them. You will make explicit why you feel it would be advantageous to see someone in addition to yourself. The most important requirement is, as always, honesty in the context of a trusting relationship. For example, if you have become worried about some aspect of your patient's life but feel it is out of your depth to help them with it, tell them so. At the same time, try to communicate that the event is not horrendous in your eyes, but that the upheaval and stresses of serious illness or major injury provoke personal difficulties (not madness) and these must be dealt with early on – in this case using the help of someone who specializes in giving such assistance. Do not, however, force an agreement to accept referral to us, the therapists, because, in most circumstances, working with people who have 'been sent' is a frustrating and fruitless endeavour. Negotiate the issue to a conclusion and accept a refusal on the idea of referral if that is your patient's sincere wish.

Will many referrals be necessary?

There is no reliable way of estimating this. At present, few referrals are made from the general hospitals because much of the psychological distress goes unnoticed and, frankly, because the pyschiatric and psychological services can be held in low regard by the medical profession. However, the general hospitals are for the physically ill and not the mentally ill. There is therefore no reason to expect that an overwhelmingly large concentration of people will need referral, although we know from Chapter 2 that there are a great many in psychological distress. The real lack at present is of *preventive* psychological care to assist people with the known stresses and demands of serious illness and injury. Properly implemented, psychological care will reduce the number of psychological casualties below the current level – the complication being that it will also lead to many of the currently hidden psychological casualties being noticed.

My own experience suggests that the numbers needing referral will not be excessive and that, as the quality of psychological care improves with experience, and the number of people offering psychological care rises, the number of cases needing referral will eventually diminish.

CHAPTER 7

Self-Care and Preventive Support For Nurses and Therapists

JOB SATISFACTION VERSUS STRESS

Having worked alongside nurses and therapists for quite a few years now, I have been encouraged to see that those who have added psychological care to their work almost always gain personally. Most noticeably there is a gain in job satisfaction, particularly where there has been an opportunity to set up a properly run scheme of psychological care. From discussion with nurses one discovers that, in the past, they were often disturbed by the feeling of incompleteness that the traditional, physically oriented style of nursing produced. Walking away from a person who is obviously ill-informed or in distress is both unfulfilling and unpleasant for the nurse with a 'whole person instinct', yet that was the daily experience of many nurses. However, the extension of the nurse's role to include psychological care offers a sense of completeness and professional direction, which most nurses with whom I have discussed the issue find to be a boost to job satisfaction. A similar point of view has been expressed to me by speech and occupational therapists.

Recently, I interviewed one of the home sisters from the Exeter Renal Unit. I wanted to learn about her experiences in helping people who had decided to give up the effort to survive renal failure and had arranged to stop dialysing. As it happened, she had quite recently been providing the psychological and nursing care for two such patients. Although the weeks leading up to their decision, and the week or so prior to death once dialysis had been stopped, were arduous for all concerned, the sister was nevertheless able to say, 'Those few weeks were some of my hardest ever, but they gave me the highest job satisfaction of my whole career'.

There is, however, another side to the story. Although providing psychological care may be professionally fulfilling and personally rewarding, we should also now recognize that it is a role which should

170

be undertaken with a degree of caution, combined with considerable concern for *self-care*. This is an awareness on my part which has sharpened noticeably during the last few years. At the time of writing the first edition of this book I was preoccupied with the psychological neglect in hospitals, and with campaigning vigorously to hasten the changes necessary to tackle the problem. We just had to get the direct involvement of nurses and therapists in psychological care work. The paradox, to be critical of my former position, was that I gave little attention to the potential impact of this work on the nurses and therapists involved. Consequently, I made only scant mention of the stresses and burdens of the work and the very great importance of self-care and support. However, since that time, various examples similar to the following have brought the issues into rather better focus, such that I now put great emphasis on self-care as a professional discipline for those giving psychological care. The case study below, involving a nurse, should be taken as a cautionary tale for us all.

Case study

Jane, a nurse of sister grade, had held her post on a general medical ward for three years. She had attended a short course in psychological care techniques and had elected to develop psychological care on her own with selected individual cases, until such time as other staff had attended courses and the ward was less precariously staffed. Over the months she began relatively long-term care relationships with several people suffering from cystic fibrosis. On the whole she worked alone, other than obtaining the occasional piece of advice from the psychologist who had run her course.

During one winter, various things came together to increase pressure on her. Sickness led to staff shortages and the ward was kept going only by involving trainee nurses at a level which Jane felt guilty about. The second sister on the ward ran into marital problems and her husband left her. Consequently, this colleague became very fragile and needed both support and a period of protection from anything other than routine work. Lastly, two cases were admitted to the ward within a short time of each other which demanded rather intensive psychological care.

One of these cases, a 30-year-old man, Paul by name and an architect by profession, had recently been married. He had received treatment for cystic fibrosis for years and had generally coped well, but a trend of deterioration had set in. It became clear to Jane that he was probably in his last months. Slowly as the weeks went by, Jane edged into a terminal care stance with her psychological work. She spent considerable time with the young couple, helping them prepare for the forthcoming death. She gave regular allocations of time to be with Paul and offer emotional care. During these weeks she talked very little to anyone else about this case nor, for that matter, about the other cases with which she was working. She tried to protect her co-sister (whom she was continuing to support) and also the trainee nurses, from much involvement with Paul's psychological care, fearing that they would be overwhelmed.

They were very busy weeks and the strain mounted. Jane was aware that she was feeling increasingly tired, and also recognized that she was becoming rather emotionally unstable herself. In particular, she was getting angry at trivial things at home and at work. Jane had not, though, sensed that she was near any kind of crisis herself. Things suddenly came to a head when, after a very stretched day, she ended her work with what was intended as a brief visit to Paul. He was very poorly with a massive lung infection. He realised that he could die and was quite clinging to Jane. She stayed for nearly an hour with him. As she arrived home (she later recounted) she stopped the car near to her house and thought to herself, 'I can't go in, I feel too tearful, I just want to curl up on the floor by the fire and cry'. She sensed that she could not deal with the normal family demands that would wait for her on the other side of the front door. There would be the usual clamour: 'What are we having for tea, mum?'; 'He's taken my ruler.': 'Can we watch *Neighbours*?'; 'Tell him he can't have my ruler, mum.'; 'Did you have a good day, dear?'. So Jane sat for quite a while outside the house. She did not cry but suddenly realized that if something did not change she was going to experience some kind of collapse or crisis herself. She had reached the end of her own emotional resources.

The immediate problem was resolved. Jane went to the nearest telephone and phoned home. She told her husband the truth: it had been a traumatic day and a traumatic week, she was feeling stressed to the point where she just needed quiet and an hour or two alone. He agreed to handle things at home. The next day she arranged a very much overdue review and support session.

STRESS IN HEALTH CARE

There are now a substantial number of publications which examine the stressful elements of the caregiving role in general. Payne and Firth-Cozens (1987), Bailey and Clarke (1989) and Burnard (1991) are typical examples. Emotional exhaustion, burnout, role conflict, organizational stresses, communication problems and work overload emerge as typical and common problems. More specifically, much has been written concerning stress in nursing. Jacobson and McGrath (1983) write on the general nature and origin of nurse stress, and Llewelyn (1989) gives a useful overview of stress in nursing related to the caregiving role. She notes that one-third of nurse trainees leave the profession before completing their course, and 10% of qualified nurses resign annually. There will be various causes for this high rate of attrition, but indications from several of the studies which she reviewed implicate stress as a major factor. Incidentally, *The Times* reports the Royal College of Nursing as estimating the cost of this loss as running at about £24 million annually (Bassett, 1991). In a similar vein, Sweeney (1991), working with occupational therapists, found that approximately 25% of her sample were significantly stressed in their work.

My overall impression from discussion in recent stress workshops is that levels of stress and stress casualties in the nursing and allied professions have increased in recent years. One of the most significant problems is that of increasing volumes of work and therefore workload. In fact, Baglioni *et al.* (1990), in a survey involving some 475 nurses of sister grade and above, showed that a heavy workload was clearly linked with mental health status, that is, high levels of anxiety, depression and psychosomatic disorders. Not surprisingly, stress in the medical profession is known to affect some 50% of junior doctors, where an excessive workload combines with high levels of personal responsibility (Firth-Cozens, 1987). Similarly, Payne (1987) found indications that surgeons were chronically exposed to moderately intense strain and, as a group, showed raised levels of cortisol. In other words, they showed stress-related physiological changes which held long-term health implications.

Clearly the issue of general work stress in health care professionals is of great importance. However, my concern in this book is to develop an approach to psychological care and, as part of that, to promote an understanding of the effect on the caregivers of giving psychological care. This is not to minimize the effects of general work stress, especially since a stressed member of staff inevitably becomes less effective in giving psychological care, but it is a huge topic and beyond the scope of this particular book. Do note, however, that while the later sections of this chapter deal with the techniques of self-care and preventive support for those involved in psychological care work, the approaches are equally relevant to general work stress in health care.

GIVING EMOTIONAL CARE: IS IT A STRESSOR?

As I hope you will now agree, one of the key elements in psychological care has to be emotional care. As described earlier, the objective in emotional care is to provide a close, safe and facilitating relationship in which patients and partners may express, explore and share their true emotional state. The nurse or therapist serves as a trusted professional companion and support figure to people in distress, so minimizing the stress of illness, injury and hospitalization.

It is a paradox, perhaps, that *the better the emotional care is conducted, the more the support figure is exposed to the distress of those receiving her support.* A distant, psychologically defended nurse in, say, a coronary care unit, remains safe from exposure to the distress of men and women who have suffered an infarct, but, at the same time, she cannot possibly be effective in giving good emotional care. This can only be achieved if she maintains an openness to the emotions of the people with whom she is working. In other words, she establishes emotional contact. *Emotional care thus inevitably involves exposure to the emotions and distress of others.*

Exposure to the emotions of others is, in itself, nothing more than normal life. *Repeated* exposure to particular types of intense emotion, perhaps several times a day on a daily basis, is a different issue. Consider, as a further example, the husband of a woman dying from breast cancer. A nurse offering him emotional care will be striving to empathize with his experience and feelings, seeking to make contact with his feelings at a depth in which the feelings are, to a degree, echoed and *felt by her.* In this example, then, she will sense his agitation and fright, together with a profound sadness at the coming separation and loss of his only true friend.

From such a perspective, it is clear that in properly conducted emotional care a nurse or therapist cannot avoid constant emotional activity in herself. She becomes a recipient for whatever emotions and perceptions a patient may bring.

Fortunately, empathized emotion does not usually have the same impact as emotion actually experienced. Nevertheless, it can create tension, lead on to an emotional draining effect and leave the person giving support with a synthesis of uncomfortable reactions. It is also to be remembered that, occasionally, empathizing the feelings of others who are in distress may bring us into contact with emotionally laden issues of our own. Herein lies the hazard: *unless the nurse or therapist giving emotional care paces herself well, balances psychological work with other duties which offer an alternative atmosphere and, above all, engages in planned self-care and preventive* support work, then insidious stress effects may take place. These stress effects are the result of becoming isolated with emotion, or becoming overwhelmed by the constant exposure to the emotion of others. In this state, job satisfaction and the sense of personal coping and worth in the role fades. So also may tolerance to other demands from patients, colleagues and family.

These are the ingredients of a destructive work stress created by emotional demand. This in turn leads to emotional drain and represents a definite risk for anyone regularly involved in psychological care. Imposing continual demands of this type may begin a slide towards stressed episodes or even a stress-induced 'breakdown'. Alternatively, there may be an unaware, defensive retreat into a distanced, 'burnt-out' state (Jackson *et al.*, 1986). I do not, as the Americans say, want to 'awfulize' too much here but, having met several serious casualties in this situation, I do want to mark it as an area of genuine risk. Some relevant research findings do exist to support these concerns. Bailey and Clarke (1989) consider the impact of caring for the dying, and also the special demands of intensive care nursing. They conclude that, in these settings, the intensive emotional contact with either the patient or a close relative can impose considerable strain on the nurse. Interestingly, the strain is increased when the other elements of psychological care are poorly done, especially informational care.

THE PRINCIPLES OF SELF-CARE AND PREVENTIVE SUPPORT

Enough of dreadful vistas. Although I could easily relate other cases similar to the one above, they are by no means everyday events. It is more important to explore the fact that, when such cases are examined in depth, they tend to emerge as having one common theme – namely, *it did not have to happen*. In short, the problems were usually avoidable and the people involved got into trouble with stress because they did not recognize the need for self-care and support. So, to you, I say *do not let it happen*. Now, having said this, I must offer you something which enables you to deal with the pressures and stresses inherent in giving emotional care.

The ground rule

I hold the view that to accept a role in health care known to be 'stress-laden' without, at the same time, maintaining a personal programme of *self*-care, is a form of self-neglect. Accordingly, it can be seen as unprofessional behaviour because it is an act which threatens to reduce the quality of psychological care delivered to patients (since a stressed member of staff does not usually give good care). This may seem harsh and rather dramatic, but it is meant in a kindly and positive way. The intention is to promote a strong argument in order to establish self-care and preventive support as important priorities, and thus part of any job involving emotional care. In these terms, some aspects of this approach, especially support work, *legitimately belong in working hours*. Without this perspective, various common and sabotaging attitudes prevail. For example, the following have all been said to me: 'It is only the weak ones who need support'; 'Unless they are a bit stressed they cannot be doing their job properly'; 'Everybody gets stressed, but we can't have half a dozen nurses sat around talking about whether they are stressed or not twice a month – what would I tell the manager?' What is the rule, therefore? In regular emotional care work you cannot do the job properly without giving time to self-care and preventive support. As far as the manager goes, it is a good investment of staff time – better a support group once every two weeks than staff regularly off sick.

The basics of self-care

The kind of stress we are talking about is to do with absorbed emotion, emotional demand, and occasional emotionally traumatic experiences. A balanced programme of self-care will therefore need to focus on the means of opposing the effects of such things.

Some aspects of self-care work are usually conducted on an individual basis, whereas others can only be set up with at least one other colleague, or better, a group of colleagues. Let's take a look at the aspects of self-care which are conducted on an individual basis first. These are, effectively, sets of attitudes, habits and antistress behaviours:

- *Learn to identify your personal stress signs and continuously monitor their levels of intensity.* This is a central skill in dealing with stress. Key stress signs are changes in one's mood and manner of interaction with family and colleagues, for example, a shift towards irritability and 'short fuse' behaviour, with feelings of being overstretched, agitated and, possibly, emotionally fragile. Similarly, signs of physical change may occur, including headaches, tenseness, muscular tension pains, fatigue, sleep disturbance and an inability to relax. An unusual proneness to coughs and colds or atypically severe premenstrual tension can also indicate a stressed state. Figure 7.1 gives you a more detailed outline which you can also use as a checklist.
- *Regulate your pace and workload and keep the content of your work balanced.* This important stress-containing strategy involves you in establishing (by trial and error over the years) a workload and pattern of work which, from first-hand experience, you know to be one you can maintain without undue stress. It requires a degree of assertiveness and compromise which is not always first nature to those in health care, especially nurses. It means being able to judge how much you can do and making sure that you are not forced into exceeding this on a regular basis. It also means planning work so that you have a variety of duties such that, as you turn from one, it gives you a rest from the other. A well thought-out strategy like

STRESS SIGNS

Emotional	tense, irritable, angry outbursts, unsettled, agitated, feeling a sense of pressure, mood swings, low feelings, emotionally fragile, tearful, resentful of demands, episodes of anxiety and/or depression
Physical	cannot relax, 'wound up', tense, headaches, back or neck aches, muscle tremors, sense of physical strain, fatigue prone, excessive sleep, increase in minor illnesses: colds, 'flu, etc. indigestion, rapid weight loss/gain, asthma, skin conditions, menstrual problems
Behavioural	rushing, lots of deadlines, overcommitted, self-neglect (missing sleep, meals) self-sedation: increase in drinking, smoking, drugs, growing inefficiency, withdrawn, sleep loss, nightmares, over/under-eating
Cognitive	poor concentration, forgetful, distractable, thoughts full of worries, perception of hopelessness or injustice, feeling trapped
Relationships	less able to cope with other people's needs and demands, behaving badly at home, impatient, intolerant, inclined to row, avoiding company, wanting to be left alone, overcontrolling towards others, needing to be supported

**EACH PERSON WILL HAVE A CHARACTERISTIC
STRESS BEHAVIOUR PATTERN OF THEIR OWN**

Figure 7.1: Stress signs – how people change under stress

this must not be misunderstood as a ploy for doing less. It is a simply good policy for your own wellbeing and also for your employers, since the product is a valuable worker who will last ten years in the job rather than two.

- *Adopt a 'credit card' style of personal stress management.* In simple terms, if we draw heavily on our physical or emotional energy, we must be reliable in paying back the 'debt' by compensating rest, a proper relaxation technique and by prearranged breaks from, say, intensive emotional care work with the substitution of other duties. This is what is meant by a balanced workload. A nurse specializing as counsellor for a breast screening unit will, for example, programme her week so that on some half days she is not working directly with women who have recently been told that they have breast cancer. She will plan in other activities such as teaching, administration, case discussion, etc. Those who do not learn this skill do not usually last very long before developing signs of burnout or stress.

- *Use the support facilities.* Obtaining support is a vital element of self-care. Although support work itself is not a skill which can be undertaken on an individual basis, the conscious discipline of using support facilities should be seen as an individual responsibility. Sometimes, when support is most needed, the motivation to engage in support work fades and we can find ourselves hiding away with private hurt. It thus requires some sympathetic and disciplined 'self-talk', a skill in itself, to find the motivation to seek support again and avoid the trap of becoming isolated with strong feeling.

Just before exploring the notion and techniques of support, a short case study drawn from recent experience illustrates the importance of these individual self-care strategies. They need to be seen as a personal *responsibility* for those involved in frequent emotional care work. If you neglect this responsibility, you put yourself at needless risk.

Case study

A newly appointed sister took on a post in a ward dealing mainly with advanced cancers. She threw herself into the emotional care work with no heed for her own care. She handled most of the cases herself and worked with great intensity, taking little break from the pressures of the work. Naturally, she had other duties, but these involved a fairly high degree of demand too – for example, assisting with the chemotherapy. The job proved a delight and more than matched her expectations. In the early months she loved being at work, because she felt the value and impact of the work she was doing. As one dying man who had derived much benefit from her psychological care work commented. 'She's an A1 lady.' There were some problems, though. Although some of the consultants involved backed her up in the psychological care work, others were dismissive and undermining. So, too, were one or two nurse colleagues. As the months went by, she worked at a hectic pace, involved with a slowly increasing pool of very sick people and very distressed partners. Friends in the hospital noticed that after about 12 months she visibly began to tire and slow down. She seemed to become more affected by non-supportive colleagues and more despondent about the treatment of cancer and frequent deaths. Colleagues began to worry about her and urged her to slow down. Unexpectedly, after 18 months, she suddenly resigned. Basically, she was totally emotionally exhausted and simply unable to carry on. It was a sad outcome because she had brought a new era of much-improved quality of care to the ward. The mistakes were obvious: no concern for self-care, no *regimen* of self-care, no regulation of pace and workload, no built-in alternative activities to allow respite, and no support. It was never a question of *will* she become stressed, but rather, *when?*

The principles of preventive support

It is a frequent experience these days to hear nurses, therapists, managers, psychologists even, talking of stress and the consequent need for support. Quite often, though, with further eavesdropping, things are said which leave no conviction that the true objectives of support are fully appreciated – or at least, the true objectives as I see them. The concept usually revealed is of a limited crisis-intervention model of support. Thus, during times of trouble, crisis or distress, staff are 'picked up and dusted down' by means of a supportive intervention and then set back to work. It is a wholly problem-centred approach dedicated to dealing with 'stress casualties'. This is a very narrow view. Certainly, crisis intervention has its place in support work because crises do happen. However, with prevention in mind, support schemes need much broader objectives. These are probably best described in terms of benefit. A properly conducted scheme of support for health care professionals should give the following 'preventive' benefits:

1. Support work breaks emotional isolation. Many professional people in caregiving work, particularly emotional care, become isolated with their burdens and difficulties, despite being in regular contact with colleagues. Isolation is destructive and has to be opposed by regular support meetings.
2. Support sessions allow the opportunity to both make contact with (perhaps to discover) and express one's true state of feeling at a particular time. This, in turn, allows emotional release. In other words, rather than holding in the personal feeling generated by, say, a week of many pressures, including emotional care work, time is set aside to identify this feeling and share it with support partners.
3. The act of self-expression yields two very valuable products. It allows *self-monitoring* of personal feelings and stress signs (core skills in self-care) and also the opportunity for a general reappraisal of the approach being adopted in work and other aspects of living. Since support work always takes place in the presence of at least one other colleague, their views can help to promote new ways of dealing with troublesome issues. Thus, preventive support provides a continuing medium for self-monitoring and reappraisal.
4. Support sessions are usually conducted in the presence of mutually caring colleagues who have equivalent issues and personal feelings

to share. This experience of mutual care and concern builds co-hesion and gives a sense of uplift. There is thus a strengthening effect.

From this, you will see that the point of attending support sessions is not just to present problems to colleagues or hear about their difficul-ties in turn: it will often be the case that you have no specific difficul-ties – things may be going well. Rather, the object is to use the safety of a support session routinely to ask oneself the following questions: 'How am I feeling, what has happened since we last met, how has this affected me and do I need to attend to any issues of self-care either in the support session or elsewhere?'. The answers to these questions may then be shared and talked through with the support partners. *Thus, the fundamental objective in support work is that of creating a safe situa-tion with one or more colleagues which allows this gentle exploration of personal feeling, i.e. self-monitoring.* Necessary self-care action can then be worked out and implemented with the intention of preventing any drift into a stressed state. Naturally, if it has been a bad week, with crises of one sort or another, then this type of meeting caters very well for that too.

The skill of receiving support

There remains one last comment for me to make in this review of the principles of preventive support. As described earlier, giving support involves a specific set of skills and attitudes (listening, empathizing, reflecting back, holding back any personal urge to give advice, etc.). It is rare to find mention of the point that *receiving* support requires a different set of skills and attitudes. First-hand experience leads me to the observation that professional caregivers tend to be very good at giving care but, paradoxically, quite poor at receiving it; clinical psy-chologists provide a good example (Nichols, 1988).

If I manage to convince you of the need for preventive support then you do need to think through your own position on the issue of receiv-ing such support. How do you respond to it? Begin by working out your reaction to your own feelings. In the busy clinical routine there is little opportunity for sharing feelings in any depth. Those who are ill at ease with their personal feeling reactions will use this situation as a comfortable smoke screen. In mutual support work, though, self-disclosure is the main means of participating and deriving benefit. Thus, when in the 'care-receiving mode', there has to be an ability to relax with and explore one's own feelings in some depth. Since this is done in the presence of others there has to be a basic respect for one's own feelings, otherwise there will be inhibiting blocks and a need to hide, or even apologize for, personal feelings.

Similarly, in this approach to support it is necessary to work with another colleague or group of colleagues. In other words, you have to be able to receive the time, attention and care of others and they, in turn, have to be able to receive your time, attention and care. Figure 7.2 gathers these views together. Thus, the use of support must be seen as a professional *strength and skill*, and certainly not something which the 'weaker ones' need – quite the opposite.

Attitude and skills required to receive support

- Understanding that seeking and receiving support is a necessary *strength* required for de-stressing

- The ability to value, identify and disclose one's own feelings

- Being able to receive the time, attention and care of colleagues

Figure 7.2: Receiving support from colleagues

Support groups and networks

Unless an outside agency is used, the provision of support is usually something which is arranged on a reciprocal basis with colleagues. It is not necessary for the colleagues to be closely associated. Sometimes, if there are interpersonal tensions in a unit or ward which cannot be easily resolved, linking with colleagues from elsewhere may be preferable. Similarly, if there are grade or role differences which seem to create a gulf, then linking with colleagues of the same grade may be of help. For example, at one unit I have been involved with, the nurses set up a support group within the unit but felt that they wanted to keep it for nurses below sister grade. The sisters were understanding of this and formed their own support network with sisters from other units. Practice or community nurses almost always have to link up with colleagues from elsewhere.

Before discussing arrangements to do with support meetings, it has to be said that the best overall foundation for support scheme is a supportive atmosphere in your ward or unit. If you are a nurse or therapist in a management position, do bear in mind that the general sense of supportiveness that staff feel is a measure of how effective you are as a manager. Where staff complain of a generally unsupportive atmosphere it is almost inevitable that their work will be affected for the worse. Furthermore, setting up support groups is likely to prove a troublesome task in these circumstances, which means that staff are placed at risk. Woodhams (1992) describes how, at Exeter Renal Unit, there is a planned strategy for maintaining a supportive atmosphere for staff. New staff are given an extended induction and training period lasting for several months. During this period, it is made clear that seeking support is valued as good professional conduct, and nurses are shown how to obtain support (who to go to etc.). There is an effective education and mentor system which means that the nurses can achieve true confidence and are not rushed into rapid independence. All senior staff make much effort to be genuinely open for, and to, communication. Thus a conscious effort is made to create a subculture in the unit which is based on sharing, openness and supportiveness. Not surprisingly, the unit does have a support group.

By far the best arrangement for support is that in which you attend prearranged meetings with a known and trusted group of colleagues, then combine this with an agreement to contact any of the members of the group between times should anything occur which is disturbing for you. They in turn will honour an arrangement to contact you or other members of the group should they run into difficulties. It is thus a mutually supporting network which also meets as a group. The scheduled meetings are for monitoring and general support purposes, and the non-scheduled meetings are for crisis intervention.

Depending on your work situation, this arrangement can be set up with, as a minimum, a pair of colleagues, but it is usually better with a group of seven or eight people. Ideally, it will be a stable group with the same people attending every time. The frequency of meetings is very much determined by circumstances. In general, once a week can be a touch too frequent in a busy health care setting, resulting in the meetings becoming a burden rather than a respite. In contrast, fewer meetings than one a month probably stretches things out too much.

Setting up a support group

How should you set up such a group and how should it be run? There are many things to consider and quite a few tips to pass on, which make it too big a task to brief you properly on the subject within the last few pages of a chapter. However, it is important to have guidance, and since this is not always easy to come by, a colleague and I have tried to create a guide to setting up such a group in a companion book (Nichols and Jenkinson, 1991). Here you will find that we see the vital foundation for an effective support group is the sense of *safety*. If the members of a support group are present voluntarily, feel completely safe in terms of status and confidentiality issues – that is, they do not feel that they are under scrutiny in a way which may affect their future – this gives the beginning of safety. In addition to this, if the other members have good listening skills and share the same understanding of what the group is for and what is supposed to happen, then the group will very likely succeed. Without this 'psychological safety', a support group will never succeed. For example:

Case study – an effective group

At the beginning of this chapter you will have read through the case of Sister Jane. Following the events recounted in that case, Jane responded to advice and linked up with a support group run for local hospice nurses. This involved a network arrangement whereby members could (and would) contact one another if they felt a need to work on troublesome issues, in which case the tendency was to meet as a pair. This was combined with a regular monthly meeting of the whole group. The meeting was led by a clinical tutor and had a fixed membership of 11 nurses, all of whom were women. They had each accepted an explicit contract which simply involved an agreement to review with each other how they were feeling and what experiences they had been through since the last meeting. The emphasis was on sharing the emotions felt and the burdens carried in as open and honest a manner as possible.

Because the membership was stable, the level of group cohesion was high and the members felt a strong sense of belonging. Thus, an attendance at a meeting was usually an uplifting event, with feelings of friendship and mutual support very much in evidence. Most times, the individual members looked forward to the meetings and recognized the importance of reviewing their working and emotional experience with trusted colleagues. The meetings also provided opportunities for personal learning in terms of increased understanding about the nature of the circumstances which caused distress to individual members. Similarly, it allowed members to learn from each other's experiences and to incorporate new attitudes and practices into their ways. Jane fitted in well with the group, although she was not solely involved in terminal care nursing. The sense of strength which she drew from the group enabled her to continue with further arduous case work without such personal stress and distress.

An ineffective support group

Despite the best intentions, the first meeting of a support group can, on occasions, be painful and disappointing. The members can seem very hesitant and tense. The atmosphere feels troubled by confusion and floundering. The more threatened members make the running, with defensive irrelevancies and false jocularity. Awkward silences raise the tension. If this happens, it is probably because the pregroup preparation has been inadequate and the members do not know what they are there for, or because the membership is unbalanced in some way. For example, a sister from an oncology ward decided to set up a support group for her nurses. No pregroup preparation was attempted except at the first meeting, and no selection for membership had been possible since all the staff were to attend – that is, trainees, staff nurses, two sisters and a nursing officer. The younger nurses (who had originally suggested the need for support to the sister) later revealed that they felt completely intimidated, fearing that they would be judged by what they said and that this might go on to their records. Needless to say, these nurses froze and the group became the opposite of a warm and supportive environment. In fact, this particular group did not recover and it foundered after three sessions. A classic example of how not to do it.

The moral to this chapter ought to be clear by now. If you are seriously thinking of taking on psychological care, then think seriously of self-care too. Preventive support is an important part of self-care and the support group is the usual way of providing this. But do not rush lightly into starting a support group. Take advice. Ask the local clinical psychologists to help you set it up. Read about support groups. Nichols and Jenkinson (1991) cover all the basic issues of pregroup preparation, membership, how to guide a group and how to avoid some common pitfalls. In my own experience, I have found that a good support group can be an incredibly valuable asset to the life of health care professionals, especially when combined with the other basic self-care skills.

CHAPTER 8

Overview and Dealing with Reality

We have worked through the aspects of psychological care which I judge to be essential for seriously ill and injured people. Of these, monitoring psychological state and informational care should unquestioningly be provided for all patients. Emotional care and the provision of basic counselling should be readily available and on offer, according to people's needs and inclination to accept help. The actual requirements for such care will, of course, vary greatly from person to person. Now it remains to join the pieces together, stand back and see what we have got, then answer some of the more obvious questions and criticisms.

The approach adopted has been to present the work of psychological care as it will be conducted by the individual nurse or member of the therapist professions. In making this presentation, the assumption has been held, as I have pointed out with some regularity, that the person involved has the benefit of an environment favourable to such work, with adequate time and facilities, together with the genuine under-standing and positive support (insistence would be better) of the medical profession, senior nurses, heads of departments, etc. I do realize that this has been an idealization, and I do know that some readers will not have the benefits of such a favourable setting. I hope, however, that you will appreciate the necessity to teach the work in its 'pure' form, that is, without dilution by accommodating possible shortages of time and staff, and without distortion as a result of impoverished understanding and inadequate back-up (or even obstruction) from colleagues. The emphasis of the material given is also clearly directed at longer-term patients, or at least those who maintain contact through regular outpatient visits, rather than those who have been and gone in the space of 24 hours. Such idealization on my part must have provoked protest in many readers, especially those who genuinely see the need for psychological care in their own work environment but find the opposite conditions to those I have apparently assumed. To you I will say, stay with me for a few pages more and then we will discuss

185

your position. Keeping the idealization alive for a last few moments, I
want to take a look at the events of psychological care as a whole.

BECOMING EXPERIENCED IN PSYCHOLOGICAL CARE

What will be the general approach of people who are thoroughly experienced in psychological care and know how to put it all together?
First, may I remind you of the role concept. Experienced 'models' will
construe psychological care as a natural and necessary extension of
their role. It will be seen by them as important, central in fact, and not
as a low-priority luxury to be abandoned whenever things are a bit
tight. In other words, it will be seen as an essential part of the professional care routinely provided in hospitals. The not uncommon, well-
intentioned but amateurish 'trying to help' behaviour will be replaced
by professionalism. These people will know exactly what they are
doing and why, in terms similar to those set out in the earlier chapters
of this book. As each patient is taken on, it will be automatic for them
to begin informational care which will be seen as essential as, say, the
physical routines of nursing. Similarly, as each patient is taken on, it
will be automatic to take up the task of monitoring their psychological
state, that is, thinking and inquiring about the patient in a psychologically minded way as well as in a medically minded way. The basic
orientation will be preventive. The stresses and harsh experiences of
illness will be countered as these people assist their patients with the
tasks of adjustment, acceptance and emotional processing. They will
offer a supportive and genuinely caring relationship, and be quick to
provide emotional care and basic counselling according to the needs of
their patients. They will always hold in mind the possibility that referral to a psychological therapist may be advantageous, and, should the
occasion arise, will make this clear to their patients in a non-
threatening, non-possessive way.

'But,' you may want to protest, 'how will I know at what stage to
offer the different parts of psychological care – how will I ever really be
sure that I am right?'

The answer is a reassuring one. Relax with it all. Be thinking, of
course, but do not turn psychological care into a ritual of strict procedures, full of stages and rights and wrongs. Accepting the premise that
psychological monitoring should go on *all the time*, beyond this there
are no set sequences and patterns to the work, which will vary from
one case to another. It is a matter of blending the various skills we
have studied in relation to the needs of each person. In psychological
care, *the master skill is that of identifying the needs of the patient and responding appropriately.* Regrettably, this ability cannot easily be taught by
written word. It is an asset acquired by experience, through spending

time working with your patients in an open, receptive way, so that they can teach you their needs. You will have to be patient with yourself while you expand your experience. Thus, one patient may find your supportive concern and informational care work sufficient for his needs; another may want to use your ability in counselling to help resolve a particular issue, but will have her needs for emotional care met elsewhere; a third person may be in constant need of emotional care throughout the span of your contact, whereas a fourth will require emotional care for brief, intense but infrequent occasions, yet draw heavily on you as a counsellor. A fifth person may need all that you can offer but decline to receive any of it. Again, I will stress the value of regular case discussions, which will accelerate your learning.

There is, I admit, an obvious flow to the 'typical' case. Initially, relationship building and early informational care work take the time available, followed by a move to check whether the patient seems to need emotional care and whether he is able to make use of the opportunity for this. Later, when things are stabilized and the relationship is formed, the contacts may well naturally turn into the counselling mode of working as the 'problems arising' are grasped. If there are medical incidents, for example a failed transplant attempt or complications following surgery, then additional emotional care work may be necessary. In this way, a man who has just suffered the traumatic loss of an arm in an industrial accident will probably need much emotional care in the early period of recovery. Later, the mode of working will shift increasingly to deal with the wider horizons involved in picking up life and work again, and the examination and resolution of personal difficulties through the counselling techniques. Possibly this will be taken on by his occupational therapist as regular contact with the nurse ends. The occupational therapist, however, will have to remind herself to check that any need for emotional and informational care is still being met, and not assume that this aspect of the case is history. Thus, you see the answer to the question, 'What do I do at which stage?' is simply *meet the needs of your patient*. Figure 8.1 suggests the type of self-image you should hold.

- Professional guide/companion
- Stable, trusted support figure
- Personal and advisory counsellor
- Advocate

Figure 8.1:   A suitable self-image for psychological caregivers

ORGANIZING A SCHEME OF PSYCHOLOGICAL CARE

Clearly the long-term objective in the development of this approach to medicine has to be that general hospital staff as a whole become more psychologically minded, and that psychological care becomes a regular part of standard practice. By implication, there will be coordinated schemes of psychological care operated at the ward, unit or departmental level. Consider, as an example, an orthopaedic ward which deals with long-stay injury and surgical cases, together with a flow of less serious, shorter-stay surgical patients. How will the psychological care be organized?

It seems to me that the precise way in which such schemes are run is really the business of those in positions of medical and nursing authority. The allocation of psychological care duties and time for psychological work, the maintenance of standards, the provision of training and support, must all be worked out to suit the situation, which will, of course, vary greatly from place to place. *The most fundamental requirement, though, has to be that someone in an executive position (doctor, ward sister, etc.) does regularly ask, concerning each person on the ward, 'Who is handling this person's psychological care and how is it going?' When such a question is heard regularly we will have entered a new era in the development of general hospital care.*

My own thoughts on how to approach some of the organizational problems are on the following lines. Initially, the sister in charge must deal with the prevailing problem of training and maintaining professional standards. She needs to use local resources to secure a standard training facility which is suitable for new nurses, and other staff who may wish to slot into the scheme. Working with the local psychologist and senior nurses in charge of training, she will negotiate the development of a training package, which will automatically be available at various times throughout the year. This will include appropriate reading, video teaching tapes on counselling skills etc., lectures or tutorials and some experiential training sessions. It may sound a lot, but a course of only several days' length along the lines of those already organized with some frequency on, say, care of the dying, ward management etc., would give a reasonable introductory training. Really, the resources are available already – all that is required is sufficient pressure to set it all in motion. Obviously, if the ward sister in our example combined with several others to say that they all needed a regular training facility of this type for their staff (twice a year, perhaps), then it would make a more powerful demand and be more sensible in terms of cost efficiency. Additionally, the sister in charge needs to create a regular case review session, once a month perhaps, where nurses and staff involved in psychological care report back, discuss and offer mutual tuition to one another. This is very important as a device to maintain psychological-mindedness, provide necessary support and keep an ongoing atmosphere of development and training alive.

The organization of training needs to be made into a permanent structure unless staffing is very stable, with few additions throughout the year. Suitable and interested new members of staff may thus be given an initial training experience and then provided with regular supervision and teaching. It would seem appropriate that the nurses who have extended their roles in this way should be referred to as *nurse-counsellors*. In a similar manner, the head of a therapist department, say speech therapy, would need to make such provision for her staff too. She might well consider joining in with training events for nurses.

A word on 'suitability' at this point. It is a large topic and my plan is to sidestep it. We must, however, at least recognize that by no means all nurses or members of the therapist professions are suitable for psychological care work. You may recall the section in Chapter 5 which gave the profile of a person suited to emotional care work. Similarly, in general terms, one is also looking for a good intelligence, sufficient to allow a genuine grasp of the principles of psychological care, and an ability to think through the issues which assail individual patients. Certain other important resources clearly include a good level of sensitivity to feeling (without oversensitivity and thus a vulnerability to becoming upset oneself), the capacity to function independently and cope with the responsibility of individual case work, general stability and an interpersonal manner which fosters good relationships (in other words, not excessively timid, insecure, trivial, cold, authoritarian, assertive etc.). How this is assessed in a reliable way is something I must leave for local discussion and experience. It is, however, important. A sister or head of department must be selective and exercise judgement on suitability.

Incidentally, I cannot help noticing that there is an assumption in the last two or three paragraphs that these basic psychological skills are not, and will not, be taught effectively in the schools of nursing, occupational therapy and physiotherapy etc. My thoughts are based on the present-day situation, and I have to say that very few people qualifying in these professions whom I have met in recent years identify themselves as adequately trained in psychological skills, although many are acquainted with basic theory. As to the future, I sincerely hope that the training schools will teach courses designed around the idea that basic nursing and therapist roles include psychological care work, and will thus make a component of their courses over to the necessary preparation.

With the preparatory aspects provided for, the sister in charge must now organize the provision of psychological care and integrate it with other ward duties. At her disposal will be a 'pool' of nurse-counsellors and, hopefully, one or two other professional staff (social workers, physiotherapists, occupational therapists) who will have declared themselves interested in participating in the scheme – obviously a little

tment drive, with the offer of training where necessary, will be a
here. Thus, as each new admission joins the ward, one of the
pool members will be asked to deal with the psychological care of that
person. Many cases will prove to be brief, light duties, involving little
more than systematic informational care, attention to psychological
state and the provision of a supportive contact whom the patient realizes can be called upon for more extensive help if necessary. Other
cases, the type that have served as illustrations throughout this book,
where disfigurement, loss and threats to security in life arise, will
prove to be longer, heavier commitments. The sister will thus have to
coordinate the allocation of psychological care duties in the same
fashion as she arranges the other routines of nursing. The monthly
case discussions meeting will serve as an evaluation and support
group, and it can also consider issues to do with referral – whether to
refer, and to whom. Thenceforth, a visitor to the ward *will* be able to
ask, 'Who is handling the psychological care of the latest admission
and how is it going?' The sister or doctor will be able to reply, naming
a member of staff, with an indication of any ongoing psychological
work.

PARTICIPATION BY THE MEDICAL PROFESSION

So far, I have omitted a vital aspect. Such a scheme will run at its
optimum only if it is understood, valued and supported by the medical
team. Although not being excluded from offering psychological care
themselves, I have argued earlier that they should be exempt from the
face-to-face care work if this is their preference, since the necessary
protective psychological defences for those in the role of hospital doctor are incompatible with the type of psychological functioning
required for effective work in psychological care. This in no way pre-
cludes the medical staff from complementing the scheme of care by
assisting in its organization – ideally *insisting* on its organization – and
guaranteeing that the information flow to the nurse-counsellors and
others is up to date and sufficiently full; information should be a
shared property.

The symptom of non-cooperating or incomprehending medics is that
the nurse-counsellor is forced to keep asking them for relevant information and is made to feel something of a nuisance for her trouble.
The sign of genuine back-up by medical staff is that *they* take the initiative and make sure the nurse-counsellors have appropriate information, so that informational care may be conducted properly. A flight
of fancy? Well, I was allowed a few last pages of fantasizing about the
ideal setting. If you are sceptically curious to discover how we will ever
move the majority of the medical profession into this position, I have

to say it makes my head ache thinking about it too. It is a strange conflict. One wants to be considerate and supportive to medical colleagues: many have a difficult and stressing job. At the same time, if they are traditionally minded they really can destroy attempts to introduce psychological care. This has to be opposed. I am optimistic for the long term, though. With a great deal of patient, hard work there will be slow improvement. Thus, it is important to be assertive and have resolve, remembering that your function is to strive for your patients, not to protect other professions.

DEVELOPING PSYCHOLOGICAL CARE IN UNFAVOURABLE CIRCUMSTANCES

The central argument of this book will not find universal sympathy by any means. However, without doubt some readers will want to add their contribution to the development of psychological care in general hospitals, and will also want to expand their own knowledge and skills in the area.

Regrettably, not all those with a positive motivation will experience their particular work setting as encouraging. In fact, the less fortunate will discover that the whole atmosphere is one which discourages psychological care, where those in leadership appear neither to understand nor to value the approach. How, in the face of such a discouraging environment, might one still make a contribution? A helpful outlook is to view the development of psychological care as at least a two-stage event. Stage one is to do with attracting sufficient support and interest such that attempts at stage two, the actual implementation of the roles, will be viable. I do not mean to imply that you should hold back from attending to the psychological needs of your patients as best you can. If it is obvious, though, that if you are attempting this in a permanently unfavourable atmosphere without the understanding and positive support of the medical staff and senior colleagues, then your work will be badly undermined and you will become despondent and resentful. Thus, for a while, you must divide your energies. Part of you must become a 'campaigner'. So, in very general terms, your contribution begins by accepting the responsibility to do something about the present situation yourself, no matter what position you have reached in your training and career. Perhaps the most important first action is to think, read and talk about psychological care, then to begin a personal campaign to 'sell' the idea to those of your colleagues who are unaware or unconvinced. To be realistic, you must be braced for brusque rejections from some colleagues. These are usually generated by feelings of threat brought about by a lack of understanding and knowledge, and your response, probably over a period of months, should be a patient, reassuring, educating flow of discussion and information. This is the foundation stone which you must work at even if it happens that you are in a junior position. (A *staff* nurse should educate a sister or consultant? Well, who else is there to do it? This is what I mean by accepting the responsibility and taking initiatives.) On the bright side, you will also meet with much agreement and support from other colleagues. Frankly, I find that by no means all nurses or therapists accept the approach or wish to be personally involved. However, it is very definitely the majority who *are* interested. The balance is bound to vary according to the specialty involved.

Let us return for a moment to the suggestion that you may be faced with a setting which is a 'psychological desert'. It will be hard to go it alone, without support, recognition or encouragement. One thing which should prove helpful, therefore, will be to track down like-minded colleagues from other wards and departments, and develop an informal special-interest group. The advantage of this, apart from the obvious supportive gain, is that it will be easier to obtain some teaching and supervision from the local psychologist or allied professions. Incidentally, never be shy in seeking training and help directly. Lift the telephone and get on with it. Most psychologists will welcome your approach, as will social workers.

Objections

I have mentioned before that I often find myself teaching psychological care to groups of nurses or trainees. Naturally, in such a setting, I come face to face with 'reality' and have to absorb the objections and criticisms of the audience. In similar style, therefore, it seems appropriate that we should give an airing to some 'popular' objections and examine the responses which can be made to these. Let's imagine we are in a seminar together. It is discussion time. Here are some of the comments and questions which are likely:

'Nurses are too busy, we just do not have the time'
Until a trained team of work-study observers conduct objective studies, we will not have a factually based answer to this. The next best alternative is to inquire of a large sample of nurses how *they* view the situation. This I do with some frequency. For our purposes, it is relevant to relay to you the opinions of several senior nurses whom I have recently engaged in conversation around this point. All have replied strongly in the following manner: 'Too busy doing what, though? A good deal of this busyness is centred on tasks of low importance. There is still a covert task-orientation to nursing, with unnecessary repetitions and rituals – it's a kind of defence'. This will sound familiar from Chapter 2, where there was a description of the defensive strategies which have

evolved in nursing as a means of minimizing interpersonal contact. The overinvolvement with tasks, the task-oriented approach, was noted as a mainstay defence. Thus, a strong possibility arises that some of the duties which still appear to weigh some nurses down and leave no time for psychological care may, at best, be low-priority, labour-intensive rituals which are related more to the preservation of routines than dealing with the actual needs of the patients.

Please understand that these comments do not come from me but are a composite of comments from various senior nurses, which I simply pass on to you.

I also want to point out that some of the important changes needed in the development of psychological care are not likely to demand much time. I refer to changes in thinking and attitude towards a psychologically minded style of nursing. Change of attitude itself takes no time out of regular duties at all, yet it can have a positive influence on the care given. Also, note that no matter what turnover and work-load exist on a genuinely busy ward, *time will already be given* to some information exchange and supportive contact – it is inevitable. As the minimum development, this time may be used in the rather more systematic and professional activities of informational care and moni-toring psychological state, together with some input in terms of emotional care. Thus, you see, psychological care may be introduced at various levels of intensity according to the time available. There will *always* be some time available, and therefore objections to its intro-duction based on the plea of insufficient time are unsound.

'With the economies and cutbacks, we do not have the staff to cope with psycho-logical care'
The same points apply to this objection as to that concerning the avail-ability of time. However, an important additional issue must be emphasized. The shift to caring medicine and the implementation of psychological care will be a slow process of change, taking place over many years. Even in the 'lean times', the work of laying the foun-dations can and should proceed, albeit at a slower pace. Since all things have seasons, the current era of cutbacks will inevitably be fol-lowed by a stable period and even selective re-expansion. It will be highly advantageous, therefore, to have established psychological-mindedness in the hospitals and to have plans for the full implementa-tion of psychological care, even though present conditions may allow only relatively reduced schemes to be introduced initially. The great need is to make the start. Remember, too, that effective psychological care is an investment – it saves money and medical/nursing staff utilization.

'If the doctors are against it, we can't just go ahead, it would be treading on

their toes. If a consultant says he does not want someone informed, you have to abide by what he says'

This is not going to be an easy debate for any of us, but the contentious issues must be faced. Issues of both principle and fact are involved. The following are my views on the situation described. Let's deal with the facts first. A medical consultant has indisputable *clinical* responsibility. He is given authority to organize and conduct the medical treatment necessary to restore or maintain physical health and, by implication, must control those aspects of hospital activity which bear a direct relationship to these treatments. *His contract of employment will not, however, instruct him to maintain moral, social, political or psychological authority over his patients.*

Now, as a power-conserving monopoly, the medical profession often gratuitously mandates itself with responsibilities in these areas and assumes decision-making authority. In strict terms, however, if the issues involved are not of a clinical nature, then the 'ice on which the profession stands is too thin'. For example, a man is being treated for cancer of the pancreas. His consultant surgeon will rightly assume responsibility for all aspects of the case management which affect the conduct of treatment and the general health of that person. If issues arise which go beyond that brief, then the consultant is exceeding the range of his *exclusive* authority. His view will be important, but the view of say, a senior nurse will have equal weight. Extending the example, what happens if the consultant opposes psychological care and plans to withhold information from the patient against the nurse's judgement? *If* he can demonstrate that there are *clinical* reasons for so doing (i.e. it adversely affects the cancer or general physical health), then he is operating within his contract. If, however, the basis on which the decision is generated is anything other than medical, i.e. psychological (for which few surgeons have had any training), social, moral or even personal caprice, then that decision cannot carry real authority. He is operating beyond his contract and has no grounds on which he may *impose* such a decision. He may, however, want to make a case for *persuasive* purposes, in which case, the only way to resolve the issue would be by consensus involving the whole team.

Many such decisions seem to me to be areas of great ambiguity, and are as much the province of nursing authority as medical authority. My motive for arguing this is not to encourage a fight, but to find ways of improving psychological care in hospitals, one way or another. If the key concern is to do with the wellbeing of the patient there will, I suspect, be few instances in which psychological care (including the informational care components) will prove injurious to the clinical conduct of a case. Opposition to it could not, therefore, be justified on medical grounds and so the decision to introduce psychological care stops being the exclusive province of the medical profession.

respect. Accordingly, the emphasis should be on a gentle, educational approach.

'To be honest, I just feel too emotionally tired. I don't think I could get involved in people's problems like this. I just want to do my basic nursing job and go home'
Honesty of this type is welcome. In the same way that people should not be forced to receive some of the elements of psychological care, neither should individual members of staff be forced to provide it. The result would be poor-quality work. A person who feels unable to participate in a scheme of psychological care because they are ill-suited is being responsible in withdrawing. The only proviso I will make is that they should still recognize the need for psychological care in hospitals and support its implementation. Their personal position does not in any way justify obstructing the provision of psychological care by those who wish to provide it.

'Some people only stay for a night on my ward. You can't do much in that time, it's not worth it'
This is so wrong. The general approach and atmosphere of doing things matters greatly in a hospital, even when intensive psychological work is not feasible. Psychological care should even pervade an out-patient clinic. In overall terms, the introduction of formal schemes of psychological care is part of a wider shift from solely technical to more caring medicine. Never lose sight of this objective. A 24-hour stay on a traditionally run ward carries the risk of some disturbing, possibly damaging, psychological experiences, whereas that same event in a ward which at least thinks in terms of psychological care has a built-in safeguard insulating people from these risks. Added to this, if the task of monitoring psychological state is conducted properly and there exist facilities for referring on, then arrangements can be made for the occasional patient on the ward who needs more extensive and longer-term care.

'We would like to do this kind of work but we have never been trained to do it'
Then take the initiative and arrange some training for yourself. Explore local opportunities for teaching and training – it's easy enough to do. Ask your senior nurse in charge of training (or head of department) to make approaches to the people you discover who could help out. Ask her to make inquiries then set something up. Note: *You* take the initiative.

'Don't you think that this will make some people worse – it encourages them to become dependent and start thinking about their problems, which stirs things up'
First, I am suggesting that what already exists in an 'amateur' way is

intensified and made professional. Surely there can be no objections to that. Secondly, dependency is not a sin, it is an emotional state. If you offer support to people in trouble they will lean on you, particularly if there is trust and you are strong. As you help patients with their reactions and difficulties you can, where necessary, include the issue of dependency as something to be dealt with, aiding them in the development of coping skills. Dependency is a natural *phase* in most instances, not a permanent feature (except in the case of highly dependent personalities who would demand much of you anyway).

As for stirring up problems, the whole spirit of this work is that of an invitation for a patient to share reactions and difficulties if he or she so wishes – the issues are at a level of conscious awareness already. Put it like this: if you were to be admitted to hospital after a serious road accident and faced permanent physical handicap as a result, if your mother were to be admitted to hospital for surgery to deal with cancer of the tongue and larynx, or if your husband had to attend a neurological unit with suspected multiple sclerosis, would you worry for yourself and your relatives in these situations *because* there were people on hand to give professional care for the inevitable emotional needs? Would you worry because the staff planned to help with any personal and psychological difficulties arising; planned to maintain a flow of trustworthy informationand also expected to give support by representing any psychological needs to the rest of the team? I doubt it. Perhaps, though, you might worry a little if this type of care was known to be missing.

IS IT REALLY WORTH THE EFFORT? RESEARCH FINDINGS

Caring medicine, with psychological care as one of its main thrusts, will need much development effort. Are we to forge ahead with this effort in blind faith, or are there encouragements from existing research which allow us to know in advance that it will be worthwhile? Fortunately, faith is not needed. There already exists a body of knowledge from independent studies which gives a good basis for optimism. I should say that it is not my intention to compile an extended review of research findings, since this book is practical in emphasis rather than academic. However, I do want you to feel assured that there is a good basis of supporting evidence and will indicate to you one or two rich sources of such evidence should you need more detail.

Evidence supporting the value of informational and educational care

For simplicity I will confine myself to one important publication dealing with this issue, although, since it is a review study, it draws on scores of research papers. The review, by Ley (1989), has already been mentioned in Chapter 4. It provides most useful findings and I recommend that you read it in full. It discusses various research studies which were concerned with the benefits of improved communication in medicine, including several based on meta-analysis. Meta-analysis is a technique for condensing the findings of many different studies together in order to assess the general trend of results. Overall trends are often expressed as 'effect size'. This is a numerical index of how powerful a procedure has turned out to be in a sample of research studies. Ley writes:

> 'The techniques of meta-analysis have also been applied to the assessment of the effectiveness of improved communication in increasing patients' knowledge and understanding. Mullen, Green and Persinger (1985) analysed a variety of methods likely to improve the communication of information. These included the provision of additional face-to-face consultation, group education, written information, and combinations of some of these. The mean effect size was +0.53. This can be interpreted as showing that the average patient who received these additional educational inputs had better knowledge and understanding than 70% of those who had not received this extra input. Thus, the provision of information increases knowledge and understanding. Also, understanding and recall can be further enhanced by the use of special techniques and by the provision of suitably prepared written materials.'

In similar manner, Ley argues that existing studies demonstrate a positive effect of informational care on:

- Compliance. A meta-analysis of studies of instructional and educational methods by Mullen *et al.* (1985, cited in Ley, 1989) showed an effect size of +0.37. In other words, if people receive this type of informational care they will be likely to comply with their treatment requirements better than 64% of those not receiving it.
- Speed and quality of physical recovery and reduced levels of distress during invasive procedures. Another meta-analysis by Mazucca (1982, cited by Ley, 1989) returned an effect size for psychoeducational techniques of +0.18. That is, people receiving this care will be likely to have better progress and outcome than 57% of those not so treated.
- Recovery from heart attack and surgery. Again, a meta-analysis, this time by Mumford *et al.* (1982, cited in Ley, 1989), showed that informational care techniques gave a significant effect size of +0.3. Thus, people receiving informational care after a heart attack or

after surgery will progress better than 61% of those not receiving this care.

- Length of hospital stay. Devine and Cook (1982, cited in Ley, 1989) also showed that informational care did have an effect of reducing the length of stay in hospital by an average of 1.21 days (although Ley comments that more recent studies return a slightly lower reduction of time, possibly because some information is almost always given now, so true control groups no longer exist).

Thus Ley concludes that improved informational care (he uses the phrase enhanced communication, but it refers to the same thing) 'leads to better understanding and recall, greater satisfaction, better informed consent, greater compliance, and better recovery from illness'.

Evidence supporting the value of emotional care and counselling

Few researchers use the term emotional care. However, many have investigated regimens which include what is effectively emotional care referred to by a different term. Support is one such term. An interesting and powerful study concerning support was presented by Speigel *et al.* (1989). Thirty-six women with breast cancer took part in group support sessions once a week for a year. The group sessions encouraged the expression and sharing of feelings (emotional care), discussions on coping (basic counselling) and a technique of self-hypnosis. Women in a control group receiving none of these had an average survival time of 18.9 months, whereas women in the support group had an average survival time of 36.6 months.

Again, there is an important review article which I will recommend to you. Davis and Fallowfield (1991) have encompassed a great number of research studies. They find sufficiently numerous and reliable studies to conclude that counselling in medicine offers the following positive benefits:

- Health care professionals with counselling training derive greater job satisfaction and experience less burnout.
- Diagnostic adequacy is enhanced when staff use a counselling style of communication in the diagnostic sessions.
- Patient satisfaction is greater when staff use a counselling style of interaction.
- Brief advisory counselling (informational care delivered in a counselling style, as it always should be) improves compliance with treatment requirements.
- Counselling intervention is effective as an aid in preventing heart disease, in reducing distress in the acute phase following myocardial infarction, and also in rehabilitation.

- Counselling intervention is of value in reducing emotional disturbance during the early stages of cancer after diagnosis. It gives positive psychological benefit during treatments such as radiotherapy and chemotherapy. It is an aid to overall adaptation and coping, and can be of benefit in strengthening the will to live, which is known to link with survival rates.

In short, plentiful evidence exists to justify the introduction of properly formulated schemes of psychological care into medicine and nursing. Without such schemes I believe it is fair to say that care can only be second-rate or, worse, open to the charge of negligence. It is for you, now, to decide on your own position. I will, however, give the very last word to a medical source:

> *'The answer is that counselling in the acute phase of disease and psychological support in the chronic may be as important to outcome as many other therapeutic measures now undertaken.'* Editorial, *The Lancet* (1985)

Epilogue: 'Alone With Illness'

Lorna A. Sealy

Author's note: in the role of a psychologist in a general hospital, one spends a great deal of time listening to detailed accounts of people's experiences. Sometimes I feel that many of my colleagues in nursing and medicine have never allowed themselves to do that – ever. It is appropriate, therefore, that we should rehearse this skill together. We will give time to receiving the experiences of a woman who nursed her husband for several years and was herself damaged, both by the nature of the event and the absence of psychological care skills on the part of the staff. We will just listen and put the effort into understanding what it was really like rather than making any comment.

I was married to a man who went into chronic renal failure. My perception of events during this time was, of course, subjective and not always easy to formulate concisely and clearly. However, I will attempt to chart out the history of my experiences without too much loss of accuracy.

We had both newly qualified as teachers and, in the last month at college, Kevin had been offered a teaching job in the south of England. We were engaged at the time and planned to marry the following summer. We moved and I found a job locally as a secretary, since there were no other teaching posts available. We had been living in the new location for a couple of months when a routine examination and blood test by the GP we registered with showed Kevin to be anaemic. On investigation, it was revealed that his kidney (he had one removed when he was five due to a urinary infection) was not functioning properly and would deteriorate until finally treatment by dialysis would be needed, probably in about twelve months. Kevin was given an appointment with a consultant nephrologist and a transplant surgeon and I, as his fiancée, was invited to attend.

We met with the two doctors and they gave us their view of the situation and offered treatment by haemodialysis, with the possibility of a transplant in the future. The other alternative, we were told, was inevitable death. We were young and he had just begun his career as a teacher. To us, the consultant nephrologist appeared to paint quite a rosy picture of the life to come, including adequate work capability, a degree of sport and a 'normal' living pattern being in reach. We were advised by him not to have a family too early in marriage in order that we could fully establish our routine of home dialysis first. If Kevin had a successful transplant he could expect normal health but would have to take steroids for the rest of his life. These could affect his fertility and present problems for conception. We left that interview with a feeling of gratitude towards the doctors and confidence for the future.

Did we only hear the things we wanted to and disregard the remainder? To a degree we probably did. However, the doctors may have found it a hard task to put a more realistic picture to two people who so obviously wanted to be reassured. Kevin's decision to accept treatment would not have been any different had he been given a more modest picture. I wish we had at least been given fuller information, and that someone had made sure we understood some of the risks and problems involved. I have no memory at all of being given advance information on the negative aspects of life with dialysis, for example the constant minor physical irritations, continual tiredness and the extent to which our social life would become totally disrupted.

The six months or so that followed were filled with the mechanics of training for dialysis and becoming self-sufficient other than dealing with accident or emergency. We attended the unit three evenings a week. Our training was adequate, although at times we found ourselves rebuked by one nurse for adopting procedures taught to us by another nurse in the preceding session. The business of informing us was haphazard – there was no record of what we had been taught and what remained for us to learn. Neither was there a system for assessing our absorption of information and, more importantly, our basic understanding of life on dialysis. We felt drawn to one or two nurses who obviously sensed our needs as 'people' in the situation. It would have been ideal if they could have been personal tutors, but as things stood this was not possible and we never knew from one session to the next which one of a dozen or so nurses we would be working with on any particular day.

With the positive remarks of the doctors still fresh in our minds, we went ahead with our marriage and the purchase of a house. In retrospect I find it staggering that we received positive encouragement to marry, rather than being advised against it in the strongest terms. Anyone with a clear understanding of what life is truly like for a haemodialysis family could never, in honesty, offer encouragement if they had the welfare of *both* people in mind. I suspect that part of the motive was to secure a stable dialysis partner for Kevin, which I became, although at high personal cost.

Dialysis equipment was installed at home and we were keen to distance ourselves from the renal unit in order to gain a degree of independence and flexibility, which it was not possible to achieve in the hospital environment. We made the transition accompanied by visits from a home sister for the first two dialysis sessions, after which we were pronounced 'capable'. For a few months all seemed well, then Kevin became ill. It happened suddenly. He developed pulmonary oedema, pericarditis and pericardial effusion. He was in hospital for the next few weeks. We had been aware that there was something wrong and had been to the GP as well as the unit. It was revealed that Kevin had become fluid overloaded (that is, he had consistently taken in more fluid than was being removed) and from then on our common experience was that we were made to feel at fault by the unit staff. Yet we felt we had never been told about the importance of the link between weight control and fluid intake. No doubt we had, but with so much information to absorb during training, much of it had been lost by this time. Thus, as Kevin had slowly put on weight over that first summer we had been pleased, believing it was the muscle weight returning which he had lost as a result of the kidney disease. In our ignorance, the link between fluid and weight had not occurred to us and no-one had checked up on what we were doing or thinking once we were at home. Kevin slowly recovered from this but my memory is that at least two years elapsed before his heart, which was badly stretched by the fluid overloading, returned to its prestressed size. Our resentment, however, never did recede. We had been striving hard but did not have the knowledge we needed, and it felt very unjust to be accused in this way.

The doctors in charge of the unit always emphasized most strongly their feeling that there was no good reason for a person on dialysis to stop work. Kevin would be seen as having failed not only himself but also the 'team' at the unit if he did so. Hence he continued to work, although it became more and more of a struggle against the exhaustion caused by uraemia, and he took increasing time off work sick. The job took every ounce of energy which he had and thus the total responsibility for the 'administration' of our lives passed to me. I can see now the damaging effect that this expectation towards normal working had on us. We were dialysing back at home again and knew few other patients to 'compare notes' with. We were effectively cut off from people who really understood what a life on dialysis meant. All I knew was that I was having to do so much whilst Kevin did proportionately less and had more time off work – a very different experience to that which he had been led to hope for. Kevin felt undermined as a man and saw himself as a tremendous burden to me. He loved teaching but knew he wasn't doing as good a job as he could (his employers, both inside the school and the local education authority were wonderfully patient and supportive – there was never pressure exerted on him by them) and he would have resigned much sooner than he in fact did, except that the idea of 'letting everyone down' filled him with guilt. I can also admit now to having unspoken feelings of resentment because I wanted to accuse him of not doing the things the doctors said he should be able to do. But I felt guilty at my resentment because I knew my husband was profoundly ill and literally disabled, something our doctors seemed to find difficult to accept.

The next couple of years passed by fairly uneventfully but the routine was unremitting. It felt as though we were becoming more and more deeply entrenched in a day-by-day existence centred on dialysis, and that control of our lives was steadily passing from us. In retrospect, this is exactly what was happening, mainly because of our lack of recognition of this change and my lack of determination to alter it. I think it was through a feeling of guilt that I allowed Kevin to adopt more of an invalid's role and myself more of a mother/nurse/housekeeper role – I found it difficult to assert equality in our relationship when there was the unspoken (and occasionally spoken) accusation of 'How can you be so hard – you don't know what it's like feeling ill all the time. You're lucky you're healthy.'

We still hoped for a transplant and during this time there were two 'false alarms', where we were telephoned and told that a kidney was available for transplantation and to ready ourselves for the operation. On the first occasion we were asked to go into the unit so that Kevin could dialyse before the operation – the kidney was still in Liverpool. By the time we arrived at the unit they had been notified that the transplant was not proceeding because of damage to the organ. On the second occasion we had come much closer. Kevin had actually finished a five-hour dialysis session when a telephone call from a Birmingham hospital came through with the news that the kidney had again been damaged in transit. That was a terrific disappointment.

Life continued. I found our financial struggling harder to cope with as the months went by. We never had any money to spare and we couldn't see how we would be able to manage if Kevin stopped teaching. We had even contemplated both giving up work just in order to reduce the stresses and permanent rushing about (for me) and throwing ourselves on the State, possibly giving up home ownership for council accommodation. We had seen the then social worker and had talked to her about various options, but she never really seemed to pick up the urgency behind our meetings. Maybe we tried to appear too bright about everything and would have been better off if we had just collapsed and relied on outside agencies to sort us out. But we didn't.

I did belong to a sports club and tried to go to it twice a week, although this was not always possible. It was the one thing that gave me social contact outside home, other than work, and was very important to me. However, some kind of holiday where I actually had a break from the routine for a couple of weeks would have been such a relief. In four years this was never to become available. First, we could not have afforded it, and secondly Kevin would always bring pressure to bear by becoming very agitated and upset at the thought of dialysing at the unit for a period of time. He disliked unit dialysis, possibly because he had much more sympathy at home and was made to do a lot less for himself than at the unit. However, whatever the reason, I was made to feel that I was 'deserting' him and putting him in an intolerable position. No-one at any time elaborated to us the benefits of a partner being able to have a break from the stressful routines, and it was only later that such suggestions were made.

Eventually another opportunity to have a kidney transplant occurred and this time the operation was carried out. Prior to surgery, Kevin dialysed at the unit. I remember very little about the time spent waiting except that Kevin slept for quite a lot of it. I don't recall much communication with doctors and nurses, although I do remember them talking to us with general encouragement. As far as transplants were concerned, we did know that 'things could go wrong', rejection could set in (hopefully being suppressed by huge doses of steroids), the kidney might not start functioning, it might work for a while and then suddenly for no apparent reason stop completely, necessitating dialysis again until the next transplant. We also knew that dialysis might be required until the kidney did work at a satisfactory level. I cannot think of any other bits of information we were given, although with all the time spent at the unit over the years I daresay we had talked about transplant surgery with patients and nurses, but only on a general level.

Other than telling Kevin that he would be taken to the intensive care unit after the operation, we were unprepared for how he might feel during the next couple of days. In fact, we knew very little indeed about the actual events following a transplant attempt. The anaesthetic used was curare-based and, shortly after coming round from it, Kevin was aware that he could hardly move at all. He could barely move his fingers and moving an arm or leg was impossible. He had not known this might happen and was not able, so soon after surgery, to understand that this was a temporary thing which would pass within a day or so. It caused him a great deal of distress and fright, which I feel could so easily have been avoided. The staff in ITU were very caring but seemed to have little in-depth understanding of the treatment of dialysis patients and transplantees. This in itself was understandable since, if patients in ITU required dialysis, a nurse would come from the kidney unit for this purpose. However, there also seemed to be confusion between the treatment of general surgical cases and the treatment of transplantees. When the two were combined, it caused real problems.

One example presented itself somewhat traumatically after the transplant operation: Kevin developed low blood pressure as a result of which his fistula (that is, his access to venepuncture in haemodialysis treatment) collapsed. The new kidney was not working yet and he needed dialysis. A temporary external access (a shunt) had to be inserted into a vein in his leg under a local anaesthetic. Within a day or so of this happening, the staff of ITU were making Kevin get out of bed and move around the room despite our anxious protests that we didn't think he should put any weight on his leg. The response was that after an operation (any operation?) the best thing was to use the body rather than lie prone. They did not check this out with anyone experienced in renal medicine and assumed that normal post-surgical procedures would apply. As a result of the transplanted kidney not working, Kevin's legs had become oedemic and being made to use his leg in this condition caused the openings for the shunt to enlarge considerably. Once he was well dialysed (since the kidney never worked well) and the oedema was reduced, he started bleeding profusely from his leg wounds whenever his leg dropped much below horizontal. I clearly remember being told by the staff at the kidney unit that what else could you expect from ITU – they didn't know about it. *Why didn't someone take the trouble to tell them?*

Another very unpleasant incident in ITU concerned catheters. Kevin had to have a catheter inserted into his bladder during the transplant operation for the purpose of preventing raised urine pressure in the bladder if the new organ started functioning quickly and well. After 48 hours or so (I think this was the approximate time period) this was removed. Kevin was being given a steady intake of fluid at the time to try, I believe, to stimulate the kidney into action. While the catheter was in place he had not been passing much urine. After its removal, the nurse who was looking after him kept asking him to try to pass urine but he was unable to do so. About four hours later a doctor came in, looked at his records and announced that if Kevin did not pass urine within an hour, she would have the catheter replaced. Kevin was very distressed at this and said how uncomfortable it had been and that when it was removed there had been blood on it and it had not come out easily. I was present the whole time and was upset at the high-handed and dismissive manner of this doctor, who virtually ignored his fright other than telling him he would have to have it put back and not to be stupid, things like that didn't hurt. I don't believe that I could be a silent witness to such an incident ever again. What I would say might make no difference but at least I would take the opportunity to express my disgust at such treatment. The deadline arrived and Kevin had still been unable to pass urine. He was in a poor frame of mind when the doctor returned. For some reason I was not asked to leave the room. A local anaesthetic (lignocaine jelly, I believe) was put onto the end of his penis and a few minutes later the doctor starting inserting the catheter. I'd seen Kevin crying from emotional distress in the past, for example when he was told that he would need dialysis and the implications and uncertainties were frightening him, but I'd never seen him cry out of pain. It was, looking back, appalling that so much fright and distress could be added to the problems of anyone in Kevin's position, especially when it was handed out by a person who would undoubtedly profess to be caring. It would have been caring to at least acknowledge the distress and take time to discuss the situation with Kevin. In contrast, the doctor attempted to ignore it, brushing it aside as a nuisance. In the end, she said the gauge of the first catheter inserted under the general anaesthetic (and also this one) must have been too big, hence the pain and bleeding, and she used a smaller one, which she fitted relatively easily.

It was a relief to get back to the kidney unit and see familiar faces. Kevin was put in a room for barrier nursing. The procedure then for entering the room was initially gowning up, masking and wearing sterile gloves. During this period, some of the staff would come into the room, in particular auxiliaries, 'just for a minute' without following the procedures. This used to cause Kevin some anxiety, especially since the kidney was not doing well and he did not want to hazard himself by possible exposure to infection. I remember one night nurse in particular who used to come into the room without masking up, despite being full of a cold and sneezing. When we complained we were told we were making a fuss. However, in the initial couple of weeks back at the unit, despite dialysis being required, we did feel very supported by the staff. They were all eager for transplants to be successful for the patients they spent so much time with, and were always delighted when people could leave dialysis behind, even as a temporary thing.

There was, though, disagreement between the doctors in charge, which came across to the nursing staff and the patients. I couldn't begin to guess at the reasons, but it appeared that personalities clashed and a new appointment had disturbed some of them. Mutual dislike was apparent and this was a very unsettling time for all concerned. We personally found we were being told one thing by one doctor which was then contradicted by another. This was confusing and upsetting. It eroded our confidence and affected the nurses, who were also receiving conflicting orders, which created tension and difficulties for them.

Kevin's new kidney struggled on for a short while but what little function it had seemed to fade, rejection being the primary problem. Eventually, after about six weeks, a biopsy was arranged and as a result Kevin had a 'blast' of steroids to try and halt rejection. Sadly this did not work and the transplant attempt was recognized as having failed. At this point we felt a subtle shift in the way the nursing staff related to us. The supportive, sympathetic attitudes became much less evident and there seemed, in the background, an air of unspoken accusation. This we found bewildering – surely *we* weren't to blame for the kidney not working? I imagine few, if any, of the staff would accept this as having happened, and probably we were in an extremely emotional, sensitive state and were looking for something or someone to take our anger and disappointment out on.

We did, however, feel as if it was 'the two of us versus the rest of the kidney unit' at that time. Kevin had a brother living nearby who spent a good deal of time with the two of us. He was the only person who made himself available to us and understood our feelings sufficiently to let us take out behaviour on him which would, outside these circumstances, have been unacceptable. He was a silent listener, someone who provided us with an outlet, and in that role he was of tremendous value to us. I don't think I ever once acknowledged this to him afterwards, probably because it felt difficult to talk about behaviour that was the result of such emotional distress, but he was very much appreciated. It seems to me, though, that such distress is an obvious and normal feature of such surgery, where the outcome could mean a change of lifestyle from one very impaired and restricted to one of comparable freedom. It might have helped if the staff at the unit had been more able to understand our needs and help guide us through the period of a failed transplant, or refer us to other help. Instead, they appeared to need to work through their own disappointment and could give little help. The decision was made to remove the failed kidney rather than leave it, because there was the possibility of some infection. Surgery was carried out eleven weeks after the transplant under local anaesthetic (epidural), and Kevin was allowed home shortly afterwards.

That whole episode seemed to take something vital away from Kevin. I think now that it was hope. His manner became much more introspective and his behaviour changed. The convalescence was slow and he saw himself as an invalid, leaning heavily on me and totally unable to do much for himself. I think I was aware of the danger in letting this become too entrenched, but again I could not cope with the accusation of being hard, uncaring and unloving. So I capitulated, thereby worsening the situation.

It was obvious that Kevin had no wish to get back to work, mainly, I think, because he saw it as unattainable. He would become easily upset if people talked about it, even though he was under no pressure. Eventually I suggested he resign and he leapt at the opportunity. It lifted a tremendous worry from him and he became much happier (at least for a while) with the sense of relief. The summer passed slowly, with little happening in our lives bar (for me) work and dialysis. With the convalescence after the transplant, my one outlet at the sports club became difficult to sustain. Kevin would complain about being on his own all day and then, on the evenings I went out, being left at night too. I stopped going. He never made much effort to get out and sustain a social life, or just go out with me, and I became more isolated. Yielding to the pressure to leave the club was a bad mistake on my part. Perhaps it would have been different if we had had much family locally, but we didn't. Being new to the area we had few friends either and Kevin resisted meeting others. He was becoming more and more difficult socially.

The mechanics of dialysis passed by uneventfully into the autumn and there was not much contact with the kidney unit, except when Kevin had problems with sleep and 'itching skin and pins and needles' – common symptoms with dialysis patients. He would contact the unit for alternative drugs, since those he was given seemed to be of little help to him. His pattern of life seemed to be changing and he would spend an increasing amount of time downstairs at night, distressed because he couldn't sleep. He found that difficult to accept and would fight it, being unable to view the time constructively and do anything positive with it. Instead it was seen as a nightmare. He would take larger and larger doses of drugs to try and induce sleep. When I left the house to go to work he would finally get to sleep and would often still be in bed when I returned home. His difficulties seemed to be compounded as he became more and more lax about his fluid allowance, often drinking way beyond what he should. His resolve to stay in control collapsed. I was quite unaware at first of the way he was treating himself, especially over the quantity of drugs he was taking. It came as quite a shock when I realized this. He was often still asleep when I got home, but in a very dopey state when he was wakened. At first, I thought it was because he was still tired but he was probably becoming toxic with the quantity of drugs he was taking. He would think nothing of taking half a dozen sleeping pills, a handful of tranquillizers, antihistamines and sometimes quite a lot more in one night. His behaviour was becoming aggressively dependent and harder to live with. I was increasingly feeling that I was fighting an uphill battle for the two of us and, instead of a sense of reward, there was only a sense of being trapped and feeling cheated. I felt a growing tension – we seemed so terribly alone with it all. Nobody knew of our daily experiences and the struggle it had become. The people at the kidney unit no doubt worked on the belief that we were doing well.

One night during a dialysis session he was very difficult. Suddenly the years of strain and fatigue seemed overwhelming and I broke down. My memory of the events that followed in the ensuing weeks is not necessarily strictly chronicled but is close enough. That night,

Kevin realized I was very upset and that perhaps he had gone too far, and he rang his brother who came round to see us. I was still out of control and one of the sisters at the unit was telephoned. She came round to the house, quite startled, I think, because no-one had suspected we had any problems. We always seemed cheerful and able to cope. She was a great help to me at the time, taking the stance of someone outside our lives who would listen but not judge. However, the next day she reported the incident to the unit and it was referred to the unit counsellor, who contacted us and arranged an interview. I remember this as being a fairly relaxed chat at home. I had not met him before and I suppose he was trying to sound us out and get some idea of how we functioned. I do know, however, that I felt quite at ease and surprised myself at how easily I had given him 'personal' information. In fact, sadly, Kevin had become quite annoyed at my openness and his response seemed to detract from the idea of having a 'combined session' to try and sort things out.

I felt much more in control of my emotions after giving some vent to them with the counsellor. However, the following week a minor incident triggered off another similar episode. I then felt I had to have a break and just get away from Kevin, dialysis and everything connected with it, so I packed a bag and went back to my parents. The staff at the kidney unit now became extremely sympathetic and quickly slotted Kevin into their dialysis programme while I was away. No magical solutions presented themselves to me, however. I was blocking my feelings and all the trip home did was to buy me three weeks' time. When I came back Kevin avoided talking about the real reason for my absence, and the only rationalization for it was that I had become over-tired and needed a rest. Life reverted back to the old routine and, literally, nothing altered to make any improvement. In fact, things actually deteriorated. Kevin had been finding his fluid allowance more and more onerous and was badly overdrinking. As a result, he was overloading with fluid again and felt ill. His solution to the problem was to dialyse more often and he would have liked to dialyse on a daily basis. I capitulated to an extent, otherwise I was faced with someone deteriorating into grave illness. He was at this stage dialysing four, sometimes five, times a week. The strain of this (about seven hours each session) after a full day at work, together with keeping the house going, was defeating me.

We were going to visit relatives that Christmas and Kevin had promised he would control his fluids closely. His resolve held for a day or so and then crumbled. A situation I dreaded most of all ensued – dealing with someone very ill who felt dreadful and who just wanted to switch off, giving total responsibility for himself to me. Our train journey home stretched me beyond my limits. It was at this point that I accepted that I could not continue living in this fashion, becoming more embittered at what I increasingly saw as the selfishness of my husband. I couldn't make excuses for his behaviour any more. I felt like screaming at him sometimes that he think about other people instead of just himself. But by then, even if he had realized the dangers, it would have been too late to save our marriage.

I talked to the unit counsellor and from that visit it was obvious to him that our marriage was teetering badly. He offered his support to both of us as individuals, but did not attempt to prolong the unsatisfactory marital situation. My need to escape became overwhelming and I left Kevin three days later. The week that followed was one of sleepless nights and tortured feelings. We were both devastated by events.

Kevin dialysed at the kidney unit where he received a tremendous amount of care and warmth from all the staff. I also received kindness and understanding from them. They finally seemed to recognize the difficulties we were having. Some months passed and Kevin converted to continuous ambulatory peritoneal dialysis (CAPD) treatment, which gave him a degree of independence he had not had for years and released him from unit dialysis. He appeared to be going through a positive phase and was planning on travelling abroad to visit friends for an extended holiday, possibly going back to college to do a further course, and his general health and sense of wellbeing was better than it had been for a long time. Again, though, outward appearances did not represent the real Kevin and on a grey, autumn day he ended his life. It was a tragic end to a life whose last few years had been full of suffering.

All of us who had cared for him were stunned. It drew us together and, when talking with the nursing staff then, I found that for the first time the isolation and distance was broken. The great tragedy is that this genuine contact between the staff and myself came only after Kevin's death – I needed them at the beginning, and all the way through.

If I am honest I have to admit that this stance might generate a confrontational situation in certain circumstances. For some members of the medical profession it will be threatening and feel like loss of power. It will tap into the 'my patients, my ward' manner of thought and provoke defensive power-conserving reactions. Attention, however, must be directed resolutely to the unmet psychological needs of the ill and injured – tending to these must take priority.

Having said this, I want to repeat the message given earlier in the chapter. Open fights are usually unhelpful. You need to be firm, thoroughly informed and negotiate from a position of strength. Also, make an effort to be reassuring and work patiently at the task of attitude change. Harmonious professional integration is your target.

(Doctor) 'Yes, probably there is a lot in what you say but I'm not having my nurses' time tied up like this until I'm sure that everything else is done properly'

The composition of nursing duties is the business of the director of nursing and the individual ward sisters. They offer a service to support the medical service, and are duty bound to maximize the effectiveness of medical treatment. However, they are not 'your' nurses, they are members of an independent, allied profession and the decision concerning what constitutes good nursing care is a nursing matter, although of course it should be negotiable. It would be inappropriate for a member of another profession to attempt to impose restrictions of such a nature that nurses were forced to conduct what, in their eyes, would amount to bad nursing. Added to which, it is an unrealistic statement, since extending the roles of nurses and staff in this way will complement and support medical treatments, possibly enhancing their effects at times. It has never been suggested that psychological care displaces any necessary nursing duties.

'It's not just the doctors. We were trained to look after people's psychological needs at the School of Nursing. Our tutors really hammered it in. But here in the hospital, the senior nurses and nursing management just will not back us up. All they seem to worry about is basic nursing duties and manpower planning'

There does not seem much more to add to this than was written a few pages earlier. If you are keen to develop psychological care but find yourself in an unfavourable setting, you must contribute initially by becoming a campaigner. If there is sufficient upward pressure directed at nursing management by a sufficient number of people, attitudes will slowly change. Some senior sisters and nursing administrators may find the whole issue threatening, since they have no training in psychological care and fear being exposed as inadequate in this

APPENDIX 1

Client's name: Homecare sister's name:

Helper's name: Primary nurse's name:

LEARNING PROGRAMME AND OUTLINE OF THE KIDNEY UNIT FOR PEOPLE ON OR GOING ONTO HAEMODIALYSIS

SECTION	SIGNATURE/DATE*

1. Introduction to The Kidney Unit

   RESOURCES

   VIDEO (1)   'Life goes on'

   Welcome to Sid Ward Pack

2. How normal kidneys work

   RESOURCES

   BOOK   'A Patient's Guide to Dialysis and Transplantation' by Roger Gabriel.
   VIDEO (2)   'The Inside Story'

3. What happens when kidneys fail?
   What has happened to your kidneys?

   RESOURCES

   BOOK   'A Patient's Guide to Dialysis and Transplantation' by Roger Gabriel.
   VIDEO (3)   'Closed for Business'

4. Principles of Haemodialysis

   RESOURCES

   BOOK   'A Patient's Guide to Dialysis and Transplantation' by Roger Gabriel.
   VIDEO (4)   'Dialysis'

   Cut-open dialyser

* The nurse-trainer signs off each lesson or event as it is completed.

SECTION	SIGNATURE/DATE*

5. Outline of water treatment equipment and its functions*
   Outline of haemodialysis machine and equipment*

   RESOURCES

   Gambro User's Manuals

   VIDEO (4)   'Dialysis'

6. Outline of the Kidney Unit and its functions

   The roles of the following:

Clinical Nurse Manager	Doctors
Pharmacist*	Dietitian*
Technicians*	Psychologist*
Nurses	Storeman
Social Worker*	Administrator*
Ward clerks	Patients' Association*

   Homecare Nurse Specialists
   Primary Nursing* – how it affects you

   RESOURCES

   VIDEO (5)   'When the Chips are Down
                 Relates to the role of diet in treatment.
   VIDEO (6)   'Keep Taking the Tablets'
                 Relates to the role of drugs in treatment.
   VIDEO (7)   'Here to Help'
                 Relates to help available from the kidney unit.

   Welcome to Sid Ward Pack

* The nurse-trainer signs off each lesson or event as it is completed.

SKILLS FOR YOU TO LEARN

	Demonstrated Signature/Date	Carried out Sig/Date	Proficient Sig/Date

Weight
  Measuring/significance
Temperature
  Measuring/significance
Blood Pressure
  Measuring/significance			

Lining up Haemodialysis Machine			
Preparing Machine for Dialysis: *RESOURCE:*			

	Demonstrated Signature/Date	Carried out Sig/Date	Proficient Sig/Date
Checklists for dialysis machine and water treatment equipment			

GOING ON DIALYSIS:

1. Insertion of needles/cannulae into fistula veins (checklist)

2. Heparin administration

3. Joining up blood lines

4. Dealing with blood pump

5. Dealing with level detector (checklist)

6. Setting and checking alarms

7. Selecting correct transmembrane pressure (TMP)

8. Management of sequential ultra filtration (UF) when applicable (checklist)

9. Management and use of filtration control module (FCM) when applicable (manufacturer's handbook)

10. Preparation of heparin and local anaesthetic injections (guidelines available)

11. Management and use of BCM and Bicart (when applicable)

COMING OFF DIALYSIS:

1. Wash-back technique

2. Removal of needles/cannulae and control of bleeding

3. Post-dialysis care of machine (checklist)

4. Reuse of dialyser using formalin (checklist)

5. Disposal of waste material and sharps

	Demonstrated Signature/Date	Carried out Sig/Date	Proficient Sig/Date

6. Cleaning of equipment and dialysis room

7. Preparation and administration EPO

OUTLINE OF NEXT SIX MONTHS

Training
Transition to homecare
Home adaptations
Telephone provision
(see guidelines)

CARE OF ACCESS

(delete not applicable)

1. *Arteriovenous Fistula (Guidelines)**
   (a) How to aid its development
   (b) Control of bleeding post-dialysis
   (c) Bruising
   (d) Infection
   (e) Clotting

2. *Arteriovenous Shunt (Guidelines)**
   (a) Hygiene and dressings
   (b) Checking patency
   (c) De-clotting
   (d) Infection

3. *Subclavian Catheter*
   See separate information sheet

4. *Francis Catheter*
   See separate information sheet

5. *Haemasite*
   See separate information sheet

DIALYSIS PROBLEMS

1. HYPOTENSION on dialysis (information sheet)

2. HYPERTENSION (+ see EPO guidelines)

3. Poor arterial blood flow on dialysis

4. High venous pressure on dialysis

5. Shivering attacks and/or raised body temperature

6. Leaking dialyser (information sheet)

7. Leaking heparin line (information sheet)

	Demonstrated Signature/Date	Carried out Sig/Date	Proficient Sig/Date
8. Leaking bloodlines			
9. Poor blood figures e.g. hyperkalaemia Video (3)			
10. Air embolus – how to prevent (guidelines)			
11. First-use reaction (guidelines)			

Polly Woodhams
April 1990
June 3, 1991

APPENDIX 2

LIVING WITH AND CARING FOR MY TRANSPLANTED KIDNEY

We have prepared and helped you to cope with life on dialysis, and now we need to prepare you for living with your kidney transplant. By caring for yourself in a certain way, you may be able to extend the length of time that your kidney works for you.

Set out below are some very important questions. Your job during the next week or so is to arrange time with your primary nurse to view Videos 3 and 4 of the series 'The Chance of a Lifetime'.

Video 3 is called 'Getting the Act Together'.

Video 4 is called 'Chance of a Lifetime'.

This will help you to obtain the answers.

(Your primary nurse is expecting you to do this).

You may have additional questions that you would like to ask us.

It is also important for you to arrange to meet with the dietitian and pharmacist to obtain information regarding diet and drugs – your primary nurse will help you to arrange this.

Before you go home, you should get your primary nurse to check through your answers. This can be your way of helping us.

Julie Butler   Polly Woodhams
Ward Sister   Clinical Nurse Manager

Q   How long will I be in hospital?

A

Q   Can I mix with other people when I leave hospital?

A

Q   What if they have a cold?

A

Q   What form of exercise is suitable for me, and how much?

A

Q   How should I treat my kidney – can I press it? What if it gets knocked?

A

Q   When can I resume driving?

A

Q   Is there anything 'special' about my diet? (Arrange for time with the dietitian)

A

Q   How much fluid should I drink? Do I need to measure and record it at home?

A

Q   When may I return to school/work/household duties?

A

Q   Would smoking be harmful to me?

A

Q   Can I have normal sexual relations – are there positions to avoid?

A

Q   Do I need to use contraception?

A
Q   What method of contraception is suitable for me? Where can I obtain advice and supplies?

A

Q   Is it possible to become pregnant/partner to become pregnant, and would it be harmful to my kidney?

A

Q   What drugs must I take and how do I get supplies?

A

Q   Are there any side effects that I may experience from these drugs?

A

Q   What observations of body functions should I make, how often and for how long? What is the normal range?

A   (a)   Weight
    (b)   Temperature
    (c)   Urine volume
    (d)   Blood pressure

Q   What should I do if the above are not normal?

A

Q How often do I need to come to the hospital for check ups and for how long?

A

Kidney Transplant Progress Monitoring

Standard frequency of follow-up:
Week 1 and 2   Daily
Week 3 and 4   Monday (clinic) Wednesday and Friday (ward)
Week 5 and 6   Monday (clinic) Thursday (ward)
Week 6 – 8   Weekly or Fortnightly (clinic)
Week 8 – 12   Fortnightly (clinic)
Months 3 – 6   Monthly (clinic)
Months 6 – 12   Two monthly (clinic)
After 1 year   Three monthly (clinic)

You should not take your cyclosporin pre blood tests

Q Does having a transplant control high blood pressure?

A

Q Does having high blood pressure damage my transplanted kidney?

A

Q What happens to my benefits now that I have had a transplant? (Arrange with the social worker if you feel it is necessary)

A

Bibliography

Baglioni, L.J., Cooper, C.L. and Hingley, P. (1990) Job stress, mental health and job satisfaction among UK senior nurses. *Stress Medicine*, **6**, 9–20.

Bailey, R. and Clarke, M. (1989) *Stress and Coping in Nursing*, Chapman & Hall, London.

Balint, M. (1964) *The Doctor, his Patient and the Illness*, Hogarth Press, London.

Bassett, P. (1991) NHS reforms – loss of nurses is costing £24m. *The Times*, October 7th.

Becker, M.H. (ed.) (1974) The health belief model and personal health behaviour. *Health Education Monographs*, **2**, 324–508.

Becker, M.H. and Rosenstock, I.M. (1984) Compliance with medical advice, in *Health Care and Human Behaviour* (eds A. Steptoe and A. Mathews) Academic Press, London. pp. 175–208.

Bond, M.R. (1980) New approaches to pain. *Psychological Medicine*, **10**, 195–199.

Brand, P.C. and van Keep, P.A. (1978) *Breast Cancer*, MTP Press, Lancaster.

Brinchmann-Hansen, O., Dahl-Jorgensen, K., Sandvik, L. and Hanssen, K. (1992) Blood glucose concentrations and progression of diabetic retinopathy: the seven-year results of the Oslo study. *British Medical Journal*, **304**, 19–22.

Brody, D.S. (1980) Physician recognition of behavioural, psychological and social aspects of medical care. *Archives of Internal Medicine*, **140**, 1286–1289.

Broome, A.K. (1989) *Health Psychology*, Chapman & Hall, London.

Burnard, P. (1991) *Coping with Stress in the Health Professions*, Chapman & Hall, London.

Byrne, P.S. and Long, B.E.L. (1976) *Doctors Talking to Patients*, HMSO, London.

Chase, H.P., Jackson, W.E., Hoops, S.L. *et al.* (1989) Glucose control and the renal and retinal complications of insulin-dependent diabetes. *Journal of the American Medical Association*, **261**, 1155–1160.

Davis, H. and Fallowfield, L. (1991) *Counselling and Communication in Health Care*, Wiley, Chichester.

Editorial *Lancet*, (1979) **1**, part 1, 478–479.

Editorial *Lancet*, (1985) **1**, 133–134.

220

Egan, G. (1990) *The Skilled Helper*, Brooks/Cole Publishing Co., Monterey, Ca.

Elian, M. and Dean, G. (1985) To tell or not to tell the diagnosis of multiple sclerosis. *Lancet*, **2**, 27–28.

Fallowfield, L. (1991) *Breast Cancer*, Tavistock/Routledge, London.

Firth-Cozens, J.A. (1987) Emotional distress in junior house officers. *British Medical Journal*, **295**, 533–536.

Gardiner, B.M. (1980) Psychological aspects of rheumatoid arthritis. *Psychological Medicine*, **10**, 159–163.

Gath, D., Cooper, P. and Day, A. (1982) Hysterectomy and psychiatric disorder. *British Journal of Psychiatry*, **140**, 335–350.

Gendlin, R. (1978) *Focusing*, Everest House, New York.

Goldberg, D. and Huxley, P. (1980) *Mental Illness in the Community*, Tavistock, London.

Greer, S., Morris, T. and Pettingale, K.W. (1979) Psychological response to breast cancer: effect on outcome. *Lancet*, **1**, 785–787.

Hackett, T.P. and Cassem, N.M. (1976) White collar and blue collar responses to a heart attack. *Journal of Psychosomatic Research*, **20**, 85–95.

Hauser, S.T. (1981) Physician–patient relationships, in *Social Contexts of Health, Illness and Patient Care* (eds E.G. Mishler, L.R. Amarasingham, S.T. Hauser *et al.*), Cambridge University Press, Cambridge, 104–140.

Hawker, R. (1983) *Interaction between nurses and patients' relatives*. PhD thesis, Exeter University.

Hawton, K. (1981) The long-term outcome of psychiatric morbidity detected in general medical patients. *Journal of Psychosomatic Research*, **25**, 237–243.

Hayward, J. (1975) *Information – a Prescription against Pain*, Royal College of Nursing, London.

Heatherington, R. (1964) Communication – some psychological aspects of the nurse–patient relationship. *Nursing Times*, 18 December.

Illich, I. (1976) *Limits to Medicine*, Penguin Books, Harmondsworth.

Jackson, S.E., Schwab, R.L. and Schuler, R.S. (1986) Toward an understanding of the burn-out phenomenon. *Journal of Applied Psychology*, **71**, 630–640.

Jacobsen, P.B. and Holland, J.C. (1991) The stress of cancer: psychological responses to diagnosis and treatment, in *Cancer and Stress*, (eds C.L. Cooper and M. Watson), Wiley, London.

Jacobson, S.F. and McGrath, H.M. (1983) *Nurses under Stress*, Wiley, Chichester.

Janis, I. and Levanthal, H. (1965) Psychological aspects of physical illness and hospital care, in *Handbook of Clinical Psychology*, (ed. B. Wolman), McGraw Hill, New York.

Johnston, M. (1980) Anxiety in surgical patients. *Psychological Medicine*, **10**, 145–152.

Kallio, V., Hamatainen, H., Hakkila, J. and Luurila, O.J. (1979) Reduction in sudden death by a multifactorial intervention programme after acute myocardial infarction. *Lancet*, **1**, 1091–1094.

Kaplan De Nour, A. (1981) Prediction of adjustment to haemodialysis, in *Psychonephrology I* (ed. N.B. Levy), Plenum, New York, pp. 343–375.

Kaplan De Nour, A. and Czaczkes, J.W. (1974) Bias in assessment of patients on chronic haemodialysis. *Journal of Psychosomatic Research*, **18**, 217–221.

Kaptein, A.A., van der Ploeg, H.M., Garssen, B. *et al.* (eds) (1990) *Behavioural Medicine*, Wiley, Chichester.

Kennedy, S., Kiecolt-Glaser, J.K. and Glaser, R. (1988) Immunological consequences of acute and chronic stressors: mediating role of interpersonal relationships. *British Journal of Medical Psychology*, **61**, 77–85.

Lacey, J.H. and Burns, T. (1989) *Psychological Management of the Physically Ill*, Churchill Livingstone, London.

Levine, J. and Zigler, E. (1975) Denial and self-image in stroke, lung cancer and heart disease patients. *Journal of Consulting and Clinical Psychology*, **43**, 751–759.

Ley, P. (1982a) Giving information to patients, in *Social Psychology and Behavioural Medicine* (ed. J.R. Eiser), Wiley, London, pp. 339–373.

Ley, P. (1982b) Satisfaction, compliance and communication. *British Journal of Clinical Psychology*, **21**, 241–254.

Ley, P. (1989) Improving patients' understanding, recall, satisfaction and compliance, in *Health Psychology*, (ed. A.K. Broome), Chapman & Hall, London, pp. 74–113.

Lief, H.I. and Fox, R.C. (1963) Training for detached concern in medical students, in *The Psychological Basis of Medical Practice*, (ed. H.I. Lief), Harper and Row, New York.

Llewelyn, S.P. (1989) Caring: the costs to nurses and relatives, in *Health Psychology*, (ed. A.K. Broome), Chapman & Hall, London, pp. 114–130.

McMahon, R. and Pearson, A. (1991) *Nursing as Therapy*, Chapman & Hall, London.

Maguire, C.P., Julier, B.L., Hawton, K.E. and Bancroft, J.H.J. (1974) Psychiatric morbidity and referral on two general medical wards. *British Medical Journal*, **1**, 268–270.

Maguire, P. (1978) Psychiatric problems after mastectomy, in *Breast Cancer*, (eds P.C. Brand and P.A. van Keep), University Park Press, Baltimore, pp. 47–53.

Maguire, P. (1985a) Barriers to psychological care of the dying. *British Medical Journal*, **291**, 1711–1713.

Maguire, P. (1985b) Improving the detection of psychiatric problems in cancer patients. *Social Science in Medicine*, **20**, 819–823.

Maguire, P. (1989) Problems in women undergoing surgery for breast cancer, in *Psychological Management of the Physically Ill*, (eds J.H. Lacey and T. Burns), Churchill Livingstone, London, pp. 193–212.

Maguire, P., Tait, A., Brooke, M. *et al.* (1980) Effect of counselling on the psychiatric morbidity associated with mastectomy. *British Medical Journal*, **281**, 1454–1456.

Marteau, T.M. (1989) Health beliefs and attributions, in *Health Psychology*, (ed. A.K. Broome), Chapman & Hall, London, pp. 1–23.

Mawson, D., Marks, I.M., Ramm, L. and Stern, R.S. (1981) Guided mourning for morbid grief – a controlled study. *British Journal of Psychiatry*, **138**, 185–193.

Mayou, R., Foster, A. and Williamson, B. (1978) Psychosocial adjustment in patients one year after myocardial infarction. *Journal of Psychosomatic Research*, **22**, 447–453.

Mayou, R., Williamson, B. and Foster, A. (1978) Outcome two months after myocardial infarction. *Journal of Psychosomatic Research*, **22**, 439–445.

Menzies, E.P. (1970). *The Functioning of Social Systems as a Defence against Anxiety*, Tavistock, London.

Miller, A.E. (1979) Nurses' attitudes towards their patients. *Nursing Times*, **75**, 1929–1933.

Moffic, H.S. and Paykel, E.S. (1975) Depression in medical in-patients. *British Journal of Psychiatry*, **126**, 346–353.

Morris, T. (1979) Psychological adjustment to mastectomy. *Cancer Treatment Reviews*, **6**, 41–61.

Morris, T., Greer, H.S. and White, P. (1977) Psychological and social adjustment to mastectomy – a 2-year follow-up study. *Cancer*, **40**, 2381–2387.

Murray-Parkes, C. (1976) The psychological reactions to the loss of a limb, in *Modern Perspectives in the Psychiatric Aspects of Surgery*, (ed. J.C. Howells), Macmillan, London, pp. 515–532.

Nelson-Jones, R. (1988) *Practical Counselling and Helping Skills*, Cassell, London.

Nichols, K.A. (1987) Chronic physical disorder in adults, in *Coping with Disorder in the Family*, (ed. J. Orford), Croom Helm, London, pp. 62–85.

Nichols, K.A. (1988) Practising what we preach. *The Psychologist*, **1**, 50–51.

Nichols, K.A. (1991) Psychological aspects of acute pain. *Clinical Psychology Forum*, **38**, 2–6.

Nichols, K.A. and Jenkinson, J. (1991) *Leading a Support Group*, Chapman & Hall, London.

Nichols, K.A. and Springford, V. (1984) Psychosocial difficulties associated with survival by dialysis. *Behaviour Research and Therapy*, **22**, 563–574.

Nursing, no. 27 (1981), Communication.

Nursing Times, **77**, (15), (1981), pp. 628–639.

O'Leary, A. (1990) Stress, emotion, and the human immune system. *Psychological Bulletin*, **108**, 363–382.

Payne, R. (1987) Stress in surgeons, in *Stress in Health Professionals*, (eds R. Payne and J.A. Firth-Cozens), Wiley, Chichester, pp. 89–106.

Payne, R. and Firth-Cozens, J.A. (eds) (1987) *Stress in Health Professionals*, Wiley, Chichester.

Pearson, A. (ed.) (1988) *Primary Nursing*, Croom Helm, London.

Petrie, K. (1989) Psychological wellbeing and psychiatric disturbance in dialysis and renal transplant patients. *British Journal of Medical Psychology*, **62**, 91–96.

Querido, A. (1959) Forecast and follow-up – an investigation into the clinical, social and mental factors determining the results of hospital treatment. *British Journal of Preventative Social Medicine*, **13**, 33–49.

Rachman, S. (1980) Emotional processing. *Behaviour Research and Therapy*, **8**, 51–60.

Rawlings, E.E. (1972) The doctors' potential for doing harm. *Psychotherapy and Psychosomatics*, **21**, 105–106.

Ray, C. and Fitzgibbon, G. (1981) Stress arousal and coping with surgery. *Psychological Medicine*, **11**, 741–746.

Reynolds, M. (1978) No news is bad news – patients' views about communication in hospital. *British Medical Journal*, **1**, 1673–1676.

Reynolds, M.P., Sanson-Fisher, R.W. and Poole, A.D. (1981) Cancer and communication: information-giving in an oncology clinic. *British Medical Journal*, **282**, 1449–1451.

Richards, C. (1981) Communication – the patients' point of view. *Nursing*, first series, no. 27, 1189–1190.

Ridgeway, V. and Mathews, A. (1982) Psychological preparation for surgery: a comparison of methods. *British Journal of Clinical Psychology*, **21**, 271–280.

Ruberman, W., Weinblatt, E. and Goldberg, J. (1984) Psychosocial influences on mortality after myocardial infarction. *New England Journal of Medicine*, **311**, 552–559.

Rutter, D.R. (1989) Models of belief-behaviour relationships in health. *Health Psychology Update*, No. 4, 3–10.

Schlesinger, H.J., Mumford, E., Glass, G. *et al.* (1983) Mental health treatment and medical care utilisation in a fee-for-service system: outpatient mental health treatment following the onset of chronic disease. *American Journal of Public Health*, **73**, 422–429.

Speigel, D., Bloom, J.R., Kraemer, H.C. and Gottheil, E. (1989) Effect of psychosocial treatment on survival of patients with metastatic breast cancer. *Lancet*, **2**, 888–891.

Stein, L. (1978) The doctor–nurse game, in *Readings in the Sociology of Nursing* (eds R. Dingwall and J. McIntosh), Churchill Livingstone, London, pp. 107–117.

Sternbach, R.A. (1974) *Pain Patients – Traits and Treatments*, Academic Press, New York.

Strong, P.M. (1979) *The Ceremonial Order of the Clinic*, Routledge and Kegan Paul, London.

Sweeney, G.M. (1991) *Factors Contributing to Work-Related Stress in Occupational Therapy: Implications for Personal, Managerial and Organisational Sources of Change.* Thesis, University of Exeter.

Tessler, R., Mechanic, D. and Diamond, M. (1976) The effect of psychological distress on physician utilization – a prospective study. *Journal of Health and Social Behaviour*, **17**, 353–364.

Thomas, C., Madden, F. and Jehu, D. (1984) Psychological morbidity in the first three months following stoma surgery. *Journal of Psychosomatic Research*, **28**, 251–257.

Tschudin, V. (1991) *Counselling Skills for Nurses*, Baillière Tindall, London.

Wai, L., Richmond, J., Burton, H. and Lindsay, R.M. (1981) Influence of psychosocial factors on survival of home-dialysis patients. *Lancet*, **2**, Part 2, 1155–1156.

Waitzin, H. and Stoeckle, J.D. (1972) The communication of information about illness. *Advances in Psychosomatic Medicine*, **8**, 180–215.

Wilson-Barnett, J. (1980) *Stress in Hospitals*, Churchill Livingstone, London.

Wirsching, M., Druner, H.U. and Herman, G. (1975) Results of psychosocial adjustment to long term colostomy. *Psychotherapy and Psychosomatics*, **26**, 245–256.

Woodhams, P. (1984) Nurses and psychologists – the first-hand experience. *Nursing Times*, 11 January, pp. 34–35.

Woodhams, P. (1992) *A support scheme for the nursing staff in a renal unit.* Talk given at a symposium on Support for Health Care Professionals, Exeter Post Graduate Medical Institute.

Wright, S. (1991) Facilitating therapeutic nursing and independent practice, in *Nursing as Therapy*, (eds R. McMahon and A. Pearson), Chapman & Hall, London, pp. 85–101.

Index

Absence of psychological care, *see*
  Neglect
Acceptance, of emotional reactions
  129
Advisory counselling
  communication flow in 143
  vs personal counselling 143–4
  see also Informational care
Advocacy, nurses' role 54
Amputation, emotional difficulties
  after 14
Anxiety
  effect on pain 42
  productive, case example 109–11
  in surgical patients 13
  see also Stress

Breast cancer patients, prevalence of
  distress in 13–14
British Association of Counselling
  160

Care
  absence of, *see* Neglect
  eductional, *see* Educational care
  emotional, *see* Emotional care
  as focus of attention 6
  informational, *see* Informational
    care
  psychological, *see* Development;
    Neglect; Scheme
Caregivers
  becoming experienced 186–7
  self-image 187
'Caring medicine' xiii, 1–2, 43–4
Case discussion meetings 138–9, 159,
  188, 190
Casualty model, psychological, 47
Challenging, in counselling 148–9
Clinical psychologists, referrals to
  164–5
Colostomy patients, prevalence of
  distress in 14
'Committed sponsorship' 23
'Committee sponsorship' 23

Communication
  absence of, *see* Non-
    communication
  as contribution to recovery 58–9
  egocentric conversation 62
  about feelings, avoidance of 24–6
  in hospitals 61, 65
  inadequacy of 64, 65
    see also Non-communication
  inadequate (in case study) 7
  need for change in attitude 64
  obstacles to success 76–8
  practical problems 61–4
  principles of 58–9
  between staff of different
    specialities (in case studies) 7,
    8, 205
  vocabulary problems 70–1
    see also Educational care;
      Information; Informational
      Care; Listening
Compliance with treatment
  difficulties of dialysis patients 40–1
  effect of informational care 199,
    200
    see also Non-compliance
Confrontation, in counselling 148
Confusion, of patients in hospital
  69–70
Consultants, responsibilities of 193
Consultations
  child patients 21
  doctor-centred style 21–2
Coronary heart disease, prevalence
  of distress in 14
Counselling
  advisory, *see* Advisory counselling
  basic supportive 154–7
  benefits of 199–200
  case study 149–53
  definition 143
  direction of information flow 143
  errors and pitfalls in 157–9
  exploring the problem 145
  as extension of emotional care 144
  facilitating action 146

226

Counselling—*cont.*
  by all health care staff? 142
  misconceptions about 144–5
  modes of 143–4
  overview 53
  personal vs advisory 143–4
  and post-traumatic stress reaction 159
  relationship with client 146–7
  research findings 199–200
  setting goals 145–6
  skills 146–9
  stages of 145–9
  targets in 145–9
  training 159–60
  see also Referrals
Counsellors
  professional and voluntary, referrals to 165–6
  self-disclosure of feelings 148–9

Defence mechanisms
  of doctors 22–4, 31
  of nurses 35–6
Degenerative diseases, death rate of psychiatrically ill 13
Denial, as feature of serious illness 12
Dependency, danger of? 196–7
Depression
  effect on pain 42
  undetected in patients 18
Development, of psychological care
  initiating support for 191, 195
  a joint approach 50
  need for explicit scheme 45
  principles 45–6
  a two-stage event 191
  in unfavourable circumstances 190–7
Dialysis patients
  check list of problems 15
  difficulties in compliance with treatment 40–1
  learning program 213–19
  partners, check list of problems 16
  prevalence of distress in 15–16
Distress
  caused by illness? 11–17
  does it matter? 37–43
  effect on doctor/nurse utilization 41–2
  effect on health and recovery 38–9
  emphasis on recognition and prevention of 45

Distress—*cont.*
  related to physical complaints 41–2
Disturbance, psychological
  caused by illness? 11–17
  definition 13
  prevalence of 12–16
  underestimation of 12
  undetected in patients 18
Doctor–nurse relationship, *see* Nurse–doctor relationship
Doctor–patient relationship
  'medical style' 20, 29–38
  trends in 36–7
  see also Consultations; Doctors; Patients
Doctors
  defence mechanisms 23–4, 31
  dread of mistakes 31
  effect of interchangeability of 24
  influence of training system 19, 30–1
  influences on behaviour of 30–2, 34
  little psychological training 17–18
  myth of infallibility 32
  objections to psychological care scheme 193–5
  participation in psychological care scheme 190
  preservation of power 33
  role in psychological care 56
  stress created by 19, 25–6
  stress in 173
  trained to objectivity 24–5
  withholding of information by 20–2
  see also Consultants; Nurse–doctor relationship
Dying, and emotional support 132

Educational care
  learning programme for dialysis patient 213–19
  overview 51–2
  research findings 197–9
  written guidelines for patient 93, 94
Emotional care
  aim of 100, 121
  assumptions, inaccurate 98–100
  basic steps 115–21
  case discussions and feedback 138–9

Emotional care—*cont.*
  communicating empathy and
    acceptance 128–9
  concepts of 97–8
  cooperation with other
    professionals 123
  core content 121
  differing needs of patients 133–4
  and the dying 132
  ending a session 132–3
  extension to personal counselling
    144
  the first session 117–21
  initiating 116–17
  laying the foundation 116
  losing objectivity 136–8
  making people comfortable 113–14
  need for self-care, *see* Self-care
  overview 52–3
  own emotions 102
  own reactions 136–7
  patient feeling safe 121
  pattern of contact 133–5
  permission for emotional
    expression 122–5
  personal preparation for giving
    100–4
  process as important as content
    132
  reactions to emotional responses
    103–4
  and relatives 136
  research finding 199–200
  setting for 117
  sharing personal feelings 129–30
  skills 121
  stress in giving 173–5
  structuring 135–6
  support for caregivers 139
    see also Preventive support;
      Support groups
  support for patients 130–1
Emotional expression
  facilitating, means of 125–7
  facilitating, reason for 127
  giving permission for 122–4
Emotional functioning 104–6
Emotional processes 107–9
  assistance towards completion of
    108
  facilitating 114
  productive anxiety 109–11
  the work of grief 111–13

Emotional reactions, to illness and
    injury 114–15
  acceptance of 129
  based on how people see
    situations 108–9
  normal and usual 99
  strength of 17
  understanding 96–7
Emotions
  in illness 114–15
  personal attitudes to 100–4
  repeated exposure to 174
  types of 99
    see also Anxiety; Depression;
      Feelings; Grief *and entries
      beginning with* Emotional
Empathy
  in counselling 147–8, 148
  in emotional care 128

Feedback from colleagues, *see* Case
    discussion meetings
Feelings
  concept of 106–7
  denial of, by nurses 27
  in doctor–patient relationship 24
  an ever-present feature 107
  opportunity to express 53
  part of an adaptive process 108
  patients encouraged to suppress
    47
  self-disclosure by counsellor 148–9
  sharing, in emotional care 129–30
    see also Emotions

Grief
  a normal process (in case study) 5
  the work of, case example 111–13

Health beliefs, influence of 74–6
Health care
  changing attitudes in 56
  nursing staff losses 172–3
  stress in 172–3
Health psychologists, referrals to
    164–5
Hospice, medical and nursing
    objectives 30
Hospitals
  confusion of patients after
    admission 69–70
  length of stay, effect of
    informational care 199
  medical style of relating in 30

Hospitals—*cont.*
  mistake rate in 32–3
  and psychological neglect xii–xiii, 19
  as separate subculture 70–1
  vocabulary problems in communication 70–1
Hospital staff, and psychological interventions 45
Hysterectomy patients, prevalence of distress in 13

IIFAC scheme of information exchange 83–4
  case example 84–7, 90–2
Illness and injury
  cause of distress or disturbance 11–17
  emotional reactions to, *see* Emotional reactions
  and experience of losses after 16, 17
  and experience of threat 16–17
Immune function, effect of psychological state 39–40
Infallibility, myth of 32
Information
  aids to retention 64–5
  censored 63–4
  distortion processes 74
  drift from accuracy 74
  exchange of, *see* IIFAC scheme
  hot-line for outpatients 95
  inadquate (in case study) 3
  inadequate comprehensibility 62
  inappropriate form and quantity 62–3
  maintenance of 65–6
    see also IIFAC scheme
  monitoring level of understanding 66, 79
    see also IIFAC scheme
  multiplicity of sources 74
  patients' wish for 20–1, 77–8
  provision of, and stress reduction 51–2
  responsibility for giving 63
  sharing of, in counselling 149
  uncoordinated 63
  unfavourable context 62
  verbal vs written 62–3
  withheld by doctors 20–2
  withheld by nurses 28

Information—*cont.*
  withholding, purposes of 75–6
    see also Communication; Educational care; Informational care; Listening
Informational care
  aims of 65
  application of (in case study) 66–7
  case example 80–5, 90–2
  effect on compliance with treatment 199, 200
  IIFAC scheme 83–7, 90–2
  lack of, examples 87–90
  monitoring level of understanding 66, 79
    see also IIFAC scheme
  overview 51–2
  planning the programme 81
  principles of 79–80
  professionalized task 79
  realistic information 90
  research findings 197–8
  responsibility in 79
  staff cooperation in 79–80
    see also Advisory counselling
Injury, *see* Illness and injury

Job satisfaction, increase in 169

Kidney failure
  case example of informational care 80–92
  partners as carers, 'Alone with illness', a case study 200–12
  prevalence of distress after 15–16
    see also Dialysis patients

Lack of psychological care, *see* Neglect
Liaison psychiatrists, referrals to 167
Listening
  in counselling 147
  difficulties when under stress 62, 71
  effect on patient 132
  need for, in inviting expression of feelings 53
  selective 3, 71–4
Losses, after illness or injury 16, 17

Mastectomy patients, prevalence of distress in 13–14
Medical inpatients, prevalence of distress in 13

Medical staff, *see* Consultants;
  Doctors
Medicine
  caring vs technical xiii, 43–4
  philosophy of 43–4
  physical treatment not enough 6
Mistakes 32–3
  communication about 23
  doctors' dread of 32
  in hospitals 32–3
  myth of infallibility 32
  nurses' concern 28
Monitoring
  of level of understanding 66, 79
    see also IIFAC scheme
  of psychological care, overview 51
  of psychological state 139–41

Neglect, psychological
  'Alone with illness', a case study
    202–12
  the 'average patient', a case
    history 1–8
  in hospitals xii–xiii, 19
  origins of 29–38
  as price of personal defences 31
Non-communication
  causing stress 21–25
  consequences of 67–8
  examples 59–61
Non-compliance with treatment 40–1
  and hospital readmissions 64
    see also Compliance
Nurse–doctor relationship 36
  and initiation of treatment 28
  trends in 37
Nurse-patient relationship
  and medical style of relating 34–5
  splitting of 27, 35–6
Nurse–relative relationship 27–8
Nurses
  and advocacy 54–5
  avoidance of clinical decisions 28
  change of image x
  clinical responsibility 35
  close contact with patients 35
  and communication 26–9
  defence mechanisms 35–6
  denial of feelings 27
  depersonalization of 27
  effect of interchangeability 27, 35–6
  as 'handmaidens' 27
  influences on behaviour 34–6
  key workers in a two-tier system
    47

Nurses—*cont.*
  lack of time? 49, 192–3
  little psychological training 17–18
  and mistakes 28
  psychological basis of behaviour 36
  and relatives 27–8
  role in referral to psychologist 54
  'standard' profile 34
  stress created by 25–6
  withholding of information by 28
    see also Nurse–doctor
      relationship; Nurse–patient
      relationship
Nursing
  changes in ix–x, 29
  features of organization 27
  interpersonal nature 35
  patient-centred 29
  staff losses 172–3
  task-oriented 27, 29, 35

Objectivity, in doctors 24–5
Outpatients, hot-line for information
  95

Pain, effect of anxiety and
  depression 42
Partners as caregivers
  'Alone with illness', a case study
    202–12
  briefing 94–5
  checklist of problems in dialysis 16
Patients
  close contact with nurses 35
  confusion of, after admission to
    hospital 69–71
  depersonalization of 27
  discrediting of 23–4
  identifying the needs of 186–7
  information wihheld from 20–2, 28
  lack of information 77–8
  need to be listened to 132
  not seen as 'persons' 24, 43, 56
  physical complaints related to
    psychological distress 41
  prevalence of distress in 12–16
  role of, in psychological care 55–6
  short-stay 195–6
  wish for information 20–1, 77–8
    see also Doctor–patient
      relationship; Nurse–patient
      relationship; Surgical
      patients

Peritoneal catheter insertion,
  example of psychological care
  preparation schedule 88
Personal counselling, *see* Counselling
Preparation schedule, in
  informational care 87, 88
Preventive psychological care, need
  for 4, 169
Preventive support, for caregivers
  benefits of 179–81
  need for 174
  objective of 180
  principles of 179–80
  receiving, skill of 181
  see also Self-care; Support groups
Probing, in counselling 147
Professionalism in psychological care
  186–7
  criteria for 10
Psychiatric approach, limitations in
  166–7
Psychiatrists, referrals to 166–7
Psychological care, *see* Development;
  Neglect; Scheme
Psychological state, monitoring
  139–41
Psychological therapy, referrals for,
  see Referrals
Psychologists
  numbers in UK 47
  referrals to 164–5
  role in two-tier system 49

Reactions
  ideal, to others' emotional
    responses 103–4
  ideal, to own emotional responses
    103
  see also Emotional reactions
Record card 139
Recovery
  aided by good communication
    58–9
  effect of informational care 199
Referrals
  many necessary? 169
  nurses' role 54
  patient's point of view 168–9
  for psychological therapy 141,
    160–1
  the system 167–8
  to whom? 164–7
  who needs? 161–4

Relatives
  distress of 16
  and emotional care 136
  relationship with nurse 27–8
  see also Partners
Renal failure, *see* Kidney failure

Scheme of psychological care
  absence of, *see* Neglect
  criteria for 10
  elements of 50–5
  fundamental requirement 188
  the ideal 9
  objections to 192–7
  organizing 187–90
  participation by medical profession
    190
  professionalism in 186–7
  training for 188–9
  the 'typical' case 187
  see also Development
Self-care, for nurses and therapists
  170–2, 174
  neglect of, case study 178–9
  a personal responsibility 178
  principles of 175–7
  reason for 175
  see also Preventive support;
    Support groups
Self-image, of caregivers 187
Self-monitoring, of caregivers 180–1
Short-stay patients 195–6
Social workers, referrals to 165
Staff, shortage of 193
Stress, in caregivers
  behaviour patterns 176
  combating 176–7
  in giving emotional care 173–4
  in health care 172–3
  in psychological care, case study
    171–2
  signs of 176
  on surgeons 31
  unrelieved, risks in 174–5
Stress, in patients
  caused by medical behaviour 19–20
  caused by non-communication
    20–4
  effect on immunocompetence 39
  effect on listening ability 3, 62,
    71–4
  emphasis on recognition and
    prevention of 45

Stress, in patients—*cont.*
  post-traumatic reaction to, and
    counselling 159
  staff-induced, causes of 25–6
    see also Anxiety
Suitability for psychological care
  work 188–9
Support
  for caregivers 54, 139
    see also Preventive support;
      Support groups
  for patients 130–1
Support groups, for caregivers 181–3
  composition of 182
  effective 183–4
  frequency of meetings 182–3
  ineffective 184
  setting up 183
  size of 182
    see also Preventive support; Self-
      care
Surgical patients
  level of anxiety in 13
  postoperative distress 14
  psychological condition 39–40

'Technical medicine' xiii, 42–3
Therapists, role of 54

Therapy, referrals for, *see* Referrals
Thinking about problems, does it
  emphasize them? 196–7
Threat, experience of, after illness or
  injury 16–17
Time
  saved by early psychological care
    47–8, 49
  shortage of? 47–8, 192–3
  wasted by non-recognition of
    psychological distress 41–2
Training
  for counselling 159–60
  initiating 196
  need for basic instruction xiii
  need for permanent structure 188
  in psychological skills 188–9
Treatment, compliance with, *see*
  Compliance; Non-compliance

Understanding
  in counselling 147
  monitoring level of 66, 79
    see also IIFAC scheme

Vocabulary, problems in
  communication 70–1